A DISTANT SUMMER

A DISTANT SUMMER

by

EDITH SAUNDERS

LONDON
SAMPSON LOW, MARSTON & CO., LTD.

First published November 1946
Second impression January 1947

Le progrès n'est point du tout une ligne droite et suivie; c'est une ligne en spirale qui a des courbes, des retours énormes sur elle-même, des interruptions si fortes qu'il ne recommence ensuite qu'avec peine et lentement.

MICHELET

MADE AND PRINTED IN GREAT BRITAIN BY PURNELL AND SONS, LTD.,
PAULTON (SOMERSET) AND LONDON

CONTENTS

LIST OF ILLUSTRATIONS

Photographs by courtesy of the *Illustrated London News*

LIST OF ILLUSTRATIONS

No One was ever in a Hurry on the Boulevards.

A DISTANT SUMMER

CHAPTER I

IMPERIAL PARIS

THE skies of Europe were blue, and Paris was a gay and prosperous city. In the gardens of the Tuileries the fountains tossed their chilly waters up into the heavy, glowing air of an August day, and children ran gaily to and fro with hoops and brightly coloured balls, with finely dressed dolls, with toy swords and drums. Newly erected railings with gilt spearheads shone in the sunlight, and here and there the Imperial eagles of Napoleon gleamed, well polished, among the dark leaves of the bushes. Inside the palace stood the Emperor himself, Napoleon III, looking across the lively gardens to the Place de la Concorde and beyond.

It was the 17th of August, 1855, and the Emperor, looking outwardly at that fair scene which ended in his uncle's Arc de Triomphe, looked inwardly at a series of personal triumphs which were about to reach a gratifying climax. For he was on the point of setting off for Boulogne to meet the Queen of England. Victoria was coming on a state visit to Paris. It would be her first visit to the French capital, which at one time she had little thought to see as the guest of this man—"whom certainly we were *not* over well disposed to"—a tyrant and the usurper of the throne of her friends the Orléans. It was not so long ago that Prince Albert had reprimanded his brother, the Duke of Saxe-Coburg-Gotha, for proposing to pay a civil call upon the new Emperor. But now things were vastly changed. Victoria, Albert and their two eldest children were coming in their turn on a visit of far greater significance.

Napoleon III, a nephew of the great Napoleon, had been a pretender to the French throne ever since the death of the Duke of Reichstadt in 1832. But he had met only with ridicule and failure until the year 1848 when, following on the revolution in France and the downfall of Louis-Philippe, he was elected president. Four years later, by means of a *coup d'état*, he had re-established the French Empire, although the European powers were pledged to resist such a restoration. Europe's divided opinions had saved him from interference; and now, only forty years after the Congress of Vienna, he ruled France, a Bonaparte and a dictator.

Everything had gone astonishingly well for him, although there had been many awkward moments since 1848. Now, dazzled by his own good fortune, and superstitious like all adventurers, Louis Napoleon believed in an auspicious star which was employed in turning events in his favour. It had pleased the irresponsible Palmerston to commit England to an immediate approval of his *coup d'état*, and then there had come the Crimean war (now in progress) which had so fortunately placed France in alliance with England. The upstart Emperor had met with a good deal of coldness and snubbing in high places at first, and the Czar Nicholas had refused to address him in the Royal manner as "brother"; but Nicholas had since died, the enemy of himself and England, and Louis Napoleon, as the ally of that most respectable monarch, Victoria, had greatly risen in status in the eyes of world rulers.

Through the machinations of diplomats and the turn of events, Victoria and Albert had been thrown into the arms of the dictator, whether they would or no; and as a military ally he had had to be received at Windsor. He had visited them in the spring with his wife, the Empress Eugénie. Now the visit was being returned. To-morrow morning the Queen's yacht would arrive at Boulogne where the Emperor would be waiting to receive her. Victoria was coming for ten days, and her visit was really the consecration of the new Empire.

For this notable event all Paris was preparing. There was a mood of happy anticipation among the people; suspicion and hostility often arose against England, but there was no trace of it at present. No reigning English monarch had been seen in Paris since Henry VI was crowned there over four hundred years ago; and no ceremonial visit had been paid by an English Sovereign to France since Henry VIII visited François premier at the Field of the Cloth of Gold. The Queen's visit meant more to the French people than the mere social recognition of the Bonapartes or the polite gesture of a temporary ally; it was regarded as a happy portent of future co-operation with a powerful neighbour, and of settled peace in western Europe. The whole city shared these feelings, and while triumphal arches and official banners were set up in the boulevards and broad avenues, the

2

poorest and the meanest streets hung out their own bright decorations and spent their hard earned sous on cheap little Union Jacks.

Later in the day, while the Emperor was speeding down by train to Boulogne, Parisian workmen were still frantically working at the far from completed decorations. Gaily painted Venetian poles were coming along in carts to be erected in the main streets; flags, oriflammes and banners were being hung out, trophies built up, the great triumphal arches painted in imitation of white marble and draped with genuine velvet of scarlet or purple, and immense eagles were being carefully reared aloft. Ionic columns, gilded trellis work, baskets of flowers, fir trees and plaster statues would arrive at a given point in carts and would be dumped down among a lot of planks and paint pots; and sooner or later there would appear, after a great deal of noise and shouting, a graceful erection based upon some decoration of antiquity and arranged with a taste peculiarly French. Emerging from the general uproar were fraternal groups, showing England and France arm in arm under striped awnings. Numerous statues of Civilization, Industry, Concord, Justice, Science and Abundance were appearing, all being set up in porticoes and bowers and archways and surrounded by Royal and Imperial initials, Napoleonic emblems, Royal coats of arms and allied flags. Emblematic pilasters stood white and clear against scarlet velvet curtains strewn with golden bees; and banners which said "Welcome to France", or sometimes "Well, come to France", were being hung across the narrower streets. Along balconies and in the trees, fairy lamps and other fancy forms of lighting were being fixed ready for the illuminations at night, although many were already up, as the Emperor's fête day had been celebrated two days ago.

The Champs Elysées were particularly gay and active. Here, midway between the Place de la Concorde and the Rond Point, France's first international exhibition was being held, following on the successful Hyde Park exhibition of 1851 and arranged on similar lines. But the Palais de l'Industrie, the main building of the exhibition, had none of the lightness and charm of the Crystal Palace; it was far more typical of the architectural taste of the day. It followed the lead of Paxton's building to the extent of having a curved glass roof, and of being metallic in construction; but the walls were of stone. The Crystal Palace had really been a vast conservatory, and as such had had the advantage of being perfectly simple; but the walls of the Palace of Industry were loaded with busts of eminent men, reliefs, medallions and edifying inscriptions; all manner of industrial figures were balanced on the main pediment, and an allegorical France stood aloft, offering to crown them with wreaths of laurel.

At the back of the palace (which stood on a site through which there now runs the Avenue Alexandre III, between the Grand and the Petit Palais) there was a big circular Panorama which until recently had contained scenes from the Battle of Eylau. Now it was joined by galleries to the Palace of Industry and to an annexe which ran along the Cours la Reine by the riverside, and it formed part of the exhibition. The centre of it had been made the Court of French National Industries: Sèvres china, and the manufactures of Gobelin and Aubusson; and it also contained the Crown jewels which were on view here for the summer. Round this central court was a circular gallery filled with show-pieces of French furniture, while outside the building were ranged open air restaurants and buffets on terraces which pleasantly overlooked the surrounding gardens. The annexe, three-quarters of a mile long, contained the machinery of all nations, all set in motion and humming away in an industrial symphony which caused ecstasies to the visitors of all nations, flocking to Paris to admire the heights to which science was leading civilization. In 1855 the whole world believed in Progress and the Perfectibility of Man, and the machine was the voice of the future.

A horticultural exhibition was being held on the other side of the Champs Elysées, just opposite the Palace of Industry and its grounds. Here were silk tents among the green trees; within there were wonderful displays of wax fruit and flowers, and outside, in the ornamental gardens with their white paths, their fountains and clipped evergreens, was a brilliant show of real flowers which was kept constantly renewed.

Carts were rumbling along the Champs Elysées now, on this Friday afternoon, weighed down with flowering trees and bushes in newly painted green tubs. In the flower beds round the Palace of Industry the gardeners were busy putting in new plants, and boxes to hold flowers were being fixed beneath windows and round entrances. The air was scented with the masses of flowers that were arriving; but it also rang with the sounds of shouting and hammering and with the chatter of spectators. There was a noisy and cheerful activity everywhere.

While both official and private enterprise were busy with the decorations, commercial enterprise was equally active. The

Queen of England was to arrive at the Gare de Strasbourg (now the Gare de l'Est) and to drive from that point to the palace of St. Cloud, outside Paris to the west, where she was to stay. Anyone with a window along the route could let seats for to-morrow afternoon at a good price and speculation was rife. Balconies were particularly sought after, and as much as 2,000 francs (or £80) had been paid for them.

Although thousands of the wealthier Parisians were away, spending the holiday weeks abroad or at the fashionable resorts of Dieppe, Etretat, Le Havre and Vichy, Paris had never been so crowded before. "All Europe is at Paris", said a letter of the day, quoted in the *Illustrated London News*, "and all the Parisians are upon the Rhine." In those happy days before the reign of Bismarck, Frenchmen were given to passing their time at Baden, Ems and Wiesbaden, and Germans sat drinking their beer outside the Paris cafés. Bismarck himself was often of their number, though champagne at the Café de Paris was more in his line. He was here now, in this month of August, amusing himself with his usual zest and little dreaming of the triumphant future which loomed up before him at the expense of this now all-powerful France.

Vast crowds of provincials and foreigners were staying in the capital to see the exhibition, and princes and diplomats from all countries had come for the Royal visit. English visitors in particular had come in great numbers. The new rich, the manufacturers and middle classes of England were beginning to feel at home on the Continent.

To-day, on the eve of the Queen's arrival, Paris was about as full as it could be; and yet each new train that arrived was crowded out. Cabs laden with visitors and their luggage rolled up to the hotels only to be turned away again, and for every traveller who found a cab a score or more had to walk.

As the day wore on, more and more people were to be seen walking on foot from door to door, carrying their hand luggage and being turned away by all to whom they appealed. For every attic, every chair, was already let at some exorbitant price. As night fell these thousands of weary visitors began to seek a resting place: any place which was just a little better than the bare streets into which, before long, the householders would be flinging their rubbish. They began to drop asleep in the stations, around public monuments and on the benches in the boulevards. Happily the night was balmy.

As these tourists fell asleep, exhausted by the hot, smoky

5

journey by train and by their search for rooms, more fortunate visitors were just beginning the pleasures of the evening. Outside hundreds of cafés the terraces were thronged, and inside the fine restaurants—La Maison d'Or, the Café Anglais, the Frères Provencaux and all the others of fabulous memory—were crowds of wealthy foreigners who had come for supper after the theatre or the fashionable stroll about the boulevards. Hour after hour the boulevards remained astir with the sound of footsteps and voices, and in other parts of the city thousands were dancing.

The hours of the night passed, and gradually the crowds dwindled away, the chairs and tables were removed from the pavements. At last only a few groups of French journalists and men of letters were left sitting here and there before some café that remained open for as long as they cared to stay. They preferred the night to the day, particularly now that Paris was invaded by visitors. They leaned back in their chairs and complained of their lot, which was really a remarkably happy one as things go in a hard world, and of the incessant turmoil which now distinguished Paris.

Into the warm, calm air their leisurely words fell. The stars shone faintly in a misty sky, and the lights of the café came through the windows on to the green tables and the glasses of dark wine. Paris was ruined, they told each other. Once the Champs Elysées had been a grove, and once the city had been the quiet and historic capital of France; now it was a commercial fair for all the world. The Emperor was rebuilding the capital from end to end; all was being changed before their eyes. The old, narrow winding streets were being levelled everywhere, and great strategic routes, straight and rigid, were being flung across Paris; and in the place of quiet old houses and secluded gardens huge shops and hotels like barracks were being put up. Commercial fortunes were being made, and France was in the hands of the men who were making them. Art was dead; and as for the stage—the stage of Molière and Racine had renounced wit and intellect for a display of legs and artificial jewellery.

So they talked and sighed through the slow mild hours of the summer night, until at last there came that moment before the dawn when the spirits begin to sink. There was a repellent chill, a silence surging upwards from the earth and struggling with human warmth, as though ghosts were walking. The few waiters left began to yawn and remove chairs with a clatter, and the journalists suddenly rose to hurry away to their homes, there to sink first into their beds and then into oblivion, until the midday sun should be shining again and the earth once more human and kindly.

But as they fled from this horrid time of morning, other men appeared, the lowest and most wretched of the city, ragged and half starved. They came up every street with flickering lanterns, with large baskets on their backs and carrying long forks. The householders had thrown out their rubbish on to the road, and carts would soon come along to collect it. But first it was turned over by the men with the lanterns; these were the *chiffon-niers* who tried to make a living by collecting paper, rag and bones and then selling it. Theirs was regarded as a regular calling, but it was followed only under the pressure of the greatest distress and ill fortune. They came from the most wretched lodging houses where they lived in overcrowded rooms, sleeping on floors and subsisting mainly on the scraps they found in the streets.

They scattered the rubbish with their forks, shone their lanterns on to it and sorted out all that was saleable. Then the carts began to arrive to clear up the streets, and the *chiffonniers* returned to their lairs to sort out their finds. The times were good; Paris was full and people were extravagant; old things were freely thrown away, and a strong energetic man, working almost night and day, could often make a few francs in the course of twenty-four hours. But most of them were human derelicts with little left of hope and enterprise; they shuffled away to eat the scraps of bread they had found, to sell their salvage for a few sous and then to buy a drink and forget for a time.

Now the sun rose to illumine the great day. It was Saturday, the 18th of August, 1855. Queen Victoria was on her yacht in the Channel, approaching Boulogne where Louis Napoleon, the Emperor, was sleeping in the best bedroom of the *Hotel du Pavillon Impérial*. Paris began to awake. The *chiffonniers* were out of sight in their own dark alleys, and another vast body of men were now coming out into the streets to do their day's work, to earn their living by their wits.

This was a glorious time for charlatans and vagrant traders. The Second Empire had been inaugurated with great balls and festivals; Paris was being rebuilt, railways were being constructed and bridges put up. Everywhere there was work and prosperity; there was confidence and people had money to spend. Crowds of visitors had been coming throughout the summer to see the exhibition, and now a week of special rejoicing lay ahead during the Royal visit. Flags, programmes, gingerbread, drinks, badges and souvenirs would be eagerly bought by the great crowds. So every smart man was up early, getting himself ready, thanking God for the settled weather and determined to make money to save. In the minds of many of them were their native villages—cottages with fertile gardens, or farms that they dreamed of buying one day—and all that modest but largely elusive longing for peace and independence which haunts the millions of the earth.

Most picturesque and gay among these diverse vendors were the "marchands de coco" who sold rather a peculiar drink. They were a diminishing band and already seemed to belong to the brighter past of Louis Philippe's reign, when summers were long, warm and dry and the world was altogether a better and simpler place. But about two hundred of them were this morning preparing for a busy day, with every prospect of doing very well for themselves. They polished the gilded, ornamental water tanks which they carried on their backs, and they polished their goblets until they shone. Then they chopped up a stick of liquorice and put it in the tank, added the juice of a few lemons, and finally poured in one or two bucketfuls of water. Now they donned their own conspicuous costume, with cocked hat and jingling bells; and as a finishing touch they fixed the allied flags on top of their metal tanks, and then set out for the sunny quays, boulevards and gardens.

Men in those days had not the uniform manner and appearance that they have now. Paris was used to variety and to eccentricity in all classes, from the Marquis of Hertford, the fabulously rich recluse who was amassing the Wallace collection, down to Mangin who sold pencils in the street. Milord Hertford with his millions might wander about among the antique shops, dressed in shabby old clothes so as not to arouse greed in the minds of dealers; but Mangin went proudly about looking like an emperor. He drove round in a carriage, dressed in a mediaeval armoured suit, a shining helmet on his head, and stopped in the street to harangue the crowds about his pencils—unique in the world—drawing as he talked, and shaded by a great red umbrella. People still remembered a quiet and inoffensive man called Carnavale who, as a young man, had suddenly lost his reason after the death of a woman whom he loved. Casting off his sombre suit of mourning with a laugh, he had donned the brightest colours, and henceforth was to be seen in scarlet, blue and yellow suits of his own making. They remembered a special sect of the Saint-Simonites, too, which had been signalized by a queer and colourful costume. And in

Afternoon in the Garden of the Tuileries.

[*Face page* 8

the streets there were always peasants up from the country in their local costumes, besides enormous numbers of nuns and priests in their ancient garb, the nuns bringing a memory of the middle ages, the monks being a link even with classical times. There was diversity on all sides.

The bootblacks of the Pont Neuf, who were now taking up their posts, not only cleaned shoes but were expert at clipping the French poodles which were then so fashionable and were a feature of the streets; their footstools were painted with pictures of these dogs, and newly sharpened scissors gleamed among their brushes and polishes in readiness for a day of brisk trade; for just as everyone would be dressed in his best, so, they trusted, the poodles would have their coats trimmed to greet the English Queen. Women with trays of cakes and chocolate, sellers of programmes of the week's events and of biographies of the Queen, were already shouting their wares in shrill tones, and an open air dentist was driving smartly up the Champs Elysées in a gaudily painted cart.

But all these highly coloured characters, though they lived on through the Second Empire, belonged to the first half of the century. With the turn of the century there had come the industrial exhibitions of London and Paris—gateways to a new and more scientific world—and the French Second Empire, the forerunner of so many nationalistic dictatorships. The real nature of the time, and the sign of things to come, was to be found in the impressive avenues, straight and broad, that the Emperor was building—in the large houses of monotonous uniformity, containing identical flats, one above the other. Gone for ever in the west were the easy days when a vagrant boy could stow himself away in Buckingham Palace, hiding by day beneath the young Queen's sofa and slipping down to the pantry at night. The age of efficiency had come; walls were spiked everywhere, and people ventured less and less from their appointed places. Eccentricity and individuality were dying, although this was not yet apparent.

It was a little later now and the water carriers were going round the streets. Dressed in green or blue velveteen, they were tramping deliberately up and down staircases, delivering water in great metal pails, filled to the brim. In this way, every flat, up to the fifth or sixth floor, had its supply brought for the day; and in the streets stood the great casks from which the pails were filled. Children stood watching the water carriers fill their pails, fascinated as they saw the plugs drawn and the water rush out through a brass-lined hole. It came out in an arched stream, round and smooth, looking like a piece of solid, polished glass. Did it move, or was it still? Imaginative children pretended not to know and tried to guess. Invariably they decided they were looking at a motionless arc of crystal. Then suddenly the bucket was full; the water, turned off, splashed and glittered in a thousand falling drops and the children would laugh delightedly.

Laughing children and a cloudless sky. The fountains were playing, cartloads of flowers were still arriving to add to the already lavish displays in the capital. Shouting men were selling cakes and flags, street musicians and conjurors were amusing the early crowds. Before long, small groups from outlying villages began to arrive in their best clothes; there were country girls with wreathed heads, escorted by *Monsieur le curé*, blandly smiling in his flat hat and black soutane, and other groups were led by the equally affable mayor. Everywhere there was an atmosphere of cheerful excitement as the streets began to fill with holiday-makers.

Yet there was a war on. England, France, Sardinia and Turkey were fighting Russia in the Crimea because of a trifling dispute that had arisen over the Holy Places of Jerusalem. It was the last of the big wars in which civilians were unaffected. Their world was stable, the ground could not be swept from under their feet. Europe was a balanced whole, and war was waged in the knowledge that a balance would be kept, and the world would continue in the same way after as before. Paris was calm and assured; in fact in the ordinary way hardly anyone gave the war a thought, in spite of the incessant military display kept up by the Emperor in his capital; but yesterday's news of a great victory had brought it happily to mind; the distant triumph was an apt accompaniment to the Queen's arrival, and everyone noted the happy coincidence of her Majesty's name.

Walking among the crowds, however, was one man whose mind was full of the war; he was General Canrobert who had arrived only yesterday from the Crimea where, until recently, he had been Commander in Chief of the French troops. He had fallen into disfavour with the Emperor, had given up his command to General Pelissier and had been recalled to Paris. But in calling to see the Emperor yesterday he had found him as affable as ever and anxious for his company during the coming fêtes.

The General had returned home ill, and had risen for an hour or two to relieve himself from the nightmares into which, having a high temperature, he sank each time he slept. Even now he seemed to see the white houses, the gilded domes and the marble theatre of Sebastopol while the brilliant Parisian streets were dazzling his eyes. The sunlight bore down as heavy as lead and the shadows were hard and rigid. Already the sightseers were beginning to seek good positions on the route of the procession; and although the Queen of England was not expected for many hours he could scarcely make his way through the amiable crowds. Even the wealthy people were arriving in the boulevards to take their places; already, at windows and balconies, there appeared ladies in elaborate dresses of billowing silk and lace, attended by gentlemen hardly less picturesque with their pale waistcoats and curled hair. And below were peasants from the provinces, groups of workmen and foreigners from all the world over, mingling with the Parisians and admiring the extravagant decorations. Family parties had brought substantial luncheon baskets with them and had placed themselves in good positions to watch the procession from the station out to St. Cloud; many excellent fat women were doing fine needlework as they sat and waited. Special deputations of working men were arriving at the Place de la Concorde, and in the Champs Elysées there stood a concourse of young girls dressed entirely in white.

Canrobert looked at the decorations; wherever he turned were the names of the few successful battles that the slow war had produced, and in which he had taken part: Alma, Inkerman, Bomarsund; and equally prolific were the banners hung out with messages of welcome to Victoria and Albert. He strolled along the Boulevard de la Madeleine; and here among the decorations was a huge pavilion in red and yellow in which were sculptured figures representing England and France in warlike attitudes, standing against an arrangement of palms and ferns. Further on he stopped to look at a full length, life-size portrait of Queen Victoria made entirely of human hair, a medium much in favour at the time for ornamental use. Then, overcome by a great feeling of fatigue, he was obliged to make his way back to his small flat and go to bed. He had been invited to dine with the Emperor at St. Cloud that night, but it would not be possible to go. The green shutters of his room were closed, but the heavy gold air of that perfect August day filtered through the narrow slits bringing in warmth and the blurred commotion from the streets. Outside people waited and watched. But the Queen's yacht had not even reached the French coast.

CHAPTER II

ARRIVAL OF THE *VICTORIA AND ALBERT*

BOULOGNE, a little cooler than Paris with its breezes from the sea, also waited. Yesterday evening the Queen and Prince Albert had gone aboard their new steam yacht, the *Victoria and Albert*, in Osborne Bay with their two eldest children and a large suite. Early this morning they had weighed anchor, and they were now making a leisurely approach across a transparent, shining sea as smooth as an inland lake.

A tremendous welcome had been prepared at Boulogne. It was popularly believed, and the newspapers kept repeating it, that this event, this state visit of Queen Victoria to Paris, was a great historic occasion which posterity would for ever remark upon. Comparisons were frequently made with the "Field of the Cloth of Gold" which was found to be a small affair indeed when set beside the material and moral splendours of the greater modern ceremony. Boulogne, fully alive to the honour of being the first to greet the Queen, had left nothing undone that could make the day impressive. Always an attractive town, with its white houses and green verandahs overlooking the sea, it was now lavishly decorated with flags, triumphal arches, and above all with flowers.

The excitement began on Friday morning when ships of the British fleet were seen advancing towards the roads. Everyone hurried down to the harbour, and watched them sail to their anchorage a mile or two out. There came first the *Fire Queen*, then the *Neptune* and the *St. George*. The *Sanspareil* followed and soon after came the *Malacca*, the *Rolla* and the *Sprightly*. Presently hundreds of rowing boats and private yachts were dancing about in the water, inspecting the British naval vessels at close quarters.

Cross channel steamers arrived, too, during the day, each bringing hundreds of English visitors, some of whom were going on to Paris, while others had timed their seaside holiday at Boulogne to coincide with the Queen's arrival on the shores of France. By the middle of the afternoon all was bustle and gaiety. "The streets were thronged," says the *Illustrated London News*, "with country visitors in every variety of costume. The limonadier, with his jingling bells and acid drinks at his back, the fisherwoman, with nets on shoulder and bare legs; the village curé with broad hat and rosy cheeks; the omnibuses, with the bells jingling on their harness; the hurrying aide-de-camp; the wandering harpist and his faded prima-donna; the tall tambour-major, the short but sprightly vivandière; the redfaced English-man, the stolid Dutchman, the vapouring Belgian, the smoking German, and the sallow Pole, gave life and variety to the picture."

When the crowds were tired of dazzling their eyes by gazing out to sea, they went to have a look at the principal hotel of the seafront: the Imperial Pavilion Hotel, the whole of which the Emperor had booked for the coming ten days. There it was, in white and newly painted splendour, bravely decorated without, and within containing a host of idle flunkeys, emotional chefs ready to commit suicide if there should be the slightest im-perfection at the Emperor's board, and all manner of self-important servants and secretaries.

The Emperor had also taken the stables at the *Hotel du Nord*, and crowds assembled here to admire the five Imperial carriages which were to convey the English Royal family and their suite from the quay to the station to-morrow. These carriages were new, and their great lamps shone in the summer light; they were panelled in green, had red wheels and poles and were lined with heavy white satin.

The Emperor himself arrived at the station at six in the evening. He was greeted by fanfares of trumpets, and by all the military display which his dignity as a Bonaparte demanded. Then, accompanied by a field-marshal and one or two aides-de-camp, he repaired to the *Hotel du Pavillon Impérial* in a fine char-a-bancs drawn by four horses. He was loudly cheered as he passed through the streets, and particularly by the peasant class which most eagerly supported him. At the hotel he stepped on to a large balcony, which overlooked the sea, to bow to the applauding crowds; and at the same time the British fleet fired a salute of guns.

Later in the evening his Majesty was to be seen reclining on the balcony and smoking a cigar. In the eyes of sycophantic admirers he was taking a well-earned rest from his dictatorial labours; but presently he was seen glancing from side to side and the word was passed round that the Imperial mind was not after all in repose but was employed in choosing sites for the disposition of the French troops round the quay to-morrow morning. Night fell, and the crowds turned their thoughts from the Emperor to the illuminations and to the entertainments that were taking place. A ball was held for the middle classes, and there was "a more select entertainment at four francs a ticket at the *Etablissement des Bains.*"

Now, on Saturday morning, Louis Napoleon could see the Queen's yacht through his binoculars. Impatiently he stepped on and off his balcony; he had risen very early and before breakfast had ridden out to one of the military camps which lay on the outskirts of the town. Now he looked down at the quay and the crowds surging about the streets; and as he watched he saw the arrival of the two thousand Lancers who were to take up positions along the route from the quay to the station. Dragoons galloped about the streets, coming and going, as if on important business, between the hotel and the station, their helmets flashing in the light, and their long horse-hair tails swaying. What they were doing, none could guess. But they were part of the new France, of that revival of so-called "glory" that had come to take the place of the sober rule of the citizen King, Louis-Philippe.

At half-past eleven, forty thousand soldiers from the outlying camps of Honvault, Ambleteuse and St. Omer marched into the town. Bands played, trumpets sounded and drums were beaten. The steady tramping of military boots and the humming of marching songs filled the air, and the Emperor appeared on his balcony once more, cigar in mouth, and clad now in a fine uniform of green and gold and wearing the ribbon of the Garter, which had been bestowed upon him last April at Windsor. The soldiers were ranging themselves in long lines around the town, and climbing the hills that overlooked it. The Queen would have an impressive vision of French strength as she arrived. How often England had looked anxiously across the channel to those splendid French camps; but now all was well, England and France were the warmest friends. The greatest enthusiasm was expressed by the crowds. "Everybody began to talk wildly of the immense significance of the day," says the *Illustrated London News* correspondent, "and of the space it was destined to occupy in history. Now the two nations were fairly allied; now Englishmen and Frenchmen were really and truly brothers. . . . Henceforth the two countries will be one."

The Emperor was now seen riding down to the point of landing to make sure that all was ready and in good order. It was already half-past twelve and the Royal yacht was due in at one o'clock. But she was still far out at sea, approaching slowly and waiting for the tide, and the Emperor turned away to canter up to the cliffs to review a regiment of *Chasseurs*.

One o'clock passed and the yacht was still a long way out. It was not until twenty-five minutes to two, that the first cannon announced that she was at last arriving.

A hundred thousand spectators were now in the streets, at the windows and upon the stands. The Emperor, still on his chestnut horse, was down at the quay with Lord Cowley, the English ambassador, and various gentlemen-in-waiting. The harbour was lined with what the papers called "noble steam-vessels" (anything that went by steam power was looked on as noble in those days of industrial fervour); there were also yachts and merchant ships about, their sails and bright flags reflected sharply in the glassy water. There were fifty thousand soldiers under arms for the occasion; the scarlet, blue and gold of their uniforms enlivened the edges of the cliffs from Ambleteuse to the fishing village of Portel, and forty thousand bayonets were flashing in the sunlight.

Municipal authorities were gathering together near the landing stage, dressed in blue uniforms and tri-coloured sashes; orderlies were rushing about with dispatch cases; uniformed official-looking persons were walking solemnly up and down with long telescopes under their arms, and a great band of drummers stood waiting on the pier head. Along the water's edge were sturdy sailors dressed in white, and near by as a contrast was a large assembly of priests in black. All manner of groups stood waiting with respectful addresses and bouquets of flowers, among them the directors of the Boulogne to Paris railway with Baron James de Rothschild at their head, and the English residents of Boulogne, led by the consul.

Broadsides from the English men-of-war now rang through the air and were answered by the shore batteries of Boulogne and by a volley from forty thousand rifles fired by the soldiers on the cliffs; the *Victoria and Albert* crossed the bar and there was a great shout of welcome from the crowds. The Emperor dismounted, the yacht glided in past the pier head, the French infantry on the jetties presented arms and the military bands played "God save the Queen". But all sounds were drowned by the continuous rolling of the drums. The English men-of-war forming the squadron of honour were drawn up outside the harbour, flying the British Ensign and the tricolour. The spectacle was a harmony of military and naval power and of Anglo-French goodwill. But you had not to be more than sixty years old at that time to have fought under Napoleon Bonaparte; there were veterans of the great war here, looking on; and one of them who had lost an arm was overheard remarking to his companion: "Did we fight like dogs only to come to this?" It is a curious reflection that there can never have been a war to which this remark was not sooner or later appropriate.

The sight which greeted Victoria, as she stood by the railings of her yacht on that cloudless day, was not exclusively military, however. "Opposite the *Depôt des Bagages*," says the *Illustrated London News*, "was seen a square pavilion, or small temple-like edifice, open at the sides and decorated in the style of the *loggie* of the Vatican." Gilt chairs and baskets of flowers enlivened this picturesque erection, and outside were ranged vases of myrtles. Although the Lancers formed a large outer square, within there was the dense mass of Roman Catholic priests, and a short distance away were columns supporting vases in which incense was burning. All this the Queen could see, as she waited for the sailors who were throwing ropes and fixing ladders, and as she smiled and bowed to those who were acclaiming her from the shore.

Now a stage was thrown on board, and directly it was adjusted the Emperor jumped eagerly on to it to meet the Queen. She came forward, in a white dress and bonnet and a blue cloak, and behind her came Prince Albert in uniform, the two children and various members of the suite. The Princess Royal, or "Vicky", was fourteen years old, a plump child who looked like a miniature woman, little younger than her smooth-faced mother, in her long, sweeping skirts and her old-looking cloak. The Prince of Wales was a year younger, a handsome, good-natured boy whose spirits were kept very much in check by parents and tutors, and whose cold tutor, Mr. Gibbs, was present to see that the coming pleasures were not without their instructive side.

Louis Napoleon, bowing deferentially, took the Queen's hand and kissed it; then coming nearer they kissed each other on both cheeks. This was merely in accordance with the Christian etiquette which supposes that all reigning monarchs are brothers and sisters. All the same, it was quite a remarkable moment. Louis Napoleon now ruled where Louis-Philippe had ruled until 1848, and he had seized power by decidedly dubious means. He was a dictator, and nothing was more against the principles of Victoria and Albert who were good Liberals. They were, too, the relations

NAPOLEON III GREETING THE QUEEN AND HER FAMILY.

and friends of the deposed Orléans family. No one had been more anti-Bonaparte than they were, no one more indignant when Louis Napoleon confiscated the Orléans estates in France. "The violent seizure of the poor Orléans' entire property is a crime that cries to Heaven," Prince Albert had written. But Victoria only ruled constitutionally and political events had forced them to swallow their feelings; the war which she and Albert would have liked to avoid was thrust upon them and with it the alliance with Bonaparte. Albert had found himself taking a trip to Boulogne to find out what the new tyrant was really like in person; and after that, since he had been able to give a more favourable report than might have been expected, Louis Napoleon and his newly married and very dazzling wife had been invited to Windsor.

The Emperor, having saluted the Queen, now turned to the Prince and shook him warmly by the hand; he then greeted the children very cordially, after which they all came ashore.

The astonishing thing, in view of all that had gone before, was that this kissing and handshaking was not a mere diplomatic formality. The Emperor had contrived to make himself liked. Even the critical Albert, although he did not in the least trust him or approve of his political schemes and ambitions, had had to admit he was the most courteous and agreeable of men; the two children, who had shed tears when he and his wife left Windsor in the spring, now tripped across the bridge full of pleasurable excitement, and Victoria was delighted. She came ashore all smiles, enthralled at the prospect of being shown round Paris by Napoleon. She had fully determined that she was going to enjoy herself and be amused; and she had brought her sketching materials and a large diary.

As Victoria stepped on to French soil, all the thousands of soldiers ranged round the cliffs and the harbour presented arms; still the drum-majors performed their prodigious roll, the cannon roared, and thousands of voices cried "*Vive Victoria*." The Emperor led her into the pavilion and she sat on one of the gold chairs on a dais to receive official greetings and flowers in jewelled holders.

But it was getting late; they were far behind the arranged time-table, and the breakfast that had been scheduled to take place at the Imperial Pavilion Hotel had already been countermanded. As soon as possible the Queen and her family were led to the carriages; the Emperor jumped on his horse and rode by his guests as an escort, and the procession moved off to the station.

The distance was short, but the spectacle was lavish; the uniforms of the fine troops—the scarlet, the blue, the flashing swords and helmets—were enough to paint the scene most brilliantly. Soldiers lined the route, and the cortège was led by Lancers and *Carabiniers*, and followed by the Imperial Guard and the *Chasseurs de Vincennes*. But there were also flags, flowers and immense decorative erections; the procession swept from the quay, past obelisks of imitation marble, ornamented with garlands of flowers and gilt devices, and then under a great triumphal arch. This arch had cost a large sum for the day, £5,000; it was seventy-five feet high and was made of gilt arabesque work; on the top of it there stood a statue of "the Genius of Civilization". On passing through the arch, the carriages came to an enclosure outside the station; here an amphitheatre of seats had been raised under a series of arches in gilt trellis work; hundreds of fir trees had been brought and set up to make a wooded background, and fine turf had been laid on the ground to create an English lawn. The seats, covered with red velvet, were occupied by "elegantly dressed ladies" as the papers put it. Wherever a good decorative effect was required, it was only necessary to put up a stand and then issue tickets to a few hundred of the ladies of leisure who were nearest to hand. They were a numerous class in these days of Europe's opulence, and if not very useful they were at least highly ornamental; they asked nothing better than to sit down on a stand, surrounded by well-dressed troops at attention and confronted by a spectacle of which they had the best view; and they could be relied on to turn up in the most charming frilled and flounced gowns of pale satin and costly lace, with well arranged bouquets in their gloved hands, tied up with pink or blue ribbon. But the fisherwomen of Boulogne also enjoyed certain privileges, and they were here too, sitting in a good central position upon rows of semi-circular benches and conspicuous in their scarlet petticoats and their neat white caps.

Now the carriages had reached the station and they drew up at the entrance to the first class waiting room. It was through this that the Emperor led his guests to the platform; but it was a waiting-room transformed and unrecognizable. The walls were covered with fluted drapery in white and rose; fine Gobelins tapestry carpeted the floor; chairs, sofas and *portières* in white and gold had been introduced; there was a white marble chimney piece, and porcelain cherubs hung from the ceiling among rare flowers, carrying lighted candles. It was all very delightful and rather incongruous, and it was a pity that no one had any time to notice it. But as it was so late the Emperor led the Queen straight to the train.

The whole station was transformed; walls were draped with purple velvet, sewn with gold bees and stars; and from the roof hung light gilt baskets, some containing flowers, and others heavily perfumed essences; sunlight was streaming in and the scene was very cheerful; the curious little engine, adorned with flags and bronze eagles, stood at the head of the train, getting up steam for the journey, and clouds of black smoke poured from its tall, thin chimney. As the Emperor and the Queen walked arm in arm up the carpeted platform the people cheered anew.

"The faces of both host and guest," says the *Illustrated London News*, "were radiant with smiles as they crossed the platform, bowing to the people assembled on either side. They were evidently delighted with the reception they had just met. His Majesty at once assisted her Majesty into the splendid state carriage; while the Prince Albert turned to Marshal Baraguay d'Hilliers, and entered into conversation with him. Judging from the pleasure painted upon the Marshal's face, and from the low bows he continually made as the Prince addressed him, he was receiving through His Royal Highness the Queen's acknowledgments for this wonderful picture of an admirably disciplined army, which he had so effectively disposed along the heights of Boulogne. These civilities having been interchanged, the Emperor invited the Prince of Wales to enter the carriage, which the latter did, with all the careless activity of a schoolboy. The Princess Royal had immediately followed the Queen. And now came a repetition of those courteous attempts to give the *pas* which charmed the people of Boulogne when Prince Albert visited Boulogne last year. The Emperor, as on the above occasion, insisted that his guest should take precedence; whereupon the Prince skipped lightly into the carriage, and was as nimbly followed by his gracious host. Then the stalwart footmen of the Imperial household scrambled into the carriages behind; a few parcels were hastily stowed away; the military band struck up 'Partant pour la Syrie'"—and the Imperial train started off on its way, not for Syria, but for Paris.

The five hour journey was usually very monotonous; nothing was to be remarked but straight, flat roads lined with poplar trees, quiet farmhouses where a few children played round the doors, cows in the dusty lanes attended by barefooted children in blue blouses, and women standing with railway signals in their hands at the level crossings. But to-day there were miles of flags and decorations along the line; and labourers with their wives and children had come from every hamlet, dressed in their best, to cheer as the train passed. The stations had been transformed into gardens; and wherever the train stopped—at Montreuil, Abbeville, Amiens, Clermont, there were troops, guards of honour, groups of municipal dignitaries standing beneath fine velvet canopies, "elegantly decorated recesses" to contain favoured spectators, and "tastefully disposed waiting rooms" in case the Queen cared to descend while the engine was being examined and refuelled. Prefects and mayors offered addresses, their daughters, all in white, and wreathed with roses, curtseyed and gave flowers; the clergy appeared in their sacerdotal robes to smile benevolence upon the scene, and professors of colleges were present in their academic gowns; the "most beautiful and elegantly dressed ladies" of the town were sure to be there, segregated on stands or in pavilions, and military bands played "God save the Queen" or "Partant pour la Syrie", the national anthem of France at the time.

Inside the train it grew intensely hot, and the Queen's face, we are told (though not in the official accounts) became very red. She was never very comfortable in a great heat. Sometimes the train would stop for a few moments near a village or country town, and a rustic group would hurry up to peer in through the open windows and to comment upon the occupants with a hearty bucolic ignorance of courtly manners; and then the Emperor would raise his voice to drown their crude observations and engage the Queen in conversation.

The Emperor was worried about the lateness of the hour; they were nearly an hour and a half behind time. The light was dazzling as the sun sank low, and the Queen became engrossed with the aspect of the countryside during the last hour of the journey. "At length," she says in her diary, "we passed St. Leu, Montmorency—both charmingly situated—then got a glimpse of Monmartre, my first sight of Paris . . . and at last we passed the fortifications and Paris opened before us."

CHAPTER III

THE WELCOME OF THE CAPITAL

THE last two or three hours had been long in Paris. By the middle of the afternoon the soldiers had taken their places; then after an hour or so their lines had begun to sag. The officers relaxed, their hands in their pockets. The crowds who had been so jubilantly excited throughout the day were now beginning to grow very tired. The ladies above at their windows and balconies leaned languidly over the wrought iron railings and yawned. Their lace and their starched frills were becoming limp and their hair was falling out of curl. The surging crowds had ceased to amuse them; they fanned themselves, they rose from their chairs, they retired into the rooms behind them, where the plush, gilt and crystal of the day provided their setting. So, hour after hour, everyone had waited through the heat of the afternoon until the sun had begun to sink.

Now the sky had suddenly become a remote, greenish blue, and the enlarged sun gilded the festoons, banners and triumphal arches with such unearthly brilliance that it seemed as though a goddess must be awaited. For a few minutes the dramatic, glowing light grew more intense. Then it suddenly faded: the sun had set and disillusionment spread through the patient crowds who had stood throughout the day; if the Queen of England did not hurry it would be impossible to see her.

Then, as the clocks were striking seven, a salvo of artillery announced that the Queen was nearing the capital. The officers braced themselves and drew their swords, the troops re-formed their lines all the length of the route to St. Cloud, loud orders flew from mouth to mouth, and the listless crowds revived.

The train in which the Royal visitors travelled now ran into the new station, the Gare de Strasbourg. The Emperor was proud to show off this fine station, which might have impressed the Queen even if she had seen it unadorned, a plain station for the use of the public—for a station was still a great marvel in those days. As it was, the Queen saw the Gare de Strasbourg, when she stepped off the train and took the arm of Louis Napoleon, as a mixture of winter garden, drawing-room and theatre. All railings and partitions had been removed from sight, and the whole place was carpeted and richly draped with scarlet velvet. Ranged round the great hall, in what appeared to be a series of Royal boxes, were hundreds of ladies of high social standing in the new régime; they were dressed in the height of fashion, and their jewels flashed under the many lighted candelabra that were suspended from the roof. Flowering orange trees, oleanders and pomegranates were there in thousands; the fabulous drawing-room was a mass of flowers. Splendid guards stood to attention, and from the roof hung innumerable flags and coloured hangings.

As the Queen came forward with the Emperor, the great hall rang with cries of "*Vive Victoria*" and the strains of "God save the Queen" played by a military band. She was followed by her husband and children; and Prince Napoleon, the Emperor's cousin and heir presumptive, came forward to greet them; Marshal Magnan, the Prefect of Police, and a group of municipal and railway officials were bowing just behind him, and Victoria accepted still another bouquet to add to those received along the route.

In the forefront of the crowd stood the notable figures of the Imperial court, and many officers from the smartest French regiments. And amid the glitter of the splendid regimentals were the court dresses of fifty ladies who had obtained leave to form themselves into a deputation to greet Victoria, although there was not the slightest reason for their doing so except to place themselves and their fine clothes in the centre of the picture, and to get a better view of the Queen than they would otherwise have had.

The members of this immaculate deputation, and the slightly less fortunate ladies in the boxes and stands round about, were gazing at Victoria with critical interest. Victoria was thirty-six years old at the time; a good and friendly expression made her attractive and all her movements were dignified and graceful. But she was short and heavy and was dressed without style. The Imperial ladies, in all their splendour, were a little scornful over the English fashions. They displayed their own elegance with superb confidence and self-satisfaction, although the credit for their surpassing distinction perhaps belonged rather to designers, lace makers and dressmakers than to themselves. Under the new Empire, women's fashions had been revolutionized by the taste of the brilliant Empress. In the reign of Louis-Philippe, thrift and modesty had been guiding principles generally accepted by Parisian women; but the Empire had brought a different stream of society to the fore, and extravagance was the order of the day. Extravagance had become a virtue; for it was a creed of Second Empire philosophy that pomp and display were an economic necessity in a prosperous state; they encouraged industry and enabled the people to find employment and good wages. The aspect of women, and their whole bearing, had changed entirely during the last two or three years in France; but the rest of the world had not yet had time to follow, and the Queen of England struck the smart Parisians as being decidedly dowdy. There was, however, an air of aristocracy about her that was lacking in the average Empire lady who tended towards a self-conscious pre-occupation with herself and her own important position in the world. Victoria was quite unassuming, although never familiar. Through her own character, and her severely disciplined up-bringing, she was great without any need to be judged by the clothes she was wearing. Not many days were to pass before all Paris admitted she had the grand manner to perfection.

Quickly, as it was growing dark, Victoria passed through the station. Six open carriages and four awaited the party, and soon they were driving off, with a brilliant accompaniment of troops. The Queen and the Princess Royal rode in the first carriage, with the Emperor and Prince Albert sitting opposite to them.

The carriage lamps had been lit, and it was impossible to distinguish the Royal persons; all along the route the crowds, who had looked forward for so long to this moment, were deeply disappointed and were rather quiet. But there was no doubt that they were very friendly; there were cries of welcome, cries of "Long live the Queen of England" and "Long live the Emperor", and there was a constant movement of waving flags and hand-kerchiefs. The Emperor was relieved, for there had been many gloomy prophets who had foretold a cold reception for his Royal guests. The enthusiasm of the country had not yet had time to make itself known, and it was not foreseen at court.

The cortège drove along the great boulevards, down the rue Royale, across the Place de la Concorde, up the Champs Elysées, under the Arc de Triomphe and along the Avenue de l'Impératrice into the Bois de Boulogne. Even the Bois was crowded with spectators. All along the route the military bands had taken up the strains of "God save the Queen", and all along were fine troops—"Artillery, Cavalry, *Cent Gardes* (who are splendid)" says the Queen's diary, "and last, but not least, to my great delight, at the Bridge of Boulogne near the village and Palace of

St. Cloud, the Zouaves, splendid troops in splendid dress, the friends of my dear Guards."

It was now, as they neared St. Cloud, that the first contretemps occurred. The Emperor called up Marshal Magnan, who was riding with the escort, and asked him to have the Empress notified that the Queen was arriving, for the Empress was waiting with her ladies at the palace. The Marshal rode forward and caught up the commander of the *Guides* and gave him the order. But in the general flurry and excitement, the clatter of horses' hooves, the acclamations and the noise of the bands, the unhappy commander misunderstood. He thought he heard the word "Emperor": "Go and announce to the Emperor that the Queen is arriving." It seemed extremely odd; but in the army the reaction to orders is quick obedience, not critical questionings. "Theirs not to reason why . . ." and thereupon the commander rode with a flourish up to the open carriage in which the Emperor rode with Victoria and Albert. It must be some ancient custom, he thought. Who could be expected to know all the awful ins and outs of Royal etiquette? It was without doubt one of those queer traditions from London, which abounded in antique practices, the use and meaning of which had been forgotten many centuries ago. The carriage slowed up at his approach; he bowed and solemnly announced, "Sire, the Marshal commands me to inform you that her Majesty the Queen of England is arriving." Whereupon the Emperor, white with fury, answered in low hissing tones that he was aware of the fact since he himself was bringing her; and the unfortunate officer realised, poor fellow, that he had made a mistake.

Time had passed this evening as wearily in the Palace of St. Cloud as on the boulevards. Here the Empress waited to receive the guests with Princess Mathilde (the sister of Prince Napoleon) and with members of her household. A journalist who was sitting in the background has described the scene in the vestibule of the palace. That famous company of Guards, the *Cent Gardes*, unequalled in the world for its fine appearance and kept for display, was being utilised on this great occasion, and the Minister for War, with a worried expression, was placing the men first in one position, then in another as he tried to get the utmost effect out of them. Finally he decided they looked best on the broad staircase, and there he placed them, one at each end of every step. Then he began arranging the Empress's ladies of honour. As he

The Royal Visitors Driving from the Station through the Decorated Streets of Paris.

Face page 24]

was doing this, a volley of artillery was heard and the ladies stood in a semi-circle while fat, elderly marshals and generals ranged themselves behind them. The Empress came in silently by a side door with Princess Mathilde, and they took their place before the assembled group. There they waited with a sense of the dramatic nature of the occasion, remembering those things the newspapers had been telling them for days past about the visit of Henry VIII; but the minutes passed; they waited and listened and nothing happened, and they began to yawn and grow restless and Henry VIII was forgotten. The Empress looked round for somewhere to sit; but no one could find any chairs. At last she sank down into a Bath chair which was in a corridor, and the whole group broke up in an anti-climax.

The cortège was now arriving, however, and the Empress was notified by the notes of "God save the Queen" which came wafting in through the palace windows. She hurried back with Princess Mathilde to the foot of the staircase. Nervously her ladies ranged themselves behind her, and the journalist and a colleague had a hurried bet as to whether Victoria would kiss Princess Mathilde. The perfect propriety of the Windsor court was famous everywhere; but Mathilde, who had been unhappily married, was separated from her husband and was living with Count Nieuwerkerke.

"In all this blaze of light from lamps and torches," the Queen's diary says, "amidst the roar of cannon, and bands and drums and cheers, we reached the palace. The Empress, with Princess Mathilde and the ladies, received us at the door."

Eugénie, the Empress, one of the most beautiful women in Europe, took both the Queen's hands in hers and kissed her; then the Queen turned to Princess Mathilde and kissed her too in the friendliest manner possible.

Everyone seemed amiable and well pleased, and the Empress led her visitors to their rooms. "I felt quite bewildered, but enchanted," says the Queen. "Everything is so beautiful."

A large and beautiful suite of rooms had been arranged for the English guests in a wing of the palace which had formerly been occupied by Marie Antoinette; they had been decorated and furnished in a most splendid manner and at a colossal expense. So that the Queen should feel at home, some of the rooms for her private use had been made to resemble the rooms she occupied at Windsor. Pictures by Rubens, Van Dyck, Andrea del Sarto, Boucher and Madame Vigée Lebrun had been brought from the

Louvre to decorate the walls. The Queen's bed was a wonderful carved affair in white and gold, hung with heavy outer curtains of pale green silk, and inner curtains of pink, covered with white muslin; the walls of her bathroom were hung with pink watered silk, covered with lace. The furniture was beautiful because it belonged mainly to the previous century, and many of the possessions of Marie Antoinette had been specially assembled for the Royal pleasure. One of these had come to disaster earlier in the day. The same young journalists who were in the vestibule this evening to watch the Queen's arrival had been allowed in the Royal bedroom earlier in the day. Calmly smoking their pipes, they had seated themselves among all the new silk and lace to sketch and describe their surroundings. As they worked they watched the Queen's bedchamber woman, who had arrived in advance, walking about in search of faults in the flawless room. Presently her eye alighted upon something: a chaste and finely executed table of Marie Antoinette's. It was too high for the short Queen, she decided; and a workman was sent for and told to saw a few inches off each leg. He dared to protest, and was told that her Majesty could not conveniently rest her arms on a table as tall as this one. Still he was unconvinced; with the French eye for form, which lived on throughout the country despite the new taste being foisted on the world by the industrialists, he declared that the shape of the table would be ruined if he cut the legs. He began to gesticulate and argue; but no understanding was to be expected from anyone capable of giving such an order; all he got was a cold glance of disapproval for his impertinence. If the Queen of England had short legs, what detriment could it be to any table to have short legs also?

So off the ends of the legs had to come, and the journalists carried away the fragments as souvenirs.

For the Queen the arrival at the palace went smoothly; every effort was necessarily directed to that end. But the almost superhuman effort thus required, in a French court without tradition, had expended itself fully upon the centre of the picture; for the suite and staff of the Queen there was a backwash of confusion and noise. The ladies-in-waiting found that neither their maids nor their luggage had arrived, and that dinner was to be served in twenty minutes' time. Nor could they begin to do anything for themselves for a host of over-zealous footmen who were bent on showing them round their apartments and explaining over and over again their anxiety to be of service. "*Madame la Marquise n'a qu'un pas à faire et elle se trouve dans sa salle de bain. . . . Madame la Marquise peut-elle me suivre par ici, par ici. . . . Absolument à la disposition de Madame la Marquise. . . . Je ne quitte pas la porte de Madame la Marquise."* Lady Ponsonby, then Miss Bulteel, has left an account of her struggles with the footman allotted to her. There was neither bolt nor lock on her bedroom door and she was never safe from him; in spite of her cries of "Don't come in now," he would sail in cheerfully—"*Mais oui, oui, oui, Madame la Marquise, il le faut, Madame la Marquise. C'est pour expliquer à Madame la Marquise . . .*" The Queen's ladies recalled a similar bustle introduced at Windsor last April when the Emperor and his wife had paid their visit to England; bedroom doors had been left open while *demoiselles d'honneur* dressed, shrieking out to each other from room to room as they did so. The trouble was that these same *demoiselles d'honneur* were of surpassing smartness, and they had to be faced to-night after a hot and tiring journey with this terrible scramble at the end of it.

Nevertheless, the whole party somehow managed to assemble at the right moment and follow the Queen into dinner. And now, there they all were—the Windsor court set down rather incongruously in the midst of the Bonaparte clan and their circle.

Dinner was in the *Salle de Diane*, a long gallery brilliantly lighted and painted across its ceiling by Mignard. Victoria found everything magnificent and "very quiet and royal"; she was complimented upon her entry into Paris and found that everyone was marvelling that so huge a concourse had appeared in the capital for the event; even to see the great Napoleon returning from Austerlitz, she was told, so many people had not assembled. In fact it was the greatest crowd Paris had ever contained, and it was particularly gratifying that people had come from every department of the country. The Queen was pleased and flattered; but she was terribly dazzled by the vast number of candles on the table before her and their heat made her most uncomfortable. It was a relief to retire to bed soon after the meal was over.

The Queen and Prince Albert retired at eleven, but all Paris was enjoying a gay festival that went on right through the night. The boulevards were illumined, the chairs and tables outside the cafés overflowed to the edge of the pavements, the street vendors were as busy as ever. The crowds were amusing themselves at hundreds of sideshows; bowls and skittles were played in some districts; in others there were shooting ranges where shots could be taken at grotesque plaster figures of the Czar, the Comte de

Chambord, or the ministers of the late king, Louis-Philippe. The theatres were full, the open air concerts were well patronised. But the most popular entertainment was dancing. In those days the people of Paris danced with an abandoned gaiety; and in the public gardens—the *Jardin d'Hiver*, the *Jardin Mabille*, the *Chateau Rouge*, the *Galant Jardinier* and a hundred other haunts, the mazurka, the polka, the waltz and the *can-can* were in full swing and the night proceeded joyously.

CHAPTER IV

CAESAR'S CONQUEST

THE Queen awoke to a radiant day; the hot sunlight was pouring through the large open windows, and Paris in the distance vibrated, blue and white, in the hazy sediment of the sky. "Slept very well and awoke to admire our lovely room," the Queen's diary says. "We have a number of rooms, *en suite*, furnished with the greatest taste, the walls of most being white and gold. In my sitting and drawing-rooms the ceilings are painted to represent sky. Next to the bedroom, are a little bath and dressing-room, with a splendid view over Paris. My sitting-room and drawing-room (quite lovely) and two more rooms, all, look out on the garden, with its fountains and beautiful long avenues of beech trees, orange trees and brilliant flowers in the foreground. Those formal old gardens are very beautiful in their way and so gay with flowers. Albert's suite of rooms join on to mine and look into the courtyard. A balcony goes all round, and there are outer shutters, as in all chateaux abroad. While I was dressing, stopped to look at the *Cent Gardes*, magnificent men of six feet and upward, ride by, and then, hearing a charming sort of Fanfare, went to another window and saw a body of Zouaves marching up, preceded by bugles. They look so handsome, and march so lightly.—At nine we breakfasted with the Children, and the Emperor, who had kindly come to fetch us. It was a room, handsomely furnished in green, on the other side of the staircase. The Emperor so very kind, amiable and quiet, seems to me in excellent spirits."

"I have such a home feeling!" Victoria exclaimed, in answer to Louis Napoleon's anxious enquiries and looking round delightedly at the surroundings which must really have been quite unlike anything in England. If only her little dog were here, she added, she would almost imagine she *was* at home. Her host said nothing, but when he left his guests after breakfast he summoned one of the officers of his household, and soon messengers were setting off in urgent haste to disturb the Sunday calm of embassy and court officials; heaven and earth were to be moved and any expense incurred to fetch the Royal pet immediately and secretly from Osborne.

The day was to be spent quietly, in conformity with the English idea of Sunday. The Emperor had suggested a drive in the park, to which his guests had readily agreed, and now at half-past nine they were ready and went out to the garden where two phaetons with bay ponies stood waiting. The Emperor invited the Queen to enter the first of these, and then sat beside her, taking the reins himself. Prince Albert and the two children followed in the other. They set off in a leisurely fashion, going up and down the seemingly endless avenues, shaded by great trees, through which were seen glimpses of the quiet countryside beyond. The Queen could not have spent a morning more to her liking; gliding about the shadowy routes of St. Cloud was the pleasantest occupation possible on so hot a day—and then the dear Emperor was so very thoughtful and attentive.

The Emperor was a man of bold methods. Aristocratic Europe had treated him with disdain after his coup d'état; and when the formidable lady of Windsor had grudgingly given way to the pressure of events and invited him to her court, he took the only course that promised social success. "With perfect knowledge of women," says Greville in his diary, "he had taken the surest way to ingratiate himself with her (the Queen), by making love to her." Having begun this in England, says the diarist, he followed it up at Paris. "As his attentions tickled her vanity without shocking or alarming her modesty, and the novelty of it (for she never had any love made to her before) made it very pleasant, his success was complete."

He certainly went to a great amount of trouble before the visit to Windsor. He had previously seen the Queen on only two occasions; once as a girl of eighteen going to prorogue parliament, and the second time at Covent Garden when she and Albert were visiting it in state shortly after their marriage. But he had had every movement of her life searched up, and had made himself acquainted with a host of petty details upon which to draw during his visit; all this personal information came out in the most spontaneous and unstudied manner possible in the course of conversation with his Royal hostess. Whereupon much exclaiming to friends and ministers on the part of the naive Victoria, who was too guileless herself to suspect guile in others, and much underlining in the Royal diary. "It is very odd, but the Emperor knows everything I have done and where I have been ever since I was twelve years old; he even recollects how I was dressed, and a thousand little details it is extraordinary he should be acquainted

with . . .'' ''That he *is* a very *extraordinary* man, with great qualities, there can be *no* doubt. I might almost say a mysterious man.
He is evidently possessed of *indomitable courage, unflinching firmness
of purpose, self-reliance, perseverence* and *great secrecy*; and to this
should be added a great reliance on what he calls his *star*, and a
belief in omens and incidents as connected with his future destiny
which is almost romantic, and at the same time he is endowed with
a wonderful *self-control*, great *calmness*, even *gentleness*, and with a
power of *fascination*, the effect of which upon those who become
more intimately acquainted with him is most *sensibly* felt.''

The Emperor had made himself thoroughly interesting in the
Queen's eye: for him an easy process, since practically all women
thought him interesting and romantic. He had a short way with
them; he fell in love with them all, provided they had a little
attraction or could be useful to him. His incessant philandering,
begun at an early age, had taught him all the tricks of gallantry
and the arts of pleasing women; and rightly seeing that Victoria's
prejudice against him could best be overcome by a strong counter-
emotion, he had been determined upon a conquest. So out of
the Imperial repertoire had come just the right kind and amount
of love to meet the rather exceptional occasion. It had, of course,
to take the form of a most discreet and respectful homage, for the
English Sovereign was a modest and virtuous woman very
happily married.

At Windsor the Emperor had been the Queen's humble subject,
kneeling not before the anointed head of an Empire but paying
court to that which he implied was infinitely greater: her own
personal charm, beauty and goodness. He managed to make
Victoria, so awful and unapproachable in her majesty, and yet so
homely and sensible in her person, feel like a Cleopatra or a Helen
of Troy. She was immeasurably flattered.

She was delighted, too, with Louis Napoleon's constant
eulogising of Albert. With Albert the wily Emperor also had the
perfect technique; he would quickly metamorphose himself into
a typical German professor when he and the Prince had a moment
together free from court etiquette; he would be ready to theorise
and point morals, and then he would jovially fall to singing
German folk songs or to reciting Schiller.

The Queen's love for Albert was deep and sincere; but this
little interlude provided an enjoyable change. Albert, although
utterly devoted to her, was no gallant knight. At Windsor he was
to be seen in their morning walks, striding ahead and not noticing

that she had almost to run to keep up with him; and he could speak of his attachment to her as being "based on reason and duty". Louis Napoleon suggested to her that there was a world in which love was based on passion and instinct; contact with such a man—one who had lived in the great world and taken its knocks in an adventurous career, and yet was now her equal, was delightfully thrilling after these many years in which no man had dared to address her as an attractive woman, and in which Albert supposed she was too reasonable to require any flattery from him.

The Emperor was eager to keep up the impression he had created at Windsor; and so now he was riding round alone with the Queen, while Albert was left to the company of the children. The Queen, of course, knew at the bottom of her mind that it was only a game; but since nothing but a friendly propriety was expected of her in response to the Emperor's gallantry she gave herself up to it with happy delight. And if anyone deserved a little harmless pleasure it was Victoria, after the heavy work, the risks and irritations of her position, the unfailing devotion to duty that had left no place at all in her life for the pleasant following of personal fancies.

If only Prince Albert could have relaxed in the same way! If only he had had the Queen's gift for leaving heavy care behind for a few moments now and then. But Albert always carried his preoccupations and his duties round with him. It is our grievous loss that the good Prince could not spare himself, that he wore himself out while still a young man. Had he lived he might well have saved Europe from Bismarck; his great influence in Germany might have weighed the balance a different way and brought about the democracy in which he believed. But his influence was removed from the world just when it was most needed.

One could wish to record that he had spent the morning in bed. But he was up and about as usual, and there is no doubt that he was improving the shining hour while Victoria basked without a thought for yesterday or to-morrow in the happy enjoyment of the Emperor's admiring glances; either he was propounding Liberal theories to the children or telling them a history of St. Cloud.

Before the morning's ride was over, the Emperor led the way through the village of Villeneuve l'Etang; he drew up for a moment to await the Prince's phaeton, and then pointed out the small country house in which the Imperial honeymoon had been

Between pages 32 *and* 33]

In the Gardens of St. Cloud.

spent two years ago. It was here, he said with a sigh, that he liked
to escape from ceremony and restraint and lead a simple private
life in the English manner. The logical Albert would not fail to
reflect that Louis Napoleon had had ample means and opportunity before he seized power to have settled himself down for life
as an English country gentleman, had he really wished to do so;
but Victoria, under the sway of her host's personality, could well
believe that he had sacrificed his true inclinations to fulfil a
mission. After this visit to Villeneuve l'Etang they turned back
towards the palace, passing through the elegant scenery created
by Le Notre and Mansard, going past antique statues and glassy
sheets of water, great fountains and cascades and all the bright
array of flowers, and presently reaching home.

Awaiting the Queen was the British Embassy chaplain with a
prosy sermon up his sleeve. The Royal family assembled with all
their suite in a room prepared as a chapel, and the chaplain
officiated at a morning service. The text of his sermon was neither
cheerful nor appropriate to so happy an occasion: "And the
Publican, standing afar off, would not lift up so much as his eyes
unto heaven, but smote upon his breast, saying, 'God be merciful
to me, a sinner'." Fortunately the discourse did not last very long,
for among all the messages and instructions sent over by the
Queen to her ambassador in Paris, prior to her own arrival, had
been the tart observation that the quality she most admired in a
sermon was brevity.

The day advanced with unclouded splendour; after lunch the
members of the household wandered out in large numbers to the
gardens, and there for an hour or so the Imperial host strolled
about with Victoria and Albert, chatting about the war—which,
with the recent news of the victory of the Tschernaya, was now
going so well for their two countries, and was approaching a
victorious conclusion—and about the future of Europe.

The Emperor, with his great tact, was quick to make his own
aims in Europe coincide with those of his guests. Leaving out
methods and details, they could all speak of the peace, prosperity
and justice that they desired. Victoria and Albert, trained to
regard themselves as the servants of humanity, found Louis
Napoleon upholding the same ideals as themselves, and just as
eager for orderly progress. To-day, with not a cloud in the sky,
how easy it was to envisage a better world, how undreamed of was
the steep descent that really lay ahead. Stretching far beyond

them, over France, over all Europe, was a blue sky above a firm earth where men had a tolerable measure of security and happiness. Truth and justice, even if seldom met with, were still unchallenged as ideals of conduct, and great humanitarian and political questions stirred the world, under a strong urge to raise civilization to new heights. The thoughts and aspirations of these princes were attuned to their happy surroundings and the general cheerfulness of the occasion; it was impossible not to have faith in a good future.

The Queen, under the spell of the Imperial charm, was far more enthusiastic as they talked than the Prince was. Fascinated by her surroundings as well as by her host, she talked eagerly about the Anglo-French alliance which she hoped would never end. After a time, as the tendency was during this visit, the Prince turned his attention to others, leaving his wife to a *tête à tête* with the Emperor. Kindly and thoughtful, he was glad for her to revel for a while in the flatteries, the rather exaggerated attentions and compliments, of which he was incapable. She was happy, and that was enough for him.

"He is so quiet, so simple, *naif*, even," the Queen wrote of their host at the end of the visit; "so pleased to be informed about things he does not know, so gentle, so full of tact, dignity and modesty, so full of respect and kind attentions towards us, never saying a word, or doing a thing, which could put me out or embarrass me. I know few people whom I have felt involuntarily more inclined to confide in and speak unreservedly to—I should not fear saying anything to him. I felt—I do not know how to express it—safe with him."

Prince Albert, on the other hand, did not feel in the least safe with him. He had sized him up at their first meeting at Boulogne last autumn and had set down his observations in a detailed memorandum. Albert had questioned and listened until he was acquainted with the whole range of Napoleonic dreams. They were rather alarming to one who regarded peaceful change as essential to progress. It was true that the Emperor also professed himself a lover of peace; discussions and conferences, he thought, could produce the highly nationalized Europe that he wished to fashion. But he was bent on frontier changes from end to end of the continent; Poland was to be restored, Italy set free, the Germanic peoples arranged in three nations, and France perhaps given better frontiers. The motives were always excellent; he wished to see to everyone's affairs and set them right; but such convictions and enthusiasms were always capable of setting Europe on fire. Particularly interesting were the Imperial wishes for Spain and Portugal; they were to be united under King Pedro of Portugal. How was this to be brought about, Albert asked, since the two countries did not like each other? Which was to dominate? Was Spain to become a province of Portugal, or Portugal of Spain? The Emperor replied that the solution was to say to Spain "I am giving you Portugal as a present," and to Portugal "I am giving you Spain." But Albert could only prognosticate trouble if any such attempt were made.

The Emperor had been, and still was, most courteous and attentive in listening to Albert and in showing appreciation of his more conservative views; he was ready to consider the opinions of others and was moderate in his expressions. But the Prince had not much faith that a dictator could remain reasonable. "The impression left upon me," he said in his memorandum, "is that naturally the Emperor would neither in home nor in foreign politics take any violent steps; but that he appears in distress for means of government, and obliged to look about for them from day to day. Having deprived the people of every active participation in the government, and having reduced them to mere passive spectators, he is bound to keep up the 'spectacle', and as at fireworks, whenever a pause takes place between the different displays, the public immediately grows impatient. . . ."

But the Queen and the Emperor strolled about in a perfect harmony of ideas, and the Queen's Ministers looked on with an amused curiosity. Lord Clarendon, Secretary of State, very much wondered what the two monarchs were plotting together. This friendship of the Queen's with Louis Napoleon, which her Ministers indeed had urged upon her, and which she had now entered into with such zeal, was a thing to astonish the world. For when all was said and done the Queen was the granddaughter of the greatest enemy of Napoleon Bonaparte. For long years and through the direst perils England led the fight for existence against the tyrant. Napoleon had carried war all over Europe, bringing untold misery to men. With his own ambitious and unscrupulous character and his horde of greedy, insolent relations, he was the scourge of the earth, and men only breathed again when they had him as a captive on St. Helena. Yet now, with many still alive who had known him, his dynasty was restored by his nephew who came, not to condemn his uncle's aggressions but to explain them away, to be his apologist and an avowed Bonapartist. "The name of Napoleon is in itself a complete programme," he said in 1849. It was as though a Queen of England should be upon amicable terms in 1985 with a member of Adolf Hitler's family, elected to power declaring that the name of Hitler was a programme in itself.

How did it come about that a second Napoleon arose to power in a world that had so execrated the first? It must have seemed in 1815 that the Empire of Napoleon would for ever be remembered as a nightmare. The answer is that a legend grew up around the Emperor's memory; there gradually developed a romantic version of Napoleon's life and character; it was the work of writers and Bonapartists and was never officially discouraged in France, but was regarded as a kind of tonic after the humiliations of a heavy defeat. Napoleon was vested by the legend with a miraculous personality which had won loyalty to the death from all who had served him. That in actual fact soldiers had cursed their lot under him and had even been known to desert in large numbers was of no account. What has a legend to do with truth? Nothing. Nor does it perish because facts are produced which contradict it. Such a legend satisfies subconscious emotions and wishes, and produces a fanatical devotion. It is a curious thing to compare the reputation of the great Napoleon, who plunged France in ruin, with that of Prince Albert who left England better than he found it. In his lifetime, Albert received only slights and indifference from the country he served with perfect integrity and self-abnegation, with a tireless devotion to all good causes and with a successful record of help given to the people. After his death the faults of this good Prince loomed large; it was mainly remembered that his speeches were dull and prosy, and that he had not had an English sense of humour. But a gift of all the virtues was made to Napoleon: a halo was placed round his head, and he became a saint who had expended his soul in "loving the people of France so well", who had sought not to plunder Europe out of a lust for conquest and the glorification of his own family, but to unite and civilize a world which had resisted him only through the blindest wickedness and folly. His gambling and adventuring, which failed more often than it succeeded, was all put down to "military genius", and the world has accorded to him a place of high and lasting historic honour not in the least deserved by one who caused little but trouble.

During his years of exile and imprisonment his nephew, Louis Napoleon, had studied and enlarged upon the legend. In 1839 he had published his book, *Napoleonic Ideas*, and it had had a large sale. When the revolution of 1848 gave him his chance to appear upon the scene he found it easy to slip into a position of power; France knew nothing about him as a man; he succeeded for nothing at all except that he shared the name of Bonaparte. How vague people could be as to what was really happening was shown by a story the new Emperor had told Prince Albert at Boulogne: he had gone with the Empress down to Biarritz, and as they travelled there the people through a large portion of southern France had acclaimed the Empress with the words " *Vive Marie-Louise*." They believed, without any realistic sense of time, that the original Bonaparte had come back to them, and they rejoiced.

Napoleon III accepted power as a man of destiny. "I believe," he said, "that from time to time men are created whom I will call providential, in whose hands the destinies of their country are placed. I believe myself to be one of those men." Later in his reign he was to make the tyrant's rôle even more clear in a life of Julius Caesar which he wrote. In the introduction to this he said: "When providence raises up such men as Caesar, Charlemagne and Napoleon, it is to trace out to peoples the path they ought to follow, to stamp a new era with the seal of their genius. . . . Woe to those who misunderstand and combat them! They do as the Jews did, they crucify their Messiah!"

Louis Napoleon was advertising not only his own dynasty, but political megalomania in general. And such exaltation of tyranny is the very breath of legends, which must always flatter the faithful: if the tyrant is a Messiah, then the followers must be something like angels or apostles. And the Napoleonic legend in the days of its fervour transformed all the old soldiers surviving from the great wars into heroic figures—miracles of loyalty and bravery. The Hotel des Invalides abounded with them: humble and simple old men who, as memory grew dim, began to remember ever more vividly the glorious past of propaganda and to grow ever more retrospectively devoted to the "General". And the country as a whole shared in their delusive memories of glory, so easily can the mind touch with magic a past that was arduous and drab in its day. But later on, after Napoleon III had failed and fallen in 1870, France had learnt its lesson and had the measure of political legends; none has been permitted to arise round the memory of the nephew. The Third Republic managed to efface his memory so effectually that to-day one can walk about Paris, upon which he left so great a stamp—that modern Paris which is largely his creation—and be unaware that he ever existed.

How little was such oblivion foreseen on this bright Sunday afternoon, as his Majesty strolled arm in arm with the Queen in the perfect gardens of St. Cloud, praised and honoured by all the world. Yesterday's copy of the *Morning Post* had said: "He is the chosen of his people. The throne on which he sits he won for himself; his sceptre is of his own fashioning; and he has this proud boast, the proudest to which a monarch can lay claim, that he is at once the founder of his own greatness and of his people's happiness. We have no misgiving of the position which such a man is destined to occupy in the estimation of posterity, for there is nothing more certain in the future than that time will do him justice. All men who, by the force of their own unaided genius have achieved transcendent eminence must expect to be traduced . . . but as surely as the duskiest rivers run themselves bright, so surely does the lapse of time restore the characters of great men to their pristine beauty and set them right with the world."

CHAPTER V

THE DEAR EMPRESS

LATE in the afternoon the Emperor took his guests for a drive through the Bois de Boulogne; and this time the Empress Eugénie was present, sitting next to the Queen in an open barouche. This was one of the very few occasions when the two ladies drove out together in public; for Eugénie did not take an active part in the fêtes of the Royal visit. "The dear Empress," Victoria wrote when the week was over, "we saw comparatively but little of, as for *really* and *certainly very* good reasons she must take great care of herself." Eugénie, in other words, was expecting a child the following March, and such care and solicitude were lavished upon her that she was hardly allowed to move.

The Emperor and Prince Albert rode on horseback one on each side of the barouche; there was a small military escort, and other carriages followed with the two children and members of the suite. The Bois de Boulogne, which they now entered from St. Cloud, had been a piece of wild, wooded country before Louis Napoleon's reign, traversed only by straight alleys and drives; but being a great admirer of the London parks he had had it laid out with ornamental gardens, serpentines and lakes in the English manner. It was a busy place on Sunday afternoons; people from the wealthier end of Paris came here to ride, drive or walk. To-day the crowds were as great as usual; everyone was out enjoying the summer warmth and the beauty of the new gardens, and wherever the Imperial carriages drove they were enthusiastically acclaimed.

With as much interest as the crowds looked at her, Victoria looked at them, dazzled by their lively foreign appearance and the sunny brilliance of the scene. The smart demi-mondaines roared up from the Champs Elysées, the postilions cracking their whips over their heads; the equally resplendent carriages of the new aristocrats of the Empire bowled round with a grand air, their footmen disdainful and impassive in the English style. Ladies in voluminous skirts rode on horseback in the company of their cavaliers, and other ladies walked or glided, among all the silk

39

and muslin folds of their wide, frilled dresses, with their husbands and children.

Against the verdant background was a fine display of fashion; skirts were veering towards the crinoline, which a few of the smartest were already wearing, although they were not yet as extravagantly wide as they were soon to become. As the Empire—and all the industrialised society of the west—grew more rich, as the people grew ever more prosperous, so dresses grew more balloon-like in size and ample in material. At the same time the silk hats of the men grew taller; it was as though the world was expressing its material wealth and progress in perpetual enlargement and opulence in fashions. In our own times, now that great wars have brought about poverty, crises and a general uncertainty about the future, the silhouettes of women are meagre, their dress is almost incredibly skimpy; and men's hats no longer rise aspiringly. But then the aspect of things was very different; there was confidence and optimism in the top hats, the billowing flounces threaded with ribbon, the heavy silk inset with bands of velvet and in the extensive use of lace.

Since Victoria had come to the throne, old London had submitted to a timely course of Saxe-Coburg culture and moral improvement. It had been thoroughly reformed and was most respectable. But compared with gay and beautiful Paris, how dull it was! Victoria, who presided over the proprieties of England, and was making herself a byword for all that was quietly virtuous, could not help responding to the vivid scene and regretting she had no place in it. She had been born with frivolous and pleasure-loving instincts, and now and then they surged up in her. She had not been quite so intensively schooled in Coburg principles as Albert had been, although in theory she had come to agree in all things with him. The poor Prince had scarcely had a chance to know what his own instincts were, so severely had he been disciplined from the beginning of his life and trained for his appointed rôle. He had come to London as a boy of twenty, fitted to improve English society, and he drove himself dutifully to the task. The pageant of the Second Empire did not appeal to him as it did to Victoria; his soul was attuned to the quiet and peaceful Germany of his boyhood, and he was beyond thinking of amusement, beyond understanding how, in a world full of trouble, dangers and urgent tasks, anyone else could pause to seek selfish enjoyment. In 1855 he was already a very tired man, and life seemed to him, as he said, a treadmill which he never left.

Victoria felt instinctively that life should be long and glorious; but Albert was rather saddened and instinctively wished to turn away from the world and all its show. "I do not cling to life," he said once to the Queen. "You do; but I set no store by it."

Victoria revelled in her holiday; although she took pleasure in the thought of coming fêtes and fine spectacles, she was also half envious of those who were rich and free enough to lead an anonymous life in this delightful Paris. There was not the same freedom for the rich in London. Freedom exists or is suppressed on varying planes. London had political freedom, while Paris was in the grip of dictatorship; but London was exclusive and undemocratic socially and was tied down with many rigid conventions. Here, while Londoners assumed Puritanical Sabbath faces, there was a lightness in the people's manner; they were enjoying Sunday afternoon, and there was an absence of restraint that appealed to Victoria; she responded to it by being very gay and cheerful herself, encouraged by the "dear Empress" at her side who talked in her animated meridional way as they drove along at a leisurely pace.

To Paris, Victoria knew, came many of her rich and idle subjects, just to be away from London society as she and Albert ruled it. In London the rich were expected to justify their existence with merit of one kind or another; but here they enjoyed a freedom that was absolute. Here they indulged in every pleasure that an artistic, gifted and obliging nation could provide for them; here they were spared all responsibility towards others and inconvenience to themselves. Such a one was the Marquis of Hertford whose "country house" in the Bois de Boulogne the Imperial cortège was now passing. This was "Bagatelle", which had been built by the Comte d'Artois in a wager with a former Prince of Wales that he could put it up within sixty days, a wager which he had won; it had been bought by the Marquis from Louis-Philippe. His other Paris house was in the Boulevard des Italiens and both were crammed with the art treasures he was collecting. The Marquis lived in perfect selfishness. He had grown very mean of late; he had always ignored and refused to help the tenants of his estates at home; now he begrudged his friends a dinner because of the expense, although, being a favoured friend of the Emperor, he did offer the Queen a cup of tea one afternoon during this week. Such terrible selfishness was deplorable, and such men usually became eccentric and half mad in the end. All the same, how very agreeable it would be to be a dissolute millionaire Marquis in Second Empire Paris for a week or two.

Past the white gates of Bagatelle, the cortège drove towards Neuilly. For Louis Napoleon and Eugénie had suggested that their guests might like to see the ruins of Louis-Philippe's favourite summer residence, the Chateau de Neuilly, which had been destroyed in the revolution of 1848.

Now they drove through the gates of the chateau, the carriages stopped and the Emperor assisted the Queen to alight. Albert had once stayed here as a boy with the King and Queen of France; now two pavilions alone remained of the building, empty and burnt out and overgrown with weeds. "Nineteen years ago," Albert wrote afterwards to his step-mother, "I was in Paris with Ernst and Papa, and I have not been there since. You may imagine what a strange impression so many changes must have produced. Neuilly, where we were then received, now lies in ruins, and the grass grows upon its site. The Duke of Orléans was then alive and unmarried; Marie and Clémentine, daughters of the house; Nemours, Aumale and Montpensier were at school; Joinville a naval cadet. All this is vanished as if before the wind, and in its stead we brought with us two children, almost fully grown."

There had been a fine library in the chateau; and the good Queen Marie-Amélie's dressing cabinet had been famous, too: here the sole ornaments had been the school prizes of her large and intelligent family, and certificates framed with branches of laurel had filled the walls. During the revolution an unruly crowd had burst into the building; there were great quantities of wine in the cellars and a terrible orgy had ensued during which some were drowned in a well in one of the cellars, and others contrived to set the house alight and perished intoxicated in the flames.

It was melancholy to reflect upon the books and treasures lost and the lives as uselessly destroyed, and the visitors turned away to look round the desolate grounds. There was a monument on the spot where a cannon ball had rolled up to the feet of Louis-Philippe, when he was still the Duke of Orléans, and where a few days later the crown of France was offered to him; there was the garden of his young grandson, the Comte de Paris, containing a botanic garden and an aviary, and there was a circular building which contained the tomb of Diane de Poitiers. But all was neglected and overgrown.

The Empress, all this time, leaned back in the carriage and studied the Queen's dress with her professional eye as the latter flitted about the shrubs and ruins, listening to Albert's reminiscences and conclusions.

In our day, almost any woman can go to Paris and feel that she looks much as everyone else does. But at that time even a foreign aristocrat could not buy clothes at home that would do her credit in Paris. The Queen of England, great and terrible though she might be, was hopelessly out of the fashion. Fashion, in fact, was a thing the Queen knew little about; and although she enjoyed new dresses upon occasion, long consultations with dressmakers and fitters seemed to her a dreadful waste of time. She was a practical woman and liked to wear her clothes out before discarding them; her admirers could applaud her good sense, but the most devoted of them could not have pretended that she had any taste; fat and short as she was, she loved to wear the rather loud Royal Stuart tartan whose wide squares accentuated her own width; and the demands of a great and ceremonial occasion, such as this present visit to Paris, she would answer with an array of rich, heavy silk and satin, lace, embroidery, feathers and diamonds, all worn with a bland indifference to considerations of line, style and harmony.

Very different was the Empress Eugénie, who was elegant to a superlative degree. It was she who set the fashions and who designed and invented most of them herself throughout her reign. As her husband dictated in politics, so she dictated fashions to a willing world. She had a great talent, a touch of unusual brilliance, for dress designing, and none at all for politics. She had the happier gift of the two. But unfortunately, in her elevated position she fancied herself as a politician, and the French have never forgiven her. She was a prejudiced woman, ambitious and reactionary, and she was largely responsible for the disastrous Mexican campaign of the 'sixties, which ended in the execution of the Emperor Maximilian. But the days of Eugénie's political influence were still undreamed of. This afternoon, as she waited in the carriage, twirling her diminutive lace sunshade, her political aspirations were only a hazy idea at the back of her mind, and she was quite content with her rôle as the world's fashion expert.

Before her reign there had been no very high standard of elegance in Europe. Frenchwomen, as always, were noted for their taste; but on the French throne there had been Queen Marie-Amélie who lent herself to all manner of trimmings, draperies and bits of false hair. She and Madame Adelaide had favoured the heavy poke bonnet because it enabled them to hide Louis-Philippe's profile from possible assassins in the street if they sat one on each side of him when driving out; and dress had been generally unbecoming in their day. But Eugénie had risen like a brilliant star, to create not only new fashions but a new taste in beauty, a new type of woman. The old type, which lingered on in England and was represented in the pages of Dickens, belonged to Europe's Romantic period and was open-mouthed, angelic and mawkish. The new type, with its predilection for blonde hair and its hard expression, is still with us. The Empress set the modern standard of highly polished perfection which is maintained to-day by Hollywood film stars and mechanically transmitted to entranced millions who follow in the measure allowed by their circumstances. To look like a film star is the dream of the present day woman of the industrial age; in 1855 everyone dreamed of looking like Eugénie.

Eugénie had a thousand moods; alternating with her flights of extravagance there came phases of extreme simplicity; no one knew better how well a severely plain dress of some quite cheap material could look if it was faultless in cut and in fitting. The great dress designers of Paris flourished in her reign, and she made the fortune of Worth. She was a fascinating creature with wavy gold hair, deep blue eyes, an oval face and the ideal features of a classical statue; her figure was perfectly proportioned, and the simplest dress or the most elaborately ornamental invention looked equally well on her. It was this way she had of seeming so elegant in anything she put on that made her such an authority. In the shop windows of European towns, in Cologne as well as Paris or Madrid, pictures of Eugénie were displayed and her fame spread about the world. But her followers seldom realised that she attained most of her effects easily, without undue expenditure. She brought in an age of great extravagance among women, but was herself less extravagant than most of the wealthy society women who sought in vain to imitate her.

The visit to the chateau was over now, and the Queen was led back to the waiting barouche by Louis Napoleon; as she approached Eugénie looked at her still more narrowly; many years later, when she was an old woman, Eugénie could still see the Queen in her mind's eye in every detail, so strong had been the impression made upon her. Victoria was still wearing the poke bonnets of Marie-Amélie's day, and was carrying a bag of such size that it accentuated her own shortness; the bag was rather startlingly embroidered, too (perhaps as a suitably topical accompaniment to a visit to France), with a large poodle. It would be interesting to record what the Queen was carrying in her large bag; but such things are among the mysteries of history. The Royal diary, perhaps, with a bottle of smelling salts and a handkerchief. Or a fan and an album for pressing flowers.

Now they drove off again, going back through the Bois de Boulogne and along the banks of the Seine to St. Cloud. Everywhere groups of people paused to acclaim them as they passed. The two ladies sitting side by side, whom the world must now regard as social equals, turned from side to side, bowing, and then talked affably with each other. The Empress's blue eyes were joyous; now she was indeed lifted to the heights; she, modest in origin, although a Spanish aristocrat, born in a narrow street of Granada and obscure enough at the beginning of her life, could now go no higher. The Empress in these golden years of her reign could never quite hide her delight. Her life was like a fairy tale, and she was jubilant.

This was the hour of triumph for herself and for the Emperor. But the Emperor never showed his real feelings. He rode now, calm and imperturbable, among his subjects who were cheering and waving so enthusiastically. Those subjects had been cold and indifferent when he married Eugénie in 1853; but now they paid homage to her, and to-day they saw that she was on equal terms with the Queen of England.

By the end of the last century the friendship of Victoria and Eugénie had become, like so much that had to do with the great Queen, a time-honoured institution which no one would have dreamed of questioning. The situation was vastly different in 1855; for Eugénie de Montijo had schemed and struggled for her position, and her marriage had created a sensation in Europe.

When Louis Napoleon had fallen in love with her he had merely envisaged her as another in his succession of mistresses. Previously his cousin, Prince Napoleon, had met the beautiful Spaniard and had had some thought of marrying her; but Louis Napoleon had discouraged him. "One loves but does not marry a Mademoiselle de Montijo," he had said at that time. The new Empire, as the Emperor well knew, needed the prestige of Royal alliances to persuade the ancient dynasties that Imperial France meant to fall in with the routine of Europe. And his Ministers were negotiating for the hand of a foreign princess while he himself was attempting to make a conquest of Eugénie de Montijo.

Eugénie, however, never left the path of conventional morality and had less intention than usual of doing so on this occasion. The correct behaviour on her part would have been to take herself away from Louis Napoleon who could not have followed her out of France. But she aspired to nothing less than the Imperial diadem.

She felt herself, in fact, preordained for this great position, for throughout her youth prophecies had haunted her foretelling such a destiny. Gypsies, priests and nuns had vied with each other in dramatic forecasts; an eagle would carry her to the heavens and then drop her, a gypsy had said; and once when, being tired of the world, she had almost decided to take religious vows, an old nun had called out to her, "Do not seek rest within our walls, my daughter. Your destiny is to adorn a throne." All the same, it was not without a determined effort on her own part that the prophecies were fulfilled. Had she let events take their course she would never have become the Empress of the French. She did not regard these signs and portents as a forecast of the inevitable but as a hint of the possible; they acted as a spur to her ambitions and led her to exert herself to the very utmost.

Far from having left Paris when the Emperor tried to seduce her, she had kept herself before him, using all her skill to charm him and increase his desire for her. The comedy was carried out with blatant publicity. Ambassadors, princes, courtiers and flunkeys watched the arts of finesse and cynicism which she displayed. They saw her provocative gaze, the display of her suggestive, easy familiarity, and then her withdrawal into icy coldness. They watched her as she sulked, they watched her agitate her Spanish fan with a thousand mannerisms. They watched her mouth open in a seductive smile, and then saw her eyes remote with indifference. Endless affectations in her dress beguiled their days; now the beauty of her figure would be freely displayed, and now tantalisingly obscured. They watched Louis Napoleon's efforts to bring about her downfall, and they watched the ease with which she evaded his ruses and ensnared him ever more deeply in his own desire. And in the end they saw Eugénie win her contest. Louis Napoleon, just the opposite of the philo-sophic Prince Albert who was now his guest, was uncommonly self-indulgent; he had never tried to restrain his instincts where women were concerned, and by the time Eugénie appeared in his life he was like a drunkard whose cravings were irresistible. Eugénie had made it clear that she would marry him but not on any account become his mistress; therefore, since there was no other way, she must become the Empress of the French. The first beautiful woman to hold herself aloof from the Emperor's wiles, his sarcastic courtiers said, was inevitably given the crown. Such was his reputation, and such was the reputation of the countless women ever falling over each other in the scramble to attract his notice.

Thus Eugénie had conquered the world. But her methods had not inspired respect and confidence; to all but the man at whom they were directed they had looked decidedly brazen. Europe had been amused and shocked, and *Punch* had suggested that the Emperor might as well marry Lola Montez while he was at it.

There were few well-wishers of the new Empire who thought her a suitable wife for the ruler of the country, for all the modesty and dignity she was at pains to assume when once her object was attained. Above all, there were many women who ground their teeth with rage over an injustice which they could hardly formulate in words. They too might have married the Emperor, for they had attracted him before she came and they were as good or better than she was. Although Mademoiselle de Montijo was a Spanish grandee, and inordinately proud of her blue blood, it had taken some painstaking and rather suspect heraldic researching to produce the titles of nobility used at the marriage. As much could have been done for any one of them. But they had not presumed to expect the crown which they felt was rightly destined for a Royal princess. They had given way to the fascinating monarch's entreaties and declarations of love, to be tossed aside and forgotten soon enough, whereas Eugénie had resisted him and at the same time had redoubled her efforts to enflame his desires. She had displayed the coldest calculation to drive a hard bargain. Was the earth to be given to a woman just for this? It was, they found; and from now on, if they wished to continue enjoying the pleasures and privileges of high society, they must bend themselves double before the successful woman, paying everlasting homage to the triumph of her ambitions.

Now the final touch was put to those ambitions. Owing to the alliance with England and the interchange of Royal visits, Eugénie was formally introduced into the illustrious circle of European Sovereigns. There were even those who said that the Crimean War had been contrived with the object of improving Eugénie's social position; this seems unlikely (although Napoleon may have been less anxious to avoid the war than his acts and deeds suggested, for deception was a natural art in the Bonaparte family); but it is probably true that on this brilliant afternoon, as he cantered home in the company of Prince Albert and their two wives, the Emperor would not have changed the history of the past two years. The war, which was inflicting untold misery upon multitudes of obscure men, had immeasurably strengthened the Bonaparte dynasty. The Emperor was kindly and humane; but it takes someone further above the average than he was to balance the troubles of unknown men against his own interest. This afternoon he could only rejoice that events had brought about the happy friendship with the Queen of England, and that the people of Paris should see Victoria's cordial manner with Eugénie.

There could be no doubt about Victoria's friendliness. Everyone knew that she did not wear any fixed, conventional smile of royalty. Although so well schooled in manner and deportment, she was at the same time all sincerity, and when she looked pleased it meant that she was pleased. With Eugénie she had been delighted from the moment when she first set eyes on her, last April at Windsor. The Empress was twenty-nine years old, an experienced woman whose life had been free and spectacular; often before her marriage (when she was "in the world" as she liked to put it—as though joining the ranks of royalty had been rather like entering some holy order) she was to be seen galloping through the streets of Madrid on a magnificent horse, smoking as she went; she was a devotee of the bull fight and would be conspicuous in her striking clothes, sometimes appearing like an Italian lady of the Renaissance with flowers and pearls entwined in her thick and gleaming fair hair, and always a centre of attention. She had travelled from country to country in her youth, getting to know a host of famous people as she did so; her sister had married the Duke of Alba, her mother had been given a high position at the Spanish court. But travelling had been their passion, and wherever they went Eugénie had been conspicuous for her originality in dress, her bold and eccentric ways and her sporting prowess. Even at Windsor such a woman is hardly likely to have felt abashed, and yet she appeared there as a shy, nervous and very delicate lady of excessive modesty. No doubt anyone really shy and retiring would have been too frightened to appear shy at Windsor and would have made prodigious efforts to seem at ease; but however that may be, the Queen was quite delighted and touched by the dear Empress's unfailing nervousness. The Empress was gentle, graceful, modest and retiring in the Queen's diary; here and in her letters Victoria could mention her only to praise her sweetness and her diffidence.

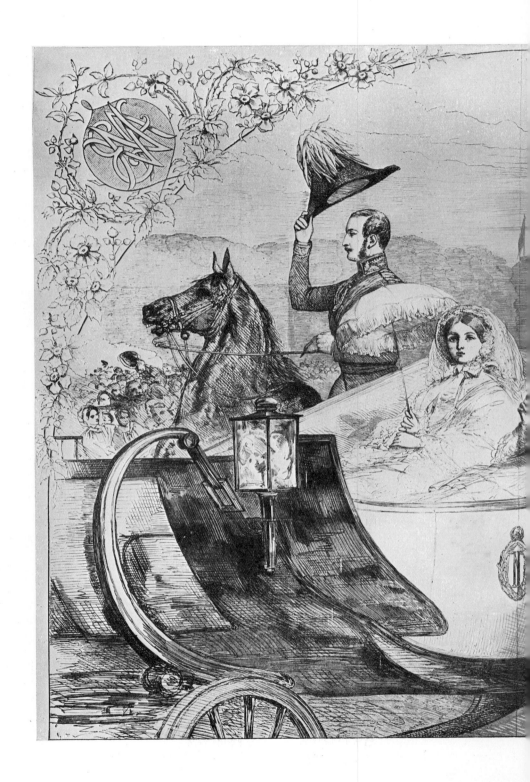

Between pages 48 *and* 49]

SUNDAY AFTERNOON. VICTORIA AND EUGÉNIE, ESCORTED BY PRINCE ALBERT AND
NAPOLEON III, DRIVING TO THE BOIS DE BOULOGNE.

Yet the Queen had heard all about her at the time of the Emperor's marriage, and she had written to Augusta, Crown Princess of Prussia, in 1853:

"*Le grand évènement du jour* is the incredible marriage of the Emperor Nap. In France it is being very badly received. The future bride is beautiful, clever, very coquette, passionate and wild. What do they say about it in Germany?"

But she had written again to Augusta after Eugénie's visit to Windsor and had said:

"The Empress is a very charming, lovable creature, also extremely tactful, yet natural in her manner. She is not actually beautiful, but very pretty, with a charming profile and figure and with a sweetness and friendliness that win all hearts. She was deeply touched by my affection and care for her. She is, alas, not at all strong."

Even Albert came ever so slightly under her spell, for Victoria said, speaking of Eugénie in her diary:

"Altogether I am delighted to see how much Albert likes and admires her, as it is so seldom I see him do so with any woman."

They were both just a little taken in, particularly with regard to her physique. Victoria told everyone how poor her health was and how careful she needed to be; but the Empress had great powers of resistance; she was a fine walker and climber and a most hardened traveller. It was the Emperor who was in bad health, though he strove to hide the fact; Eugénie's own rude health led her to be less sympathetic with him than she should have been, and to drive him off in 1870 at the head of his troops when he was only fit to be in bed. She herself died in 1920, having lived for the best part of a century, for she was born in 1826. But no doubt when at Windsor in 1855 she pleaded illness to avoid coming down to Victoria's early breakfasts, taken by draughty windows opened to let in the cool air and the strains of bagpipes.

CHAPTER VI

THE CRIMEAN WAR

GENERAL CANROBERT, still feeling far from well, had managed to ride out to St. Cloud for the evening. The war, although ordinary civilians could live their lives without giving it a thought, was never long absent from the minds of Victoria and Albert, and they were above all things anxious to talk to the man who, until recently, had commanded the French army, and who had only just arrived home from the Crimea.

It was late afternoon; the sun was still blazing down on to the dry and overheated earth and courtiers wandered in and out of the palace, uncertain where the temperature was more bearable. The General was greeted by various friends and he strolled about the terraces with them to await the return of the Imperial carriages. Here also he caught sight of some of his enemies; every honest man had enemies at this court of opportunists, where the majority sought to discredit virtues which might show up their own vices to disadvantage. Only a month or two ago the General, who was the most loyal and honest of men, had attempted to commit suicide by exposing himself to the view of Russian sharp-shooters. He had been so persistently slandered in Paris that the Emperor had been turned against him and had written an abusive letter to him. The letter, finally, had not been sent; but Canrobert had heard about it and, with that high-spirited, keen sensibility which exists in the French army, had forthwith decided to make an end of his life. But he was happily prevented from carrying out his intention by some of his subordinates who dragged him forcibly to safety; and after this outburst of despair the mood passed. He resigned his post to Pelissier and remained to lead a division until he was recalled to France.

Even before he came to write this unjust letter the Emperor had been making Canrobert's life a burden to him. Louis Napoleon's curious methods are well shown in his handling of the Crimean War. Last autumn at Boulogne Prince Albert had noted his eagerness in perusing secret correspondence from his agents, and his disinclination to trouble himself with serious documents

50

or even the daily newspapers. The Emperor was never happy unless he was scheming, and he spied even upon his own army. His conduct was the opposite of the Prince's. The latter in the course of the war penned no less than fifty volumes of memoranda, and did not fail to read a single dispatch. With his vast knowledge and common sense he discussed the campaign openly with Ministers and made suggestions that were efficient and worth attending to. But the Emperor could not bring himself to act openly.

It was of vital consequence to the Emperor that the Crimean campaign should succeed. It was France's first serious affray at arms since the great days of his illustrious uncle, and he counted on its victories to atone for the memory of Waterloo, the greatest defeat of French history. He knew, too, that his own dynasty was not yet so well established that he could afford to lose the war, and he had become fidgety and anxious over the long, drawn-out siege of Sebastopol which had begun last autumn. At first he had satisfied his desire to be active by a host of military inventions and experiments. It was a part of his great inconsistency of character that, although the sight of human suffering plunged him into real distress, he could yet lend himself with enjoyment to the hateful occupation of devising weapons of destruction. A carbine that he had invented was in use in the Crimea, and throughout the war he was carrying out experiments to perfect a new and unpleasant weapon, the rocket, which could already rise to twenty thousand feet. But as time went on he felt a desire to exercise a more strategical influence on the course of events; and he began to send out agents of his own to spy on the Crimean generals and collect information of all kinds. These agents and correspondents went out under varying instructions, and in ignorance of each other's missions, and the information they gathered was often of a contradictory nature.

The Emperor next decided that he must repair to the Crimea and lead the French and English armies to victory in person. Cries of horror went up from the English government: how could Lord Raglan and his colleagues, so many of whom had served under Wellington, be expected to take commands from Napoleon's heir? The alliance was tricky enough without that. But these cries, though translated into the most judicious of diplomatic terms, had no effect. All was fully prepared for the departure of the rather burlesque Bonaparte in search of a revival of glory. A couple of thrones covered with scarlet velvet and gilt tassels and fringe were set up in a palace at Constantinople, whither the Empress was to accompany him, and trainloads of *pâté de foie gras*, preserved woodcock, fine wines and liqueurs, assassins and would-be Dubarrys stood ready to leave the stations of Paris. But at the last moment Napoleon was forced to change his mind; there was no one in his entourage sufficiently trustworthy to hold the reins of government at home during his absence. Friends and relations were all equally ready to stab him in the back.

At this stage the Emperor consoled himself with the electric telegraph. This wonderful new invention gave him tremendous pleasure; since the spring a cable had connected his rooms in the Palace of the Tuileries with the army headquarters in the field. He now proceeded to madden Canrobert with a flow of instructions. The English and French generals planned their actions together, so that it was quite unreasonable on the Emperor's part to send out orders to Canrobert which had no bearing on the plan that he was following with Raglan. Louis Napoleon could exercise no authority over Raglan, and he contented himself by referring to him as an old woman in his own intimate circle, although he praised him inordinately in public; but he was determined to keep his own Commander-in-Chief under strict surveillance. The unhappy General was deluged with commands from the Palace of the Tuileries. These commands were suggested to the Emperor by his agents; in particular he had sent out a favourite aide-de-camp to spy out the land, decide upon a plan of action and submit it to his Sovereign who would then impose it upon General Canrobert. The Commander-in-Chief was thus in the absurd position of being directed by an officer who was without command.

Canrobert was constantly finding himself forced to back out of engagements solemnly undertaken with the English. For although he was an excellent general he lacked the Nelson touch: he had not the courage to disobey the Emperor's orders. Inevitably he lost the confidence of the English generals for having let them down; but he consoled himself by imagining that the Emperor whom he served so devotedly must understand the embarrassing position he was in and must be grateful to him for his obedience. But it was at this point that he learnt of the Emperor's anger against him and tried to commit suicide. Pelissier, his successor, was a doughty man who found it easy to be ruthless; he soon put the Emperor's aides-de-camp in their place, and he had a large waste-paper basket for the Imperial telegrams. He got on with the war in his own way, and the war was now being won; after frantic but wasted efforts to get him to attend to the telegrams, the Emperor had recently given up, and had devoted himself instead to decorating the Queen's apartments at St. Cloud and to planning festivals.

In spite of the underhand treatment that had driven him to despair, Canrobert was ready now to pay court to Louis Napoleon. The very weakness that had forced him to obey the Emperor against all reason now led him to forgive him. The Emperor had greeted him effusively on Friday; whatever he might say behind a man's back or write of him, to his face he could seldom be anything but genial and kind; it was part of his treacherous make-up, or else part of a dual personality: he was the kindliest and most generous of men, and yet he had the hard, unscrupulous side to his character that drove him to seize power violently, to scheme and to mislead others. Faced by the monarch's affability, Canrobert had not steeled himself to remember his injustice. Perhaps he was not sorry that his enemies should see that he still enjoyed the Emperor's friendship in spite of their active malevolence.

Now there was a stir among the courtiers; the return of the Sovereigns had been announced and everyone strolled to the edge of the terrace to watch the carriages driving up. General Canrobert was most interested to see Queen Victoria; during many long inactive hours in the Crimea he had listened to his English colleagues while they talked of their country, its system of government and its Sovereign; now the great Queen was stepping from the carriage, and fascinated he watched her.

"I can still see her," he wrote as a very old man at the end of the century. "In spite of the great heat, she had on a massive bonnet of white silk with streamers behind and a tuft of marabout feathers on top. Her face struck me as being amiable. Her dress was white and flounced; but she had a mantle and a sunshade of crude green which did not seem to me to go with the rest of her costume. When she put her foot on the steps she lifted her skirt, which was very short (in the English fashion, I was told) and I saw she had on small slippers tied with black ribbons which were crossed round her ankles. My attention was chiefly attracted by a voluminous object which she carried on her arm: it was an enormous reticule—like those of our grandmothers—made of white satin or silk, on which was embroidered a fat poodle in gold. The Queen seemed very small to me; but of a most amiable appearance; above all, in spite of the shocking toilette, I was struck by her dignified air."

The Sovereigns went straight to their apartments, and Canrobert continued to talk to those about him. In particular he questioned the ladies and officers of the household who were in waiting on the Queen during her visit. They told him about the fêtes arranged for the coming week, the chief of which was to be a ball next Saturday at Versailles, the first to be held there since the days of the *ancien régime*. They described the decorations of the Queen's apartments in glowing terms, saying how much of his own time the Emperor had given to the preparations, and they gave details of the pictures and tapestry that had been brought to the rooms, the glorious heavy silk that covered the walls of bathrooms and boudoirs, and the splendid furniture that had belonged to the princes of the last century and was now assembled for the visitors' use. Having been much with the Queen they could tell him of her reactions to her reception; she was really delighted with the beautiful suite of rooms prepared for her, they said, and with all the attentions she was receiving; the beauty of St. Cloud and of what she had seen of Paris had astonished her. But what pleased her most of all was to be with Louis Napoleon who had won her heart last April when he went to England. "The Emperor's unaffected conversation," Canrobert was told, as he records in his memoirs, "his pleasing voice, his little attentions, his absence of hauteur, his simplicity, and then his goodness of heart which shone through every act, in all his words and in his expression—all these filled the Queen with enthusiasm; she had felt herself attracted, then conquered, and now saw in him a hero of romance, a fairy prince."

It was now dinner-time and the courtiers stood waiting in a large salon; the Emperor and Empress came in with their Royal guests, and everyone bowed low. The Queen went straight to Canrobert. "You are General Canrobert?" she asked. "Yes, madam," he replied. "I am glad to see you," said the Queen; "I have heard so much about you that you are already an old acquaintance of mine." "Well, madam, I am almost one of your Majesty's subjects," said the General, "because I belong to the Fishmongers' Company of London. These worthy merchants made me a member after Inkermann." The Queen laughed and said that she wanted to hear all about the war, and had asked the Emperor to put him beside her at dinner. Prince Albert

Salon in the Apartments of the Queen.

[*Face page* 54

now came up and joined in their conversation until dinner was announced.

Sitting beside the Queen, Canrobert was able to study her more closely. She had changed into a white evening dress, cut very low, and, he says, "she wore geranium flowers placed here, there, and everywhere. She had plump hands with rings on every finger, and even on her thumbs; one of these contained a ruby of prodigious size and of a superb blood-red. She found it difficult to use her knife and fork with her hands thus laden like reliquaries, and even more difficult to take off and put on her gloves. On her head was a diamond aigrette, pushed well back; and she wore her hair in long loops which fell over her ears. Her eyes were beautiful; they were straightforward and intelligent, and she had a sweet expression which filled one with confidence. She had a good complexion; but her mouth rather spoilt her face which was otherwise pretty."

As they talked together the General was struck by Victoria's air of greatness; he felt an almost indescribable aura about her that isolated her from the common run of men, and she seemed to him worthy to rule over her millions of subjects. She spoke his language as well as he did himself, and he found her extremely well informed on world affairs as well as humane and intelligent in her judgments.

The Queen led the talk to the Crimea and they had a good discussion about it throughout the leisurely dinner. Canrobert began by complimenting her upon the courage of her soldiers and telling her of his friendship for those English officers with whom he had come in contact. This was not mere flattery, for the French officers had liked their English colleagues to a surprising degree, considering England and France had fought each other in well-matched contests throughout the centuries and that the present alliance was too recent and unprecedented to seem quite credible. But the courtesy of the eighteenth century still lingered on at this time, and good manners easily bridge misunderstandings.

Without this tradition of politeness on both sides the situation might often have been impossible. When the war began, the English looked back to their last war, which had been against France and had ended about forty years ago; Wellington was dead; but those of his staff who still lived were now brought out of retirement and put in command. They came out to the Crimea, to the surprise of the French officers, in the uniforms of half a century ago, with shirt collars as high as their ears and voluminous cravats; clean-shaven, and with their silver hair dressed *à la Chateaubriand*, they were reminiscent of the Marshals of the First Empire against whom they had fought, and their conversation constantly went back to that period. Now that they found themselves in uniform again and heard the roar of cannon, they seemed to be back in their youth and to be fighting the Peninsular War against Bonaparte. As likely as not, when referring to the enemy at a conference with his allies, Lord Raglan, the Commander-in-Chief, would speak of "the French". But he was quick to ridicule himself for his mistakes and to follow them up with graceful compliments; and the French, with their sense of humour, took such things in good part.

"*Les généraux anglais sont tous des gentlemen,*" said Canrobert to Victoria. He told her much about the last days of Lord Raglan, who had died barely two months ago, and then he talked of various personal friends he had made, among them Sir George Brown and Sir Colin Campbell. With Sir George Brown he had made an immediate friendship; the English General was seventy years old, and liked to talk to him about Paris as it was during the allied occupation. He had been there in 1818, which had been Canrobert's first year in Paris as a child of eight. Sir George had been wounded at Inkermann last autumn and had given his sword to Canrobert who was to keep it as a valued possession all his life.

"Sir George Brown," Canrobert now said to the Queen, "has told me about your Majesty's interest in her troops. He told me, too, that he was present while your Majesty and Prince Albert reviewed the troops at Windsor on the occasion of the Royal betrothal."

"I remember that day very well," said Victoria. "It was terribly cold, and the wind drove the snow into our faces. I still rode on my old horse, Leopold. I had put on my military costume, with my Windsor toque, an enormous cap with a no less enormous peak. I had pulled it right down on to my head to keep me warm. It was scarcely elegant. And Albert had wrapped me in his overcoat; but I was afraid he would catch cold. He was still wearing his Saxon uniform; he was in full dress; the uniform was all in green, and he had high boots. How handsome he looked! But this will show you what he was like at that time." And Victoria showed the General the Prince's miniature on a bracelet, and added, "This never leaves me."

The Queen asked many questions about the war and particularly about the trials of the soldiers; they spoke of the difficulties of the campaign, of the climate, and all the blunders and faults that had so greatly upset the English public at home. While he satisfied Victoria's curiosity with words suited to courtly ears, many dark scenes hovered at the back of the General's mind. He spoke of the terrible epidemics, of the lost hosts of brave and patient men whom the doctors could have saved had their urgent requests for medical supplies not been ignored: for this was common knowledge; but to speak the whole truth would have spoilt the Queen's appetite and his own reputation as a man of the world. These dark, suppressed scenes remained as the sombre background to the polite and brilliant present; they showed men with cholera thrown together in the crudest shelters with re-signation and silent despair on their emaciated faces, the living contaminated by the dead, the dead buried secretly at night so that the extent of the havoc could be hidden. They showed ghastly summer days when the temperature rose to a hundred and thirty degrees, when stricken men were rigid and cadaverous as corpses and, in the confusion and haste of those who remained upright amid the general desolation, were often thrown alive and conscious, together with the dead, into the hurriedly made pits. And they showed a bitter winter where men who survived the heat, the insects and the disease of the summer were forced to endure a cold no less frightful, to live in soaking garments, to exchange swamps only for ice. It was not a horror of deadly weapons that haunted the General, although he had been wounded in the arm; it was a horror of heat and flies, cold and frostbite. The cold had been as ugly as the heat, and in the end had dragged men down in demoralising, frozen chains, lower and lower until they were half as monstrous as itself, until they were goaded into tearing the very corpses from the ground to rob their livid members of the damp and rotting clothes they wore.

Another scene, not terrible but very strange, he was to remember all his life. Near the French encampment was an ancient mon-astery; it resembled a Florentine building of the Renaissance and was adorned with Byzantine mural paintings. Through the vine leaves now covering the walls archaic figures still showed, with elongated eyes, and stiff clothes symmetrically pleated. All round the monastery were terraced gardens and dense woods, and beyond was the sea. The Russian monks had asked for Canrobert's protection, which had been given. Here went the soldiers for a change from military scenes, and here the English found a piece of ground for cricket. In an isolated corner of the garden was a hut and in it there lived a hermit in solitude. For more than forty years he had been there, silent and lost in thought; all day long he sat in meditation, gazing across a sea that was sometimes calm and heavy under a massive sun, sometimes dark and turbulent under a freezing sky. There he remained unmoved throughout the war, seeking for mastery over himself while rulers fought for material power and the mastery of others. The General, with death all around him, had liked to speculate within himself as to who this man might be who was searching for the secret of life. He never discovered the answer to his questions, however.

But here was the glitter of Caesar's table: the gold plate, the red wine in sparkling glasses, the lighted candles and the hot-house flowers—and he was telling the Queen about the Battle of Balaclava, the most picturesque action of the war. It took place on one of the loveliest days of autumn, he told her, and the sun was mild; the landscape was vast and splendid and the uniforms of the soldiers filled it with brilliant colour. The distant sea was a deep blue, the violet summits of the mountains were lost in a hazy sky, a lake splashing in a light breeze showed a thousand gold reflections as bright as the polished helmets of the English Guards. The Russians—Cossacks, Uhlans, Dragoons and Hussars—were moving about at one side of the field and the allies at the other. The Scots Greys in scarlet, with their enormous white kid gloves, were like young giants on horseback. The Inniskillings and Dragoon Guards formed another scarlet line, and sent out dazzling flashes from their highly polished head-dress. And the chief aesthetic contribution of the Russians was a regiment clad in sky-blue with silver ornaments. The Highlanders marched to and fro to the hypnotic strains of their pipes, inspiring all and sundry, the enemy included, to martial courage; and all around stood a host of interested spectators, for the ground rose so that one could watch in perfect calm and safety: the combatants would naturally follow the rules of the game and not let their shots stray among the non-combatants. It was half dress-display, and half circus; and soon the spectators watched the Russian Cavalry advance in two groups. One of these groups was soon put to rout by the Highlanders, while the onlookers cheered as at a cricket match.

But the main group of attacking Russians swept on, and now the English Heavy Cavalry Brigade charged at them. And this, Canrobert said, was more like some vision of an antique legend than like reality. Swords flashed, and the brilliant colours of the uniforms merged together; then the Russian Cavalry turned and fled with the English in pursuit. The rest watched the coloured groups trotting off elegantly among the winding valleys of the landscape, now cut off from view by a hill, and now coming into sight again further off and raising clouds of dust. And then, when the Russians had gone a certain distance and were evidently not intending to return to the field, the English wheeled round in beautiful formation and cantered back to take up their original places.

There was a general movement all over the field; columns of different regiments moved about, the picturesque *Chasseurs d'Afrique* came on the scene. Horses whose riders had fallen in the charge were galloping terrified to and fro; a few puffs of smoke appeared here and there and cannon balls occasionally rolled along the ground, like croquet balls, ready to injure or destroy the unwary who happened to be in their path and neglected to jump aside. But the scene gradually calmed down, and the opinion spread about that the battle was now over. Everyone relaxed and stood about, talking; the journalists and artists were in groups, General Bosquet was having a long discussion with Layard, the archaeologist who had recently obtained the great Assyrian sculptures for the British Museum, and Canrobert talked to Lord Raglan. Only the latter remained uneasy, as he watched the Russians removing a few cannons which they had forced the Turks to abandon earlier in the morning; and it was now that he sent out the famous note to Lord Lucan, ordering the charge of the Light Cavalry Brigade.

Now the astonished spectators saw the Light Cavalry line up to charge a semi-circle of Russian guns. Ten paces before them was Lord Cardigan, upright and solitary on a splendid horse, a spectacular figure in the dress of the Hussars; he led the brigade off at a trot and then changed over to a gallop. They rode straight at the mouths of the Russian guns which now opened fire; no one swerved out of formation; swords flashed in the air and puffs of smoke emerged from a row of polished, copper cannons. On they rode, with flawless courage, to dash themselves to pieces against the indifference of artillery. The ancient traditions seemed to be meeting the new age and demonstrating that the days of tournaments were over. They were inevitably mown down; but still a remnant rode on in order. Those who survived owed their lives to the French who hurried in to cover their retreat. It was mad and useless, but many were moved to enthusiasm by the courage and calm obedience of the brigade, and a French colonel, who was also a thoughtful scholar, had dashed in eagerly to join the charge out of a sympathy for men ordered to their death.

The Queen listened enthralled; she loved to hear about soldiers and had developed a real passion for uniforms since the war began. Her enthusiasms on this score were sometimes just a little irritating to her ladies-in-waiting. Some of these ladies had husbands out in the Crimea, where so many men were perishing, and felt impatient with her sentimentality; she realised so little, they thought, what it all meant. For she had complained terribly last autumn when Albert had left her for four days to visit the Emperor at Boulogne. They had only been parted once before in all their married life together, and that had been in 1844 when the Prince went over to Coburg after his father's death. The Queen had thought herself very badly done by over this second short parting, and had expected a sympathy she would not have spent on her ladies though their hearts were weighed down with constant anxiety and they had been parted from their husbands for many months; they felt she should have been more grateful for her immunity from their worries. But the Queen was not at all consistent; she would wave to the departing troops with tears in her eyes; but instead of being thankful that Albert was not torn from her to defend the country far from home she was distraught when he left her for four nights to go to Boulogne; she spoke of being forlorn and melancholy, and of being in need of comfort and support. But she was in the habit of considering herself as being in a category apart; what happened to her was not to be judged from quite the same standpoint as if it had happened to someone else: hence the awful, the unutterable catastrophe that was made out of the Prince's death when it came, although she firmly believed in his survival in a spiritual world. She had known and accepted the fact that everyone must die, and had cheerfully brought children into the world to live a life on these terms; yet when Albert died hers was a bereavement such as no one else in her household could conceivably have given way to. She would not have put up with it.

All the same, she very firmly believed in the sincerity of her own feelings for the troops. "Noble fellows!" she had said a month or two ago when she had been distributing medals to them. "I own I feel as if they were *my own children;* my heart beats for *them* as for my *nearest and dearest.*" And these men, loyal and brave in the simplicity of their hearts, were more than satisfied with their

Queen whose picture they so often took out with them in their pockets to the Crimea. They knew the war was no fault of hers, and would have felt rewarded for what they were enduring at the moment had they known that Victoria, during her gay Parisian holiday, was constantly speaking of them and that they were never far from her thoughts.

When the dinner ended the Emperor led the Queen from the room, followed by Prince Albert with the Empress and by all the courtiers; they went to one of the salons and sat down to listen to a concert of sacred music given by the artistes of the Conservatoire. Prince Albert had been asked to arrange the programme in advance.

An unusual Sunday evening calm now settled down upon the frivolous Imperial court. The Empress, feeling dreadfully bored, assumed a most interested and pleased expression; Louis Napoleon, to whom all music was a mere noise, sat impassive; the courtiers stifled their yawns, the Queen dreamed of the soldiers and the heroic events of which her mind was full. Only Prince Albert sat with peace and radiance in his soul, transported for an hour to the world of music where he felt at home.

CHAPTER VII

THE FINE ARTS

"To-morrow the Parisian campaign begins," Prince Albert wrote on Sunday, and when Monday morning arrived both hosts and guests steeled themselves to face the day with whatever it might bring. For now the Queen was to spend the day in Paris, and as well as visiting fashionable districts was to take an extensive drive round working class quarters. Would the welcome of Saturday be maintained? It was possible to feel uncertainty, for Anglophobia had been aroused easily in France since Waterloo, and had been rife even in the earlier months of the year when there had been a suspicion that France was fighting in the Crimea for English interests. Who could really tell how things would go, and how the masses would respond to this visible sign of the Entente Cordiale?

But it was clear from the rising of the sun on this happy day that all would be well. By seven o'clock crowds were pouring out of Paris towards St. Cloud in order to watch the procession leave the palace and drive down to the exhibition; people went by train, by omnibus, and by boat along the river; others were walking on foot up the Champs Elysées to line the route. In other districts the workmen and their families were up and in their best clothes, willingly sacrificing a day's wages to do honour to the Queen of England.

There was an enthusiasm that was rare in Paris, even in those far off days before a series of disasters had destroyed the buoyancy of French hope and faith in others. It seemed that all past misunderstandings were for ever cleared up now that the English Queen had broken the ice of centuries by coming to Paris; great was the joy, as great as it would be to-day if suddenly there was perfect accord among the great powers and a certainty that they would henceforth work together for the prosperity of their peoples.

The liveliest scene of all was in the Champs Elysées which was thronged, in the words of the *Morning Post*, with "elegantly dressed ladies and gentlemen". All the way down the Imperial Guard and the Infantry were stationed, spread out, however, in such a way that they would not interfere with the view of the crowds or their free circulation. Beneath the shady trees, behind the troops and the promenading crowds, the toy stalls and the cake and lemonade stalls were already opened, and vividly painted roundabouts and aerial ships were waiting to attract the children. A host of itinerant traders had arrived on the scene, too, and were crying their wares at an early hour.

The guests at St. Cloud were also up betimes. "A lovely morning," wrote Victoria in her diary—"pleasant air with a bright sun, and the delicious fountains playing. Further satisfactory accounts from the Crimea. . . The Emperor came to fetch us to breakfast as before. The coffee quite excellent, and all the cooking very plain and very good. . . At a quarter before ten we started for Paris with all our suite. The Emperor has pretty barouches, rather smaller than ours; the livery dark green, black and gold, with red and gold waistcoats."

The Queen was to pay a visit this morning to the fine art section of the exhibition; this was in the Avenue Montagne (which was still often called by its old name of Allée des Veuves), just off the Champs Elysées. The cortège of nine carriages, each drawn by four horses, was escorted by outriders and a guard of Cuirassiers. It drove through the Bois de Boulogne, along the lovely Avenue de l'Impératrice, still unfinished and in the hands, not of builders but of gardeners (this is now called the Avenue Foch), and then through Napoleon's Arc de Triomphe and down the Champs Elysées. Victoria now saw the measure of the French people's welcome; all along the route there were friendly, smiling faces; the crowds acclaimed her joyously and flowers were cast before her in the road. The drive was a happy triumph.

The carriages turned into the Avenue Montagne and drew up before the Palais des Beaux Arts. The scene was most lively here as great crowds had gathered near the entrance, and the Queen received a tremendous ovation when the Emperor assisted her from the carriage. The hemicycle before the building was ablaze with flowers, and all round stood poles ornamented with escutcheons, flags and oriflammes of the French and English colours. Victoria, holding Louis Napoleon's arm, and followed by her husband, the two children and their suite, stepped forward towards the door. She wore a dress of Royal Stuart tartan and a white mantle, or so says the *Morning Post*. The *Illustrated Times*, on the other hand, says; "The Queen was attired in a grey silk dress, a simple white bonnet, and wore a mantle of the same colour, *doublé de rose*." The *Morning Post* version seems more suited to the general vigour of the scene: the canopy at the entrance was of scarlet velvet, trimmed with "massive gold bullion", and was surrounded by gilt decorations in the form of great Royal and Imperial crowns. On all sides were mounted Guards in fine uniform; and military bands, their instruments flashing in the sunlight, played the English national anthem. Why should the Queen, the centre of all this splendour, be dressed in grey? The gentlemen, however, were in morning dress, and Vicky, the Princess Royal, wore a simple dress of green silk beneath a white lace mantle.

Victoria was surprised and dazzled by the applause of the crowds and by the brilliance of the scene. She walked radiant and smiling towards Prince Napoleon who, as president of the exhibition, waited at the door to receive her. Stimulated by the gallantry of her very attentive host, she seemed to have recaptured the gaiety of youth; her staid maturity had dropped from her and she was like a girl, a decidedly plump but pretty and light-hearted girl. Finding herself the object of Napoleon's admiration she became in response more lively and interesting than usual; this week in Paris brought out all that she had of latent charm; in a way she seemed to be metamorphosed by the situation; for there were those who met her at this time and called her witty. Wit is a quality for which the good, downright Queen is *not* famous; but all manner of unsuspected qualities can be brought to light on rare occasions under a very propitious stimulus. Such a stimulus the Queen now had; and away from the responsibilities of her own court, she could give herself up to it in the bracing air of Paris. "We never beheld," says one of the newspaper reporters who watched her walking into the building, "a countenance in which joy and contentment were more evidently depicted." As for the wily Emperor, who was buying decisive powers in Europe by the exercise of his charms, his eyes were veiled, as usual, and betrayed no gleam of triumph; he was a slightly ridiculous figure from the standpoint of the camera, with his short legs and awkward bulk, his waxed moustaches and his very immaculate black suit; yet his courtly bearing and faultless manners dominated his appearance for those who actually saw him.

Prince Napoleon was bowing, and the commissioners behind him bowed low. There was a surging of the crowds towards the entrance, and the police struggled to hold them back. "One rather large gentleman," says the *Illustrated Times*, "was pushed off an iron chair on to which he had climbed. '*Vive l'Empereur!*'

Between pages 64 *and* 65]

THE QUEEN IN THE RECEPTION ROOM AT THE EXHIBITION.

he cried as he fell, and he disappeared with a fashionable oath."
Continued acclamations followed the Queen as she was led into a
salon prepared for her reception.

Here she sat down for a time, and various members of the
Commission were introduced to her. A bust of her Majesty stood
prominently on a pedestal in the centre of the room, and the
walls were covered with modern works of art. Horace Vernet,
Ingres, Baron Rothschild, Le Play and Arles Dufour were conspicuous among the French commissioners; Germans, too, in
view of Prince Albert's presence, were well to the fore; and among
the Englishmen Victoria and Albert found many old acquaint-
ances formed in the course of preparing the Crystal Palace
exhibition. Here again was the intrepid Henry Cole who had
worked untiringly with Prince Albert for the success of that
exhibition, and here was his friend Digby Wyatt. They were
both taking an important part in the English section of the Paris
exhibition.

While Prince Napoleon was presenting the commissioners
to the Queen, Prince Albert engaged Henry Cole in conversation; this was always an agreeable and profitable occupation
since Henry Cole was as bent upon improving people's minds
as was the Prince himself, and was a fertile source of inspirations.
"I told his Royal Highness," says Cole, writing of the occasion,
" the outlines of my exhibition plan." With the substantial
profits made by the Crystal Palace exhibition, thirty acres of
land had been bought at South Kensington, and Cole, under
Albert's directions, was thinking out a vast scheme for turning
it into a magnificent centre of scientific and artistic education.
But difficulties were always arising, and the Prince talked of the
attempt that the Treasury was making to defeat a proposed grant
of fifteen thousand pounds for Kensington, and of how he would
need to use all his influence to persuade the Chancellor of the
Exchequer that it was a sound policy to make this educational
grant. His life was one incessant struggle to surmount the
opposition that always arose against his constructive plans.

The Queen was now ready to begin her tour of the picture
galleries. Arm in arm with the Emperor, she was led first to the
court of Prussian paintings. This seems from all accounts to have
been but a bleak display of talent; but the merits of the works
were pointed out by one Dr. Waagen, and the Queen stood to
admire the most conspicuous object in the room, a huge statue
of St. George and the dragon, by Kiss, whose work had been

much noticed in the Crystal Palace. The Belgian pictures were next visited and "the illustrious party proceeded to examine them with as much care as the circumstances rendered possible." But the circumstances were far from propitious as the room was terribly overcrowded.

At the Queen's request, the public were being admitted to-day as usual at the price of one franc. The result was that a vast throng was surging about the galleries and corridors. "More persons," says the *Illustrated Times*, "were anxious to have a peep at the Queen than her Majesty had any notion of; the building was so crowded that the temperature was raised to the heat of a vapour bath, and it was almost impossible to move about." There were constant cries of "*Vive la Reine!*" to which Victoria was obliged to respond by bowing, and the officials accompanying the Royal visitors had great difficulty in keeping Albert and the two children (who tried to while away the time by looking at pictures) from getting lost in the crowd.

At last the Belgian pictures were given up, and the party was led into the more spacious main gallery of the building, which contained French paintings. But all the public rushed in the same direction, their enthusiasm getting the better of restraint. And now the illustrious persons found the common world fairly falling on top of them; the curious, even if willing to keep at a respectful distance, were powerless to do so; they were flung forward by the eagerness of those who pushed in the rear. All the police in the building strove in vain with the unruly throng, and for a time there was a fine French scrimmage with much loud exclaiming and some danger of disaster. But in the end, with the arrival of a body of *sergens de ville* urgently called from outside, order was restored, and Royalty emerged, shaken but safe, smiling and admirably self-controlled.

"Anyway," Prince Albert said, laughing, as the crowds were roped off and the great ones moved into an adjoining and empty room, "if I were a king I would rather be killed by a crowd than by a bullet." In those days a German had not to apologise or explain himself for such a sentiment; it sounded natural.

Somehow or other the police had removed the public from several of the rooms, and the visitors were now able to study French paintings at their ease. There was an interesting and comprehensive display of work. At the Crystal Palace there had been plenty of sculpture but no paintings; at the Paris exhibition which followed it so quickly, there were many improvements and new ideas; the chief of these, as befitted a country of artistic supremacy, was the great attention paid to the fine arts.

Two gigantic figures dominated the Palais des Beaux Arts, Ingres and Delacroix. Ingres was seventy-five years old, and much of his life's work was here on view. His technical ability, the dignity of his subjects, his balanced and orderly compositions and the clear perfection of his drawing, combined with his long years of fame to make him revered both by public and critics. His faults—the silly, vacant faces of his young women and the cold emptiness of his conceptions—were sufficiently in the taste of the time not to detract from his reputation. Theophile Gautier saw in him a god-like figure, "seated at the summit of art, on that gold and ivory throne where, crowned with laurels, the immortals rest after their glorious accomplishments." Ingres was as much a French asset as the Sèvres china that was so liberally strewn about the Palace of Industry, the Royal palaces and the museums. He was the ideal official artist. No other state could produce a painter who came anywhere near him as an impressive figure of wholly acceptable genius.

Delacroix, eighteen years younger, was the leader of the Romantic school and as such particularly hateful to Ingres. The Romantic movement had been a revolt of the early decades of the century against the passion for the antique which dominated the schools of art. "Who will save us from the Greeks and Romans?" had been the watchword, and the Romantics had turned away from classical subjects to medieval and modern historical scenes and to a riot of glowing colour. It would seem to us now, looking back with the dispassion of those not in any way concerned, that there could very well be some artists painting in the Classical manner and others following the Romantic school; but at the time feelings ran very high and Ingres, the classical painter par excellence, took it as a slight to himself that the agitated canvases of Delacroix should have their following.

Although these two artists were universally respected, they were not truly popular. Ingres, with the measured repose of his compositions, was too remote from the world, and Delacroix was too passionately turbulent to put the world at its ease. The Second Empire public, and the Victorian visitors to Paris, really preferred Decamps, Meissonier and Horace Vernet. They loved to be impressed by canvases of enormous size, as supplied by Vernet, or to be equally impressed by the miniature but elaborately detailed and overworked paintings of Meissonier. Rosa

Bonheur was another popular painter of the day, and the sycophantic graces of Winterhalter called forth loud admiration.

Delacroix was brought forward to be presented to the Queen
after she had admired several of his finest canvases—"*La Barque
de Dante*", "*Les Femmes d'Alger*", and "*Les Croisés à Constantinople*"
—and the visitors then went to the court of sculpture. Here were
works, admired in their day, by men since forgotten: Rude,
Duret, Dumont, Simart, Frémiet.

The next visit was to a gallery devoted to the works of Horace
Vernet. Here the Queen was truly pleased, for the walls were
hung with huge military canvases and she could enjoy the
uniforms and the sight of "splendid fellows" in heroic action.
Some time was spent in gazing at triumphant scenes of the First
Empire, and the Queen turned to Horace Vernet, who was
present as one of the deferential band of commissioners, to con-
gratulate him and tell him how much pleasure his work gave her.

After this the visitors went to the court of Ingres. Here were
cartoons, drawings, portraits and many of his most famous
pictures, including "*L'Apothéose d'Homère*", "*Le Voeu de Louis
XIII*" and "*L'Odalisque*". It was a comprehensive exhibition
of his work which marked the climax of his successful career,
and was one of the notable events of 1855.

Napoleon and his guests now sat down in a vestibule while a
choir of workmen sang a chorus to them. The theme of "God
save the Queen" was introduced, and the *Morning Post* records
that her Majesty appeared to be greatly satisfied. This pleasing
interlude over, the Queen was shown an exhibit that was being
much talked of by the newspapers. It was a reconstruction of a
statue of Minerva by Phidias. The original had been in the
Parthenon and was known only through the accounts of the
classical writers; but nothing daunted, the sculptor Simart had
undertaken to reproduce it from the descriptions left by Pausanius.
There it stood, nearly eight feet high: the head, hands and feet
made of ivory, the eyes, necklace and ear-rings of precious stones,
and the drapery of silver-gilt. It was a painstaking, Industrial
abomination, a mawkish Victorian governess in a top-heavy
helmet. Only the nineteenth century could possibly have imagined
that it had any resemblance to the art of ancient Greece.

From the vestibule the party was led to the collection of English
works. This, one gathers from the glowing descriptions of our
own Press, was just like every Royal Academy show from that
day to this.

The Royal visitors were now taken upstairs, and "a fine bust of the Emperor at the foot of the staircase was particularly remarked by her Majesty." The upper galleries contained the water colours, miniatures, engravings and architectural drawings of all nations, and a good deal of time was spent examining them. Eventually the party came downstairs again; and the last room to be visited was the large French gallery where the interruption had occurred. It was now kept clear, and the Queen was led up to the *pièce de résistance* of the exhibition: Winterhalter's famous group of Eugénie with her court ladies. A chair was placed before it, and the Queen sat down to examine it at her leisure.

Winterhalter was a German, but in those easy days, before Europe had been bedevilled by the spirit of nationalism, a man thought it nothing amiss if he was counted among the subjects of another country. Winterhalter, painting at all the courts, lived chiefly in Paris and so appeared now among French artists. In his large painting the ladies-in-waiting are grouped around the Empress, bearing witness to the reputation they enjoyed of being the most exquisitely beautiful of women. They look strangely unlike the court groups taken by the forthright cameras of the time which hardly bear out that fabulous reputation. The Empress is raised just a little above her ladies, and is suitably above them, too, though ever so slightly, in beauty and nobility of expression. She is far removed from the factual Mademoiselle de Montijo who so energetically set out to ensnare the Emperor. All the figures are gracefully posed, and in their lovely, rarefied clothing are sweet and angelic beyond words. But if they are not of this world, neither are they of the ideal world of great art; they belong to the world of artistic opportunism, of official propaganda: they are busy telling the public that those whom Bonapartism has raised up are all goodness, charm and innocence. "Winterhalter's court group," said one of the papers, "seemed to wear a new charm after the Queen had sat a few minutes before it to contemplate the many good portraits it includes."

On each side of the group were portraits of the Emperor and Empress by the same artist. These three pictures the Queen studied admiringly, but after this she stopped to see no more, and the party left the building. Henry Cole asked the little Princess Royal as they were leaving which pictures she had liked best, and she replied with patriotic fervour: "The English ones, *of course.*"

CHAPTER VIII

A TRIUMPHANT AFTERNOON

THE Emperor and his guests stepped out of the Palace of Fine Arts into the dazzling sunlight. Crowds were rushing towards the entrance and there was a chorus of "*Vive la Reine!*" Cabs and carriages which happened to be passing drew up and their occupants leaned out; little street boys were clambering up the trees. The Queen, still radiant and untired, paused to look round at it all and to bow. The acclamations became louder than ever, the Emperor discreetly stepped back a pace to disassociate himself from any share in the triumph and the Queen smiled in the friendliest way possible, looking surprised and really touched. This response to their applause caused the greatest delight to the crowds, and the kindliest comments were made on all sides about *la bonne reine*. The Emperor now assisted her into a carriage, and he in his turn was loudly cheered. Prince Albert had his share of the ovation, and the children were much admired. One old woman serving drinks at a lemonade stall remarked loudly that the Princess Royal was charming, and as like an ordinary man's daughter as one pea to another. In which she was mistaken, as Vicky, though simple in appearance as she gazed about her with open-eyed astonishment, was very much the daughter of an extraordinary man, a real prodigy of learning, good sense and serious tastes.

The party were now going to the Palais de l'Elysée, the Elysée Napoléon as it was called at that time, which was only a short distance away. A different set of perfectly new carriages awaited them for this journey. "We drove to the Elysée in Town Carriages," the Queen's diary says, "ours very handsome, lined with white satin and gold. We always have an escort, either of *Cent Gardes*, or *Cuirassiers de la Garde*. The Elysée is very pretty, but the decorations, excepting in one or two rooms, are not nearly finished, and it is a small building. Here again, rooms were prepared for us, in which there were many souvenirs of Napoleon, la Reine Hortense, etc. Then we took luncheon in a room in which hung portraits of all the contemporary Sovereigns."

Afterwards the Queen held a reception for the corps diplomatique. While this was taking place journalists hovered about observing the scene; in the courtyard that looked on to the rue du Faubourg St. Honoré carriages were arriving; the fine white gravel which had been strewn about crunched beneath the wheels and flew up from the hooves of prancing horses. "Those invited," says one of the papers, "were dressed in every variety of gorgeous costume. Now an aged general in his rich gold-embroidered coat, crept slowly up the steps, leaning on the arm of his aide-de-camp, or a young officer of hussars, nearly covered with gold cord, ran quickly up and was in the interior of the palace before the carriage door had slammed. There were blue trousers with gold stripes and cream coloured ones with silver stripes. Red coats and blue coats with wonderful buttons and still more wonderful buttonholes, and magnificent hip, shoulder and breast embroideries . . ."

In the gardens behind the Elysée the Emperor was strolling about with the little Prince of Wales and smoking a cigar. Something was amusing them, for it was noticed that they laughed a good deal. "The scene is most brilliant as the weather is magnificent," said the *Morning Post* correspondent, sending his midday despatch to London.

Suddenly there was a great stir in the courtyard. The Emperor had ordered his private phaeton and he jumped into it with the Prince of Wales, took the reins himself and drove off at a brisk trot. He raced down the Champs Elysées and across the wide Place de la Concorde, and then drove rapidly along the rue de Rivoli. The arcaded street, with its façade glowing gold in the strong sunlight, held a lively concourse of people and was full of colour; deep blue shadows were cast rhythmically along the pavement by the colonnade, and the decorations—the flags, the gilt ornaments and the festoons of flowers—were resplendent. Pedestrians, hearing the clatter of a smart equipage driven fast, turned round and then smiled and called out their acclamations; visitors from many countries turned from the shop windows; shopkeepers came to their doors; foreign princes and politicians looked down from their hotel windows and wondered what the Emperor of the French was saying to the future King of England.

The Emperor drove up to the Palace of the Tuileries, and soon he was to be seen strolling up and down the terrace, talking to his young guest and still smoking. He continued to be very cheerful; he was, in fact, at the top of his form, and having a natural love for children was well able to delight the little boy at his side.

Louis Napoleon had every reason to feel extremely cheerful. The triumph of yesterday afternoon was surpassed by that of to-day; the atmosphere of the whole city was charged with a positive current of goodwill and pleasure, the Queen's visit was a tremendous success. That meant that all was a success. Let the war but be won—and victory was certain now—and the future was his. No one, indeed, doubted him any longer, and his enemies were quite confounded. His position now seemed unassailable.

He knew that henceforth he could be the arbiter of Europe, and he looked ahead with triumphant confidence. Yet the strains of an adventurous career—for he was getting on towards the age of fifty—had made its impression on him. The brilliant mind that had carried him through years of neglect, failure and imprisonment, to the highest of places, had become less sure, and at the same time problems and difficulties which only a keen brain could overcome pressed on him incessantly. Already his doctors saw the signs of the disease which was overtaking him and which was likely to affect his character and will; and even now he was sometimes in great pain, and then he would be a prey to doubts about the future: could he survive until he had a grown-up son to leave behind him? How fortunate were Victoria and Albert of England; more than ten years younger than himself, they had eight fine children and their eldest son, this attractive boy beside him, was almost fourteen; as for himself, even if the eagerly awaited first child of Eugénie should be a son, he must be nearly seventy before his heir could rule. Any time before then he could hardly dare to die. Besides, the child might not be a boy, and it would be idle to suppose that the more ornamental and emotional Eugénie would have Victoria's solid capacity for providing a large family in a short time. The future of the dynasty seemed uncertain at times.

But now such doubts were forgotten. All was triumph. The boy at his side made him anticipate joyfully the day when he would walk here with his own son. He looked at the flowing river and at the gardens where the public strolled about and children played. The kingdom of France was a happy one; how great a heritage awaited his unborn son. Already the wheels were set in motion that were preparing a welcome lavish and extravagant enough for so great a mortal, a welcome reminiscent of that which awaited Napoleon's son, the King of Rome, forty years ago.

But this child would wear the crown of France, this one would be Napoleon IV ruling his country in a newly organised Europe of free nations.

With such seemingly benevolent warmth the sun fell on the terrace, the water shone with such brilliance and the voices of children fell so merrily into the summer air, that anyone might easily be taken off his guard, might give himself up to illusions about the nature of things and believe that fate itself was like the August sun, that it just shone and smiled on human needs and wishes, and that doubts and fears were nothing but ingratitude and pessimism. From the fleeting pleasure of such a mood Louis Napoleon had no wish to escape; he gave himself up to it as he talked gaily to his young guest.

The Prince of Wales looked down enchanted from the terrace of the Tuileries. The sights, the sounds, the smell of Paris filled him with a delight that always haunted his mind afterwards. He saw the animation of the rue de Rivoli and dreamed of the thousand pleasures of this gay and beautiful city; he looked to the left at the river where sailing boats and barges suggested a fascinating unknown world that lay beyond the capital. Straight ahead and barely visible in the August haze was the Arc de Triomphe through which they had all driven this morning, and before it in the middle distance stood the Egyptian monolith set up by Louis-Philippe thirty years ago: relic of an ancient civilization, honoured with a distinction and sense of fitness known only to France. Paris, where beauty is respected by instinct, whose avenues were conceived in the broad dreams of princes—Paris, the earth's most fair city, its foundations in the ancient world of Greece and Rome and its head reared high in modernity,—this brilliant city lay spread before the Prince of Wales, half seen and half divined, utterly unlike anything he had known before. And there, half way back in the last century, in the delight of a boy of thirteen, much subsequent history was born. The Crimean alliance was all too soon to give way to animosity between England and France; but Edward's feelings never wavered. His family and his country might be anti-French and pro-German; but the affection of Edward VII was given to France during this week, as he avowed later in his life, and it was never shaken. The man at his side, the creator of so much of modern Paris, had a great share in this moment that foreshadowed the future. He had every quality to appeal to the child; how much nearer in sympathy and taste he was to the boy than was Prince Albert.

Victoria and Albert were conscientious and decidedly heavy parents; never before had their son careered through the streets like this at the side of a man with a great cigar in his mouth. One of the first principles put forward for the child's education by Baron Stockmar, that guide, philosopher and friend of the Saxe-Coburgs, was that he must associate only with persons of elevated character and intellect. As disease is avoided in pure air which harbours no microbes, so moral faults were to be avoided by exclusive association with men of irreproachable character. The adventurous Napoleon was as far as possible from conforming to this standard of moral perfection; the baron had always disapproved of him, and he was the opposite of the men chosen to form Bertie's disposition.

The Prince of Wales, this heir to a great kingdom, was the object of extraordinary care and attention. Albert, so coldly treated by England, never ceased to labour for the good of humanity, and he wished above all things to give England a conscientious and enlightened ruler; to that end his son was being drastically trained. Men were desperately struggling at that time to bring about a better world order; not merely was there a great movement to bring about socialism, but equal efforts were made in high places to develop a finer society. "Upon the good education of princes, the welfare of the world greatly depends," said Prince Albert. He considered that the troubles of the world, and particularly the horrors and cruelty of war, were due to the egoism and corruption of the rulers of men. Cruelty and misery must be deplored by all decent men, and by all those, whether decent or not, who are its victims; and as everyone is a potential victim of an evil man it follows from any point of view that rulers must be good men. To be wise enough to rule, a man must be specially trained and educated. Not that this idea originated with Prince Albert or at the time; it is the old idea of the philosopher-king that the ancient Greeks talked of and before them the Egyptians. It was very much alive when the Prince of Wales was born. Men felt themselves on the eve of a new and better age; for the first time in history a world-wide movement against slavery was setting men free, and rulers now seemed determined to be done with international wars.

It was natural in such an age that the early training of England's future king should attract much attention and that good advice should abound. It was Baron Stockmar whose counsels were chiefly followed, and who laid down the Liberal principles to be adopted. The boy was to be prepared for the inevitable changes of history, not taught that existing institutions were sacred and that to resist change was to serve the cause of God and his country. In all subjects a strictly disinterested outlook was to be taught, and it is strange indeed to think now of all the enlightened memoranda that followed each other thick and fast from Germany to England in the cause of the philosophic ideal. An anonymous pamphlet appeared before the Prince was two years old, in which it was suggested that he should never wear military uniforms lest the dreams of a conqueror should stir in him.

The ideals were great, and the education made its mark on a tolerant king who loved peace. But the prevailing mentality of the time was the opposite of that of to-day; the true values of life were understood to a great extent, but of the psychology of infants men knew nothing and cared less; it was the age of the grown-up. And the more his ambitious tutors tried, the less they succeeded in making their Royal pupil enjoy his lessons; through their inability to present them in the right way, they aroused a good deal of opposition to all the ideals of wisdom and goodness that they taught; and the writing out of excellent moral sentiments served mainly to associate those sentiments with boredom in his mind. He was not a natural scholar; science, music and politics were all distasteful to him, and for all the prodigious efforts made to transform him, he remained a dreadfully normal child who preferred play to work. Some parents would have been well enough pleased with him, for he was an attractive boy with charming manners and was clever at languages. But Victoria and Albert, who expected perfection from him, were bitterly disappointed and let him know it. It seemed an outrageous thing to Victoria that her eldest son should miss the heaven-sent opportunity of taking after the father whom she in her wisdom had given him, and Albert was often in despair when he saw how unresponsive the boy was to the intensive training that should have made him another Marcus Aurelius. He himself had accepted all the disciplines of training as a boy, why should Bertie not do so? He could no more understand his eldest son than the boy could understand his intellectual father; to Bertie the efforts at king-making of which he was the object seemed little less than a piece of calculated persecution devised to make his life a burden. Baron Stockmar had pointed out before his arrival that his education would begin on the day of his birth, and it seemed to the boy as he looked back that it had done so. Almost fourteen solid years of education lay behind him, and he could remember no time when he was not oppressed by many cares. Not that his life was dull; amusements were plentifully provided for him; but the watchful eye of hypercritical parents was always there, and he could hardly blow a whistle without a memorandum being produced to state the exact amount of stimulus to work that the relaxation might be expected to afford.

And now, reasons of state had caused him to be thrown into the society of a man with whom, in the opinion of his mentors, he should have felt nothing in common. The little boy liked him as much as he liked Paris. It was natural enough. Louis Napoleon might be the rogue that Baron Stockmar, Uncle Leopold, Prince Albert and the Orléans family thought him; he was ambitious, he was untrustworthy, he had the blood of a street massacre on his conscience and he was terribly self-indulgent. And yet he was a charming, kindly and civilized rogue. If he was not to be trusted it often seemed to be because he had too many good ideas at once. And if he had human blood on his conscience at least his conscience pricked and he was sorry ever after; he did not, as do the really wicked, disclaim all feeling of guilt and project the sin on to others. In adversity his first thought had always been to save his friends, and in success his greatest pleasure was to forgive old enemies. He could even love his enemies like a Christian, and in this he beat the philosophical Prince Albert himself, for although the latter might treat those who hated him to a certain amount of disdainful pity, he professed no affection for them. Out of his wide experience the Emperor, although of a strangely inconsistent temperament, had developed a strong human sympathy for all men; the little boy, so repressed at home, felt the warmth of his understanding and the broad tolerance of outlook that was also innate in his own character. How easy and pleasant it would be to live with a man like this who liked enjoying himself and didn't seem particularly good, someone who smoked cigars and never talked about music.

Up and down they strolled, until the Emperor threw his cigar away and suggested they should return to the Elysée. "You have a nice country," said the little boy, looking again across the park. "I would like to be your son." And now they were in the phaeton again, driving back along the Faubourg St. Honoré; and the people stood as they passed, raising their hats, waving and cheering.

At the Elysée the Queen's reception was ending and it was time to prepare for the next event of the day. Soon the carriages were assembled and the cortège set off on a drive round Paris, in the course of which Notre Dame and the newly restored Sainte Chapelle were to be visited.

Escorted by the *Cent Gardes*, whose helmets and cuirasses were flashing in the sunlight, the brilliant procession swept along the Faubourg St. Honoré, across the Place de la Concorde and down the rue de Rivoli. It was three o'clock; the route of the drive had been announced and it was lined with an immense throng of cheering people. "People rushed to the windows," says the *Illustrated Times*, "servants and masters mixed together—indeed the servants sometimes got the best places and stuck to them until the carriages had passed, when they began their 'thousand excuses'." The cortège crossed the Pont au Change and stopped before the Palais de Justice, which was so covered with flags and velvet hangings that hardly a stone was to be seen.

As they crossed the bridge the Emperor pointed out the Conciergerie to Victoria and said, "That is where I was imprisoned." And, indeed, fifteen years ago Louis Napoleon was languishing there in a cell, watched day and night by three gaolers. This was after his second attempt to seize power from Louis-Philippe. After the first attempt he was let off lightly; but in 1840 his plot was regarded more seriously, and when his trial came in September he was sentenced to imprisonment for life. It was six years later that he escaped from the fortress of Ham, dressed up as a workman, and fled to London to resume his plotting. The Queen was tremendously thrilled as she looked at this most adventurous, romantic and *truly marvellous* man who was now at her side, so calmly carrying his honours as her equal, so neatly dressed and so full of admiration for herself. "Strange contrast," she says in her diary, "to be driving with us as Emperor through the streets of the city in triumph."

The pavement was now a mass of spectators; windows and balconies were crowded, and ladies in white lace dresses seemed to dominate there. Men in black and brown had clambered on to the roof tops and were, the papers say, "clinging to chimney pots and resting on gutters." The carriages drew up, and the visitors were taken through the Palais de Justice to see the Sainte Chapelle.

"It is impossible," says the *Illustrated Times*, "in a few lines to give even a notion of the beauty of the Sainte Chapelle. One gentleman has endeavoured to do so in a book of 900 pages and failed for want of space. The rich colouring of its pillars and walls, the elaborate carving and costly gilding, make you almost melancholy from their extreme perfection; for the work appears so delicate, that you feel a dread lest it should fade and be destroyed. When her Majesty entered, the sun was shining brightly through the stained glass windows, and she had to walk through a shower of the most brilliant colours, which touched her white mantle with a thousand hues."

When the Queen had finished looking at the chapel, Louis Napoleon escorted her back to the carriages which now drove on to Notre Dame. Here, in the large open space before the cathedral were assembled all the workmen of the district in their blouses and casquettes, with their wives and children in their best clothes. These gave the Queen a welcome that the papers found "polite, manly and really astonishing": for the bourgeoisie and upper classes were decidedly nervous about the working classes in those days and always seemed amazed and relieved when, as was usually the case, they found them quiet and well behaved. To the left, as the visitors walked up to the cathedral, was the large hospital, the Hotel Dieu, on the steps of which were ranged the sisters of the order of St. Augustine; very picturesque in their white robes, they all bowed low as the Queen and the Emperor passed. The Archbishop of Paris, dressed in full magnificence, stood waiting at the door of the cathedral, and he greeted the Queen with an address of welcome and then escorted her round the building. "Her Majesty," says the *Illustrated London News*, "was evidently struck with the solemn beauty of the noble building, and seemed almost unwilling to quit it." But the Queen says in her diary that, although the outside was magnificent, "except the beautiful carving of the Choir there is nothing particularly to admire in the interior."

The carriages drove back to the quay on the north side of the river, and then went along a fine new avenue which was only just opened, and which still has the name which it was given during this week: the Avenue Victoria. Passing the Hotel de Ville, the carriages continued along the rue de Rivoli, which (apart from its western end from the Place de la Concorde to the Palace of the Tuileries) was a new street, and into the Quartier St. Antoine to the Place de la Bastille. From here they went up the Boulevard du Temple past the Place de la République, along the Boulevard St. Martin and then along the whole series of the great boulevards, back to the Champs Elysées. They had now been through large working class districts, where the pavements had been filled to capacity. An astonishing enthusiasm had met them everywhere. There had been the same genial smiles, the same heartfelt ovations as in the west end of Paris this morning. The truth was that a wave of high hopes and enthusiasms had swept over the city. There were great ideals in the air at that time; it was true there was a war on, but it was far away and almost won. Peaceful, orderly progress towards a higher civilization seemed to be only round the corner and to be inevitable if England and France worked together. When Winston Churchill proposed a union of England and France in 1940 he was returning to an old idea; the Comte de Saint-Simon had proposed it early in the nineteenth century. From time to time ever since, the idea has had its popularity; and there was a revival of enthusiasm in France in this summer of 1855. Charles Duveyrier, a Saint-Simonite who had the confidence of the Emperor, was preaching the advantages of such a union which, it was thought, would open new markets to the skilled artisans of France, and lead to a colossal turnover of wealth and exchange of ideas. The same hopes of an altogether better age were alive in England. The days of enmity between England and France were over, said the *Illustrated London News* at this time; "and it will be their task to extend the blessings of the happy peace which subsists between themselves to the whole of Europe—to attract other nations to their alliance, and, when the sword has done its work, to make even Russia herself sue for admission into the great Commonwealth of Europe. . . ." It was in the hope of a new era of peaceful development towards prosperity, which seemed to be symbolised in the Royal visit, that the people cheered the Queen of England during this week.

The drive had also enabled the Royal visitors to see something of the vast replanning and rebuilding of Paris that was going forward with such incredible speed. Napoleon I had had great plans for transforming Paris into a city of fine, broad thoroughfares, filled with splendid monuments and large buildings, of making it the "unique town of the world"; a beginning had been made during the First Empire, and the work had been continued very slowly under the various succeeding régimes. Now the nephew was bent on finishing the work in his own reign, and an astonishing transformation had already taken place. Paris, a city of ancient, narrow streets, was being turned into the city we know, a well-planned, orderly town of spacious avenues, which has remained adequate even to twentieth century traffic. The transformation has been very much criticised at all times, and it is undeniable that Baron Haussmann, who was given the task of carrying out the plan, was heavy handed and went roughshod over history, destroying much that was beautiful and irreplaceable. The real motive of the work, too, whatever might be said officially, was to put an end to the frequent revolutions and political disturbances of Paris. The Parisians had been in the habit of fighting any hated government in the narrow streets which were easily barricaded; but when the new Paris was completed the army could easily control the city, and cavalry charges could sweep rioters aside. The Emperor was safeguarding his dynasty by the building of strategically planned roads of magnificent open width. There was something grandiose and empty about Baron Haussmann's personality, and the Boulevard Haussmann is a fitting monument to him; but he had the driving power and determination that carries a great scheme through without faltering, and however one may regret the things that are gone and the opportunities lost for doing something better, it has to be admitted that Paris is a fine and charming city, and that the work is impressive.

Enthusiasm was general in 1855, and the critics made no impression on public feeling. The French people were impressed by the great prosperity it was all bringing, and the English could not cease admiring and exclaiming, denouncing each other for the dingy inconveniences of London, complaining of its traffic blocks and clamouring to have it transformed in the same way. There was quite a chorus in the English press when Victoria had made this extensive drive round Paris. Now she will see what a big city should be, was the general tone. Now perhaps she will realise that London is hopelessly inadequate to a large modern community. The papers were more outspoken in those days. "Here in this ugliest of great cities," one of them wrote, "bestridden by the foulest nightmare of municipal misgovernment ever tolerated by an intelligent people, we ought certainly to feel glad that our Queen can at last see for herself what has lately been done to improve Paris." One wonders what they thought the Queen could do; if she had made any attempt to refashion London in the thorough-going way that they were all admiring, it would have been as much as her throne was worth. At the first decree for demolishing a street the owners of the property would have been up in arms and the scheme would have had to be dropped. One cannot have it both ways. Paris had its dictator

Between pages 80 *and* 81]

PROCESSION ALONG THE BOULEVARD DES ITALIENS.

and its fine, agreeable city; London muddled along under the conflict of everybody's interest. On the other hand, France's dictatorship led to a national disaster, whereas England was so constituted that if no one could do much good, no one could do much harm either.

The cortège now drove quickly up the Champs Elysées, then out through the Bois de Boulogne to St. Cloud. The Emperor, as usual, led the Queen to her apartments.

An excited yapping greeted Victoria as she entered her rooms, and there was her own dog straight from Osborne. Great was the wonderment, the delight, the laughter, and Napoleon III stood by, mysteriously twirling his moustaches which swept out from his face like the whiskers of a cat.

It was six o'clock; the greetings, the remonstrances and the thanks over, Victoria took out her diary to record the events of this "most interesting and delightful day". "We passed along the Boulevards," she said, when writing of the afternoon, "by the Porte St. Martin, and Porte St. Denis, along the rue de la Paix, rue Castiglione, full of shops and fine houses, by the Place Vendôme, and the Place de la Bastille, where the Colonne de Juillet is placed, the fountains and the Chateau d'Eau, and then home the usual way, by near six. Everything so gay, so bright, and though very hot, the air so clear and light. The absence of smoke keeps everything so white and bright, and this in Paris, with much gilding about the shops, green shutters, etc., produces a brilliancy of effect which is quite incredible." The Queen ended off a little oddly by saying, "No one can be kinder or more agreeable than is the Emperor, and so quiet, which is a comfort on all, but particularly on such occasions."

General Canrobert, who had been requested to call this evening, was announced and Albert went off to talk to him. But the light of a lovely glowing sunset was beginning to illumine the rooms and Victoria seized her paint box and hurried to the balcony to do a sketch. Below here was the white avenue, lined with trees; in the distance there rose the Arc de Triomphe with Paris very blue behind it. She sat, happily absorbed, until she remembered that she had to bestow the Order of the Bath upon Canrobert; whereupon she rose, prepared for dinner and then went into one of the adjoining rooms where her husband was talking to the General at a table upon which a map of Sebastopol was spread out.

Victoria glanced at the map and began to talk about the great siege that was then in progress. "At the end of a few minutes," the General records, "I was quite stupefied by her knowledge of the siege. She had a most exact memory for all names and incidents. The position of the trenches, the camps, and batteries —all were fixed with an admirable precision in her head. She was as familiar with the siege in all its most minute details as I was myself, and I could not help expressing my admiration."

Victoria then conferred the Order upon the General, and thanked him for his friendship for her own soldiers. They then settled down to a long conversation about Lord Raglan, of whom Canrobert had much to say, since he had known him well. After that Victoria questioned him about the organisation and administration of the French army, which he explained to her until the rather late dinner was announced.

After the dinner, or banquet (for many society people had been invited), was over, there was a theatrical performance in the palace. Alexandre Dumas' *Les Demoiselles de St. Cyr* was played by the artistes of the Comédie Française. The audience in the little theatre was brilliant; fine uniforms abounded, jewels sparkled, arms and shoulders were bare and white, silk gleamed and immaculate curls, both dark and fair, framed male and female faces. The programmes were printed in gold upon white satin. The newspapers printed long lists of great names in the morning, and after the performance was over the Queen had to stand in one of the large salons of the palace while all the guests were presented to her. Then refreshments were taken, and at last, very late, Victoria and Albert retired to their rooms for the night.

The great windows stood open; it was a soft, velvety night, so warm and still that even after so long a day they were reluctant to leave it for insensible sleep. They stepped on to the balcony and stood leaning on the railings, looking down and watching the carriages drive away.

CHAPTER IX

VERSAILLES

ON Tuesday the Queen went to Versailles, and the ghosts were regaled for an hour in an unwonted manner: for Marie Antoinette's idyllic hamlet was roused from obscurity and decay, from its long years of neglect, to be the setting once again of a *déjeuner champêtre*, enlivened by military bands.

The party left St. Cloud at half-past ten in a light-hearted cavalcade. The Queen was in the usual elegant open barouche with the Prince and the Emperor; other carriages followed, and there were two brightly painted chars-a-bancs, each drawn by six horses whose harness jingled with bells. With the outriders in the Imperial livery, the postilions in powdered wigs, and the military escort, the cortège was very brilliant, and it swept off rapidly to the Ville d'Avray, under arches of evergreens and on to Versailles. That weather which always smiled so radiantly upon the ceremonies of Victoria, as one imagines it must have shone upon Augustus in his golden age, was at its best to-day. It was an ideal morning. There was a light breeze and the sky was a dark and vivid blue; rounded white clouds like small pieces of cotton wool went sailing across it.

All Paris was at Versailles to meet the Queen. From an early hour people had been pouring out of the capital; Paris, the papers say, was a deserted city, its boulevards were like the streets of a quiet provincial town. The stations of the Versailles line were in a turmoil; railway carriages were densely crammed and were like ovens. "*Mon dieu, quel chaleur!*" was the general cry as people stepped from the trains. But in the pleasant breeze that was coming across from the gardens they soon revived and changed their tone to "*Quel beau temps!*" Dresses were shaken out, and after an iced drink they set about seeking a good place from which to view the Royal persons.

Versailles was lavishly decorated and all was in perfect readiness; it is an amiable characteristic of the French never to be ready on time, so that the compliment on the present occasion and the effort that had been expended were very great. The municipal authorities had, in fact, kept their workmen hard at it all through the night, promising them everything under the sun and keeping up their energies with numerous *petits verres*. A fine arc de triomphe, made entirely in white and gold, now stood in the Place d'Armes, at the entrance to the courtyard of the palace, and near was the crimson velvet estrade on which the civic authorities waited with the Prefect of the department at their head. White gravel had been thrown down on the broad roadways, tall red masts had been fixed along the avenues and from them streamers and oriflammes hung. The flags of England and France hung from the houses, moving lazily to and fro. The Guards standing immovable at their posts filled the old courtyard with a touch reminiscent of the great days of *le roi soleil*.

Now those who watched on the boulevard heard a distant clatter, and presently there came a fine body of mounted Sappers with long black beards. Afterwards came the Imperial carriages and chars-a-bancs, followed by a detachment of Guards. The concourse of people cheered loudly, and the cortège paused at the gates of the palace so that the Prefect could step down from the crimson velvet stand and deliver his address of welcome. Then the carriages moved on again and crossed the courtyard. The Queen had pulled down her green veil and was vainly trying to protect herself from the burning rays of the sun with her fringed parasol. She did not appear to great advantage to-day, in the opinion of her ladies, having insisted upon wearing one of the "lilac cravats" of which she was so fond and which looked rather old-fashioned. But the Prince Consort, says the *Morning Post*, "wore a light summer suit which, from its unpretending neatness, gained the admiration of all the ladies, and from its coolness, the envy of all the gentlemen."

The party alighted at the entrance of the palace which they were to have to themselves, for the public had been excluded, although they were being admitted to the gardens. Entering the building, they now began a tour of those interminable galleries which Louis-Philippe had had filled with paintings of French history. The visitors were first led to the "Coronation of Napoleon" by David, then to the "Distribution of the Eagles to the Legions" and after that to the "Battle of Aboukir." There now came seemingly endless portraits of Napoleon and his generals, and after examining all these the visitors went to the huge Gallery of Battles, to make which a number of rooms had been sacrificed by Louis-Philippe. Here they viewed many hundred feet of dreary canvas, showing French victories from some battle or other fought by Clovis in the fifth century up to the battle of Wagram. The Queen stopped to admire the "Battle of Fontenoy" where the English were being put to ignominious rout, and the Emperor very politely apologised for the picture. "You see," he said tactfully, "it's a subject that's rather scarce with us." To which the Queen replied that she wished battle scenes had been scarcer still.

After the Gallery of Battles came the Empire Gallery where hundreds of Napoleonic exploits had to be passed and praised; then there was the Crusaders' Gallery where knights were hard at it in a series of colossal pictures. There came next all the victorious onslaughts of the *roi soleil* and an immense array of Algerian battle scenes, painted by the energetic Horace Vernet. Most appropriately, it was while the visitors were among these martial canvases that a telegraphic despatch was brought to the Emperor with news from the Crimea; he passed it to Victoria who read it delightedly: the news was excellent.

At last the visitors turned from the pictures to visit the historic rooms. "We saw Louis XIV's rooms," says the Queen, "with portraits of his family, his own room and bed, the hangings of which embroidered by les Demoiselles de St. Cyr—Louis XV's small apartments—Madame de Maintenon's, with her '*oratoire*', —the rooms of poor Louis XVI, and Marie Antoinette, from one of which she made her escape; *all* intensely interesting, instructive and melancholy."

Most beautiful of all was the Hall of Mirrors, into which the sunlight swam torridly through the seventeen great open windows, adding to its glowing splendour. The last place to be visited was the chapel where they were greeted by loud strains of "God save the Queen" on the organ. Having listened and admired, the visitors then left the palace.

They stepped on to the terrace, and there, stretched before them, was that vast garden of formal alleys, statues and fountains. The Queen, with her amazing gift for reducing the stately and the spectacular to the most homely proportions, commented in her diary, "The garden is very pretty, and the Emperor picked me a flower to dry".

The Emperor was now going to show his guests the great fountains, and the carriages were re-entered. They moved off at a walking pace, accompanied by their military escort, and as they began their drive the waters of the *grandes eaux* started to rise in the air. When the cortège reached that part of the garden where the public was assembled, there were prolonged and deafening cheers, and an immense concourse began to follow them on foot.

Here and there in the great park were military bands, and occasionally a few strains of "God save the Queen" might be heard in a pause between the cries of the crowds. In these conditions the Queen surveyed the magnificent but rather neglected park. The *Bosquet de la reine* was pointed out to her, and then the *Bassin du miroir* and the *Jardin du roi*. They all glanced at the *Bosquet de la colonnade*, an Ionic rotunda in marble with a fountain playing beneath each arch and a statue in the centre, showing the rape of Proserpine; and then they reached the fountain of Apollo and paused to admire the view of the grand canal. From this they went to the fountain of Enceladus, where the carriages stopped. Surrounded by a square, clipped screen of evergreens, the giant Enceladus was shown buried in fragments of rock, having been hurled down from heaven which he had tried to conquer. From his mouth there rose a column of water to the height of sixty feet. The crowds sent up a hearty cheer as the Emperor and his guests watched the fountain admiringly, and with this and the heavy roar of the water, the horses in the carriages began to snort and prance with nervous anger and the grooms had some trouble in keeping them quiet.

Up and down the carriages went from one great fountain to another, and all around them the friendly public surged. "We drove about the curious old-fashioned gardens," says the Queen, "to see the waterworks, which are wonderful and endless. The effect of the innumerable *jets-d'eau*, with the bright sunshine, the bands (of which there were four) playing, the multitude of people, and the numerous equipages going in and out of the small avenues, and winding along the *bassins*, was very fine." Beyond the amiable crowds was a vision of marble staircases and dark yews, of bronze vases, nymphs of stone in agitated water, fountains rising towards the Italian sky, and formal alleys overgrown with weeds, where statues of all the gods and heroes of antiquity looked down indifferently at the modern scene from their weather-beaten pedestals.

The last fountain to be visited was the *Bassin de Neptune*, the most splendid of them all. Here was a tremendous throng of people waiting for the carriages to arrive, and once again the Queen had a rousing welcome. In very different circumstances the Empress Eugénie sometimes saw these great fountains playing. She would be moved to go to Versailles on a fine summer night when the park was closed and empty, and then she would order the fountains to be turned on and would wander among them, dreaming. Most glorious must Neptune and Amphitrite be in the moonlight with their nymphs, tritons and sea-monsters, with water rushing high in the air on all sides: glorious and yet terrible. It would take courage to wander alone with one's thoughts under the stars in this fabulous garden, here where the dreams of kings turned to dust and ashes.

The carriages turned round now and drove more quickly down the Avenue de Trianon. The waters subsided. The display, always a costly one, was over. There was a brief visit to the large palace of the Trianon, and then everyone alighted at the Petit Trianon. Here there was perfect quietness as, from the grounds of this palace, the public was excluded. Lunch was to be taken in the hamlet, and the guests wandered off in that direction. But the Emperor had a surprise for the Queen inside the small palace. "The two Sovereigns entered this interesting building alone," says the *Illustrated London News;* "and, when her Majesty was seated, her Imperial host informed her that he had ordered Marie Antoinette's old furniture to be recovered from the *Garde Meuble,* and restored to the place it occupied during the unfortunate Queen's time. Here the two Sovereigns sat alone for some time in conversation." After this they strolled across to the hamlet. Here, in the delightful little *Maison du Seigneur,* the largest of the thatched cottages, the Empress awaited them; she was very beautifully dressed in a gown of exquisite lace, and had a rose in her hair.

The *Maison du Seigneur* had been cleaned for the occasion and fitted out with furniture of the Empire style; here the company now sat down to an excellent lunch, served with a disarming air of rusticity. The meal proceeded merrily, although the conversation would certainly go from time to time to the tragic figures of Louis XVI and Marie Antoinette which seemed to haunt the place. The great revolution with its reign of terror was still a vividly remembered episode; those present at the luncheon party were a good deal nearer to the *ancien régime* than they are to us. But the meal was a cheerful one, and past tragedies seemed only to make the present glow in a more brilliant contrast of secure and peaceful happiness. The agreeable idea of a meal at one of Marie Antoinette's cottages was no doubt the Empress's; she had developed a cult, almost a mania, for Marie Antoinette and loved every yard of the Queen's domain, the Petit Trianon, at Versailles.

The Petit Trianon was built by Louis XV and was made notorious by Madame du Barri. Louis XVI gave it to Marie Antoinette and here she spent her most happy and carefree days. She grew weary of the grandiose palace of Versailles, of its ceremonial, its dreary etiquette and the eternal gossiping and mischief-making of idle courtiers. At the Trianon she lived as she pleased; she was the mistress of a small country house and of a garden. Compared with life at the big palace, life in the little Trianon was very simple; its supreme elegance came from perfect taste rather than from luxury. Although festivals were occasionally held there, it was in the main a retreat for the Queen, her family and her personal friends; she would turn her back on Versailles whenever she could, and go there attended only by two or three ladies, dressed like herself in muslin gowns and straw hats.

On the gardens, however, fortunes were spent. Marie Antoinette was always in the height of fashion, and the fashion of the day was for wild romantic charm. The Queen was bored with the great formal Italian gardens of Lenotre, which were like reason and logic expressed in terms of horticulture. She wanted a natural garden where paths led to the unforeseen and round hedges were not made square. And so the most exquisite landscape was fabricated by artists and gardeners in a hybrid style called Anglo-Chinese. Water was brought from afar in pipes to make streams and ponds, hills were raised, woods planted and rustic grottos created. Nothing was straight here; the brooks and paths wound and curved and meandered. In this delightful setting the hamlet was constructed. The simple life of the peasant was a popular theme with writers, and the theatrical, idyllic village was a reflection of this fanciful return to nature.

In the hamlet was a miniature farm with barns, hayricks and dovecotes; there were several cottages, a water mill and a little tower. The buildings were thatched, and poverty was indicated by the skilful hands of artists who painted cracks in the plaster, rifts in the walls and chipped and broken edges to the bricks. A handful of favoured peasants were brought to play a part in the poetical scene. Butter and cheese were made, lawns were mowed and scythed, washer-women washed clothes in the brook, and a few well-trimmed animals wandered about. Sheep were led to the pasture by silk ribbons, cows were milked into beautiful porcelain pails, and butter was made in an exquisite small dairy faced with marble.

Here Marie Antoinette dreamed she was living the life of the "good people"; that in her white linen dresses she was tasting the poverty dear to heaven. And all around, in that fair kingdom of France of which she remained so completely ignorant, the people groaned under feudal tyranny; had she gone a little way to see what the good people were doing she would have found them in the last stages of misery, she would have seen ragged, hungry children and mothers in despair, and behind it all a mounting anger nearly ready to explode.

One of the cottages was kept for the Queen herself to use; it was called the *Maison du Seigneur*. Superbly designed as an exquisite and impractical trifle, it stood before a small lake. Here Marie Antoinette could survey the life of her toy village, and here she often dined with the King and their family, in much the same way as Napoleon III and his guests were doing to-day.

The Empress Eugénie, with her sentimental imagination, was pleased to envisage herself as another Marie Antoinette. "Doña Eugenia," wrote the Austrian ambassador to France, "is convinced that she will die on the scaffold. She has said so herself to me more than once, and when I smiled she was really annoyed. As absolute proof of the tragic destiny that awaits her, she tells me that while she was making preparations for her marriage she was shown a lace veil which the Queen had worn; she would have loved to have it, but could not afford to buy it. But what was her surprise—both happy and sad at the same time—when, on opening a casket from her fiancé she found it contained the same veil."

Eugénie was a keen Bonapartist; when she was a child Beyle and Merimée had fired her imagination with stories of the great man and all his military triumphs. But she also loved the prestige of legitimate monarchy and believed in the justice of inherited privilege and authority. It was a source of the greatest disappointment to her that the legitimist nobility of France ignored her.

Her cult for Marie Antoinette began when she married. She was proud to ascend the magnificent throne of France, that fateful throne of "the Austrian"; one of her first acts after marrying was to go to the *Conciergerie* to see the Queen's farewell letter, written in her last hours; and at her wedding she enjoyed wearing a string of pearls after her friends had begged her not to do so, since, they said, it would bring misfortune. Her honeymoon was a pilgrimage to the haunts of the Royal victim whose possessions she eagerly collected. She had built a model dairy at Villeneuve l'Etang, and hung up a portrait of the Queen in her bedroom.

Now the Royal party, their meal over, came outside to drink their coffee beside the lake, and to wander about examining the features of the place. Eugénie pointed out to the Queen the Temple of Love, the groves and grottos, and the stables, now so still and mournful, where once the courtiers had played at being the farmer's boy. They glanced into the dairy, full of cobwebs and old planks, where Marie Antoinette in her muslin dresses had made butter, and at the mill where the King himself, it was said, had worn a corduroy suit and carried the miller's sack on his back while the Comte d'Artois acted as bailiff of the village. They returned to the lawn before the cottage where Marie Antoinette had once danced with her courtiers, while her ladies were swinging idly in the trees in the manner of a Boucher painting. And Victoria told Eugénie of an indirect contact of her own with the ill-fated Queen which she loved to recall; how once as a girl she had danced with old Lord Huntly who as a young man had danced a minuet with Marie Antoinette.

The military band played—here, where the courtiers of the *ancien régime* were wont to listen to Grétry and Mozart, and the sun bore down in full brilliance; but there remained a haunting desolation about the scene behind the laughter and indifference of ladies and gentlemen in waiting. Louis XIV's dream of the mounting splendour and dignity of French royalty had faded, and this too, this fragile illusion of the simple life, had turned to dust and ashes.

Victoria, who never wasted time, took out her paints and brushes and a sketch book. It was these, perhaps, that the large satin bag accommodated. She was attracted not by the relics of the past, but by the fine Imperial uniforms of the soldiers, and it was these that she painted. "After luncheon," she says in her diary, "we sat for some time under the trees listening to the fine band of the *Guides*, and I made some sketches. The sun shining through the trees on the band, the ladies and gentlemen, the escort (Cuirassiers of the Guard) and the postilions and horses, with the music, and the occasional tinkling of the bells of the horses of the *chaises de poste*, made the prettiest effect possible."

Eugénie leaned back to dream of the past, and of herself in the tragic rôle of Marie Antoinette. There was something theatrical and false in this desire for a martyr's end; certainly Marie Antoinette never wished to be the victim of a revolution, and Eugénie was quite unlike her in dwelling on such a theme. But the Empress, in seeing herself as destined for a similar part, was like an actress wishing for the rôle of tragedienne in some great play. She really dreamed of being another Rachel and taking the world by storm with intense, inimitable pathos in the centre of the stage. There was no reality in the hollow pretence. For when the terrible storm did break in 1870, and she found herself at last in the midst of a revolution, she did not wait to see whether it would bring a new reign of terror and allow her to join the Royal martyrs of history. She was quickly across the Channel and in England, forgetting her former dreams in the search of a prosaic but comfortable exile. She was fortunate in not having to meet the anger of the French people; for they blamed her for their troubles as they had once blamed Marie Antoinette, and they were right in supposing that she had had a share in bringing about the disasters of the Franco-Prussian war.

Victoria, so innocently painting, has been blamed, strangely enough, for having a hand in those French disasters that the future held and that were so little expected on this glorious afternoon. She is supposed to have set in motion, in this year of 1855, the unfortunate train of events that led to 1870; this she did at Windsor during the visit of the Emperor and Empress. "In two or three days," says André Bellesort, in "*La Société Française sous Napoléon III*", "Queen Victoria did us all possible harm, though quite unwittingly." At that time the English government was most anxious to prevent Louis Napoleon going out to take command in the Crimea, and Victoria took Eugénie on one side and begged her to use all her influence to this end; she went further, according to this writer, and urged the Empress to take a part in the government of the Empire. The advice arose from the Queen's inability to judge character, particularly in a foreigner. She thought Eugénie good and kind, and endowed with a fund of common sense lacking in the Emperor himself who, even if fascinating, was an unaccountable being, all reserve and mystery, and much in need of the right guidance. Such counsels had a strong appeal for the ambitious Eugénie.

"The Eugénie whom England sent back was not the same one who had gone there," says Bellesort. To begin with, Eugénie had seen the Queen in a costume of the Hussars, and directly she was back she ordered for herself a uniform of the Imperial Guard, with a bodice of blue embroidered with gold, and a red skirt; she also ordered a beautiful Spahi outfit in which the jacket was red embroidered with black, and the skirt was pale blue. And she soon began to work for political influence; she got her way in due course through being "a woman of scenes", for her husband was definitely a man of peace in domestic affairs.

It was one thing for Victoria to wear a uniform; this was merely a part of ancient pageantry, signifying nothing. The Queen had a passion for uniforms and for well-dressed troops, and she was quite upset during this visit to Paris to see how much smarter the French soldiers were than those of England. But all her life she was on the side of peace; that the "noble fellows" should have to fight was always a distressing thought to her. It was another thing entirely with Eugénie; born in that fierce and vivid country, Spain, and with a million notions of personal grandeur surging in her soul and a strong taste for bull fights—when such a woman is mounted in a dashing uniform on the parade ground, she creates a different picture from that of good, domesticated Victoria reviewing her troops.

Eugénie became the advocate of war in later years; she had no compunction in seeing armies sent off to destroy each other. She had been born and educated into that peculiar continental tradition—so incomprehensible to those who do not share it— that sees glory in war and craven decadence in the wish for prolonged peace. She always acted in what she believed were the interests of France, she was always genuinely anxious to bring about good ends. But she was passionate, personal and prejudiced to a degree, and was quick to translate her own desires into terms of historic necessity.

She loved the heroic rôle, and no doubt she was greatly impressed to see Victoria presiding over a council of war at Windsor. On such occasions Victoria sat, thoroughly informed of everything down to the smallest detail, sober and conscientious: not seeing herself as playing a brilliant part, but genuinely believing herself to be responsible before God for the welfare of her people and the good of mankind. The Empress's turn was to come, and she had a baleful effect upon the course of political events. But Victoria, utterly honest herself, was not suspicious. Eugénie came to Windsor looking like an angel; when she talked she was all goodness and sweet reasonableness. She seemed just the person to exert a soothing and beneficent influence on world affairs.

Good advice, from all accounts, was lavished upon the Empress at Windsor; for not only was she inspired with dreams of exerting herself in the political sphere, she owed her pregnancy to the advice of the Queen of England. At the time of the visit she had been married two years and still had no child; rather than as a Marie Antoinette, she was seeing herself almost as another Josephine about to lose her position through divorce instead of on the scaffold. But the Queen's counsels had led to the desired result.

Since the ladies met for the first time at Windsor, and the visit lasted only four days, the conversations seem to have been remarkably fateful. Victoria, whatever result her influence may have produced, shines in her relations with Eugénie, so rare is good-hearted simplicity between women, at least in the annals of the famous. How many princesses in that great palace of Versailles behind them, and how many Bonaparte ladies, had been ready to scream with fury at the sight of a younger and more beautiful woman who by those very attributes was an inevitable rival? What calumny, what infamous hostility a Marie Antoinette aroused in court ladies by her light-hearted beauty alone. But Victoria could be with Eugénie, her junior by seven years and a very goddess of beauty, and never feel a trace of envy. Eugénie was always "the *dear Empress*"; seeing her radiance and her surpassing elegance, the Queen was all smiles and admiration.

The day of corrupting power was still far away from the Empress; she did not meddle in the Crimean war, and her interest in it produced little more than consultations with the spirits at table-turning, which was the craze of the hour in all the salons of Paris. And presently the Queen and the Empress entered a carriage together for the return journey to St. Cloud. They may well have discussed the latest forecasts of the spirit world if their minds were not too full of Marie Antoinette; for England too shared the passion for table-turning, and the Queen was much interested herself and would be very ready to hear what Saint Louis, Bossuet, Pascal and Rousseau had to say about the prospects of the fall of Sebastopol. To-day there was no cloud on the scene; beyond vague feelings of pity roused at the Trianon for those who lived in the bad old days, and sympathy almost equally vague for the men on the distant battle scene, there was little to detract from perfect peace of mind. And the only things that caused any shadow of annoyance were the heat and the dust.

Dinner was a quiet meal that evening and was taken early; when it was over the Emperor and Empress left the palace with their grown-up guests for a state visit to the opera. The twilight was fading as they drove through the gates, and when the cortège in all its pomp swept into the Bois de Boulogne the stars were already reflected in the still and silent lakes. The Imperial equipages—the Emperor's closed town carriages—drove at a trot down the Avenue de l'Impératrice and then roared under the Arc de Triomphe. Here could be seen, down the two mile extent of the Champs Elysées, the long line of street lamps that was so new and astonishing at that time. The lights of a thousand carriages going up and down were also seen, and other lights sparkled in the trees.

The wheels skimmed smoothly over the road, and above the ringing of horses' hooves and the occasional crack of a postilion's whip there came the steady hum of voices from many thousands who walked to and fro in the pursuit of pleasure. Some were going to the *Bal Mabille* or the *Jardin d'Hiver* to dance, some were about to dine at one of the restaurants, others to sit down at a *café chantant*. Beneath the trees was a perpetual fair. Music and laughter, animated talk and the passing of carriages filled the soft, warm air with sound, and the perfume of violets was wafted about the avenue from end to end. Among the many prophecies made to the Empress when she was a girl had been one foretelling that violets would be the symbol of her success and happiness. Violets were one of the emblems of the Bonapartes, and after the prophecy Eugénie went to great lengths to obtain these flowers to wear at all seasons of the year. Violets were definitely her flower, and she always had a profusion of them in her rooms. It went without saying that violet perfume was now the popular favourite of the day, and that one met it wherever one went.

Anyone could stroll up and down the Champs Elysées, whiling away this lovely summer night, says the thrice fortunate *Morning Post* correspondent, "in the conviction of the happiness of all surrounding him." One can imagine this writer, following the Queen to the Opera House, and then sitting on a terrace after midnight, his glass and his notebook before him, wondering how to express in adequate words the dazzling ceremony of royalty against the background of a whole city of happy people. And in the yellow, brittle pages of the surviving copies of the *Morning Post* there lingers a faint hint of the magic of that velvety summer night when all the great avenues and boulevards and all the streets were astir with life and gaiety, and no threat of any kind loomed up to disturb the peace of man.

The Imperial cortège drove across the illumined Place de la Concorde, up the rue Royale, past the Madeleine and into the boulevards where the street lighting that gleamed among the leafy trees was lost in the gold glare of a thousand cafés whose terraces were thronged. "Away up this broad scene of splendour, amid the ringing cheers of the motley and merry thousands" the carriages drove until they reached the rue Lepelletier, at the end of the Boulevard des Italiens, where, in those days, the Opera House was situated. From balconies on the tall white houses there hung paper lanterns, and the great ornamental arc de triomphe outside the opera, with its Imperial bees, its flags and fraternal groups, was illumined with a gigantic chandelier as big as a balloon. The carriages stopped, the Royal persons stepped out on to carpeted pavements, and there was a commotion among the crowds, a neighing of horses, a hissing of gas jets and a loud shouting of commands to soldiers. The façade of the building was decorated with a great display of fine flowers, and with shields, eagles and flags. A row of gas jets flared along the frieze, and the Royal and Imperial initials were also outlined in flickering gas. The place was "an object of wonderful beauty", the papers say; and the gas lamps, placed at the corners of the street, "threw out innumerable flames of light and rendered every object as clear as day".

Napoleon, his wife and their guests entered the building and passed through its halls; here columns were entwined with garlands, walls were hung with velvet and gold and floors were covered with Gobelin carpets. They went up the staircase and along corridors lined with mirrors. Masses of flowers were ranged along the walls and the most extravagant dresses and spectacular uniforms were on view; on to all this there fell the glowing light cast by dozens of crystal chandeliers, containing wax candles.

The interior of the theatre, wrote the *Morning Post* correspondent, was "a spectacle of glory". It was a scene of red velvet and gold tassels, flashing jewellery, superb dresses and bouquets of flowers, all lighted with the high-pitched glare of hissing gas jets. Tall motionless guards stood on the stage, others were below the Imperial box. And now Royalty arrived in all their splendour. The house rose and cheered, then cheered and cheered again. The orchestra waited impatiently for a chance to begin; but it was long before the vivas subsided and "God Save the Queen" could be heard. The Emperor led the Queen to the front of the box where she curtseyed to the audience;

95

and now they all sat down in a row: Prince Albert, Princess Mathilde, Louis Napoleon, the Queen, the Empress and Prince Napoleon. Behind them stood the ladies of honour and officers of the court. Victoria and Eugénie wore white satin dresses and many fine diamonds; the former wore the Ribband of the Garter, the latter the Cordon of the Order of Isabella the Catholic. It was noticed that the Queen was particularly lively and talkative, but that Prince Albert was the least animated of the group. The Queen held a bouquet of most rare and perfect exotic blooms; they were in a holder of pearls and precious stones and had been given to her by the Emperor just before they left the palace.

The six centre boxes had been thrown into one for the night; its aspect, says one of the papers, was of a "severely noble character". Its gilt chairs, covered with crimson satin, were so large as "almost to constitute thrones", and all its elaborate ornamentation, its gilded carving, velvet hangings and coats of arms, were dominated by a large Imperial eagle with outstretched wings. The paper adds that the other boxes were "filled with all that Paris possesses of loveliness, wealth and high position", that "tier after tier vied with its neighbours in the beauty and grace which it displayed", and that the prevailing colours of the ladies' dresses were pink and white.

It had been hoped to give a performance of the opera *Santa Chiara* written by Prince Albert's brother, the Duke of Saxe-Coburg Gotha, who made a hobby of this kind of thing. But it had not been possible to produce it in time, and so a series of operatic selections was given instead, followed by ballet dancing. First there was a trio from *William Tell*; there was a duo from the *Reine de Chypre* and the bolero from the *Vêpres Siciliennes*. Various other airs were sung in costume, and the *Morning Post* correspondent declared that "their Majesties appeared much gratified". But the Queen wrote in her diary that it "was not a very happy arrangement". A ballet of *La Fonti* followed, the chief dancers being Rosati and Plunket; but this was described as being far too long.

Finally a drop screen of Windsor Castle appeared, with a painted Napoleon and Eugénie arriving at the door for their famous visit of the spring. Aloft was a great gilded crown, and "protecting genii hung suspended from the clouds, the youngest and prettiest dancers of the *corps de ballet* having been selected for the purpose". On to this splendid tableau there now fell, to the general wonderment, a cold and harsh illumination made by electric light. And "God save the Queen" was now sung with a truly melting, operatic fervour by Alboni and Cruvelli. The entire audience rose and turned towards the Queen, and there were cheers and cries, with much bowing from the Royal box. The national anthem was sung a second time, and before it was finished the Royal persons gracefully retired. Altogether a really dreadful evening.

But a triumphant evening, all the same. Outside great crowds were assembled to cheer them on their way. The night of pleasure was in full swing all over Paris; the roar of applause continued all along the boulevards as the cortège drove back to the rue Royale; it was taken up in the Champs Elysées, and only dropped as the Arc de Triomphe was reached and the carriages turned into the quiet Avenue de l'Impératrice. The lights were passed now, and the bright moon could be seen; they entered the silent Bois de Boulogne and arrived at St. Cloud at a late hour.

The Emperor was very cheerful, the Queen records, and when they were back in their rooms, he and Albert sang German songs to each other. "He is very fond of Germany, and his old recollections of it," the Queen says, "and there is much that is German, and very little—in fact, nothing—markedly French in his character."

Back in Paris the crowds continued their nocturnal amusements. But gradually the paper lanterns hanging from balconies caught fire and dropped silently to the ground.

CHAPTER X

TEMPLES OF PEACE

ON Wednesday morning the Industrial Palace was to be visited, and this was the main interest of the Parisian holiday for Victoria and Albert. For the Industrial Palace was inspired by the Crystal Palace which was Albert's own triumph and the Queen's happiest memory.

The original idea of an international exhibition had been French. The French Minister of Commerce, returning to the Saint-Simonite dreams of the 1830's, had wished to ask all nations to participate in the Paris exhibition of 1849. He had, however, been overruled by the Chambers of Commerce, who were anxious to maintain protectionism, and by the manufacturers who feared foreign competition. But Henry Cole and Digby Wyatt, members of the Royal Society of Arts, had gone to Paris to see the exhibition and had joined in discussions about the rejected proposal. It seemed an extremely good idea to them; they were immensely impressed by the fine quality of the French national industries, and decided it would be good for certain rather complacent British manufacturers to see their products side by side with those of France. Why should not England, recently converted to the principle of free trade, hold an exhibition in which the products of all countries could be compared? The idea was taken back to Prince Albert, who was the president of the society, and he adopted it at once with the greatest enthusiasm. It was a scheme that lent itself admirably to his wish to see the abolition of war and a definite system of world co-operation established. There should be an exhibition in Hyde Park, and, in his own words, it would be "a step towards the unity of mankind".

It seems natural enough to us, a hundred years later, to hold an international exhibition; but at the time the idea was too original to be taken calmly. The Prince delighted in novel and progressive schemes; but insular, early Victorian England did not always share his taste and an astonishing chorus of wrath fell upon his head. This plan to encourage foreigners and the working classes to assemble in their thousands in Hyde Park heralded nothing less than the doom of the British Empire. God would be offended, and the tone of London's pleasantest residential district would be lowered. Newspapers and politicians joined in the clamour against Albert, and abusive letters reached him by every post. Happily England was also a land of great enterprise and endeavour, and the Prince had his ardent supporters. These, after a long struggle, emerged triumphant from the fray.

The fear of foreigners was caused to a large extent by the fact that in 1848 all Europe had been rocked by revolutions, only England standing firm. The nervous feared that hordes of assassins and revolutionaries would pour into London and enflame the passions of the English working classes. But it was not only the English reactionaries who opposed the scheme; the great continental rulers stood coldly aloof, and at the opening ceremony the foreign ambassadors as a body refused the Prince's invitation to present an address to the Queen. The scheme appeared dangerously Liberal.

Louis Napoleon, however, who was president of France at the time, applauded and encouraged it. French in conception, it was very close to the wishes of a big section of his people, and one of his first acts on coming to power was to authorise the holding of a similar exhibition in Paris to follow up the one in Hyde Park. Thus England and France, popularly regarded as natural enemies, tend to work together. And so it has been for many centuries. Behind the surface rivalries and the well-matched contests of history there is a long and ancient association of the two countries in every branch of civilised development. By instinct each takes heed of every tendency of the other.

In Prince Albert's opinion the exhibition of Hyde Park was an answer to the world's discord. He wished to demonstrate that salvation lay in industry and peaceful co-operation, not in blood and iron. This gathering together of representatives of all races would give the world a new start after the recent disturbances. "It will give us," he said, "a living picture of the point of development at which the whole of mankind has arrived . . . a new starting point from which all nations will be able to direct their further efforts."

The Hyde Park exhibition had been a most brilliant success. Here came not scheming politicians but rational business men from all over the world. The greatly dreaded anarchists did not, after all, put in an appearance, and the working classes, instead of creating disorderly scenes, quietly enjoyed the simple pleasures provided for them. All passed happily and harmoniously, and the Crystal Palace, that "blazing arch of lucid glass" as Thackeray called it, with its fountains, its cobalt blue framework and the leafy trees round which it had been built, became the symbol of universal peace. Popular imagination was caught; from a dread of the foreigner there was a violent swing over to the conviction that the age of permanent friendship with each and every foreigner had dawned. Moreover, owing to Albert's very efficient handling of its finances, the exhibition was remarkably profitable. Critics were silent and mollified, and for a time Albert, who had been generally slighted in England since his marriage, was well thought of.

Nevertheless, hopes had run too high over the Crystal Palace. The dream of the new age of peace soon faded. The exhibition was barely ended at the end of 1851 when Louis Napoleon staged his *coup d'état*. Bonapartism was re-established in France and lent a new military tone to all the continent. Liberals everywhere were shaken. The Empire was proclaimed; and although Louis Napoleon might declare that "the Empire means peace", knowing that this would be pleasing to his hearers, the truth remained that he was a military dictator, and that military men predominated at his court. The French had thrown out their constitutional monarchy; and in exchange for Louis-Philippe, who had been given to pottering about among the shops of Paris with a big, unfurled umbrella beneath his arm, they now had Bonaparte's heir at their head who, far from pottering unassumingly in their midst, appeared abroad only to cut a fine figure, usually that of a general. He loved to appear on a prancing charger. "He is proud of his horsemanship—in which, however, I could discover nothing remarkable," says Albert, sarcastically, in one of his memoranda. But Louis Napoleon represented a reactionary turn of events in Europe which Albert was always hoping to be rid of. He knew, and he was always saying, that there could be no headway made towards a happier world without a complete turning away from the old ideas of selfish national aims. Bonaparte, although so excessively helpful and friendly, had destroyed a dream which, if France had been differently led, might have become a reality. Albert, although he was far too kind to spoil Victoria's pleasure by not attending to her gushing commentaries upon the Emperor, and although outwardly upon very friendly terms with him, did not like the man.

The Crimean War had quickly followed the proclamation

of the new Empire, and it was in full swing when the Paris exhibition opened. Undaunted by this, however, the Emperor had declared on the opening day: "I have pleasure in opening this Temple of Peace which invites all peoples to join in unity." And it was typical of the spirit of the times that, despite the war, Russia had been invited to send in entries, although she had not availed herself of the offer.

It must be remembered that the Second Empire—epoch of strange contradictions—was intensely nationalistic and yet at the same time shared the international aspirations which were surging up everywhere among enlightened men. The Imperialistic aims of Bonapartism existed side by side with the strong following of the Comte de Saint-Simon, the chief originator of French Socialism. Saint-Simon had died in 1825, but his ideas were growing in influence. He desired an industrialised state directed by science, with war abolished by international agreement, and society organised for productive labour with the aim of creating prosperity and ease for all men. The amelioration of the existence of the poorest classes was the most urgent concern of society and was to be dealt with first. The idea of unity with England, to which few listened in his day, he declared to be inevitable at some time or other in the future. His teaching became rather fantastic when he transformed it into a form of religion in which the spiritual direction of society was to be in the hands of the men of science.

Saint-Simon's last instructions were left to Olinde Rodrigues and Prosper Enfantin; the revolution of 1830 encouraged the movement which was joined by some of the ablest men of France; they advocated community of goods, the abolition of the right of inheritance and the equality of women with men. But in the end the followers of Enfantin, who was a prominent business man, became a mere sect and the more serious members retired. The rest led a communistic life at Menilmontant, marked by very unconventional moral standards and an eccentric dress consisting of white trousers, red waistcoat and a violet-blue tunic. This dress was symbolic. White stood for love, red for work and violet-blue for faith. It meant that the Saint-Simonite was supported by love, fortified his heart with work and enveloped himself in faith. Furthermore, the waistcoat was laced on in such a manner that the wearer could not do it up for himself, and this also meant something: "You have need of your brother; never forget that he also has need of you." Hat and cravat could be chosen according to taste; but it was compulsory to have one's name in large letters across the chest. A necklace of triangles, circles and diamonds was the finishing touch, all with some inner meaning. But the edifying costume did not remain in use for very long. It scarcely suited the Industrial Religion, which of its nature leads to an ever greater hustle and vortex of affairs, and hardly lends itself, as might the quiet cloisters of the older religions, to calling in one's brother to the dressing-room before one can be ready to go out.

The great manifestations of international industry, which appeared first in Hyde Park and then in Paris, were conceived in the dreams of the Saint-Simonites. They inspired semi-religious feelings. The Crystal Palace had opened to the sound of the Hallelujah Chorus and long prayers from the Archbishop of Canterbury. Albert, deeply religious, had regarded the enterprise as an offering to God in humble thanks for the wonders of science which had been revealed for the making of a better world. Victoria had called it the *most beautiful* and *imposing* and *touching* spectacle ever seen, and had added, "Many cried, and all felt touched and impressed with devotional feelings . . ." The Industrial Palace in the Champs Elysées was also a kind of bustling cathedral of modern faith, and its organisation had been in the hands of Saint-Simonites. Frédéric le Play, Arles Dufour, Michel Chevalier and the banker Pereire were all friends of Enfantin or followers at least in part of the doctrine. Up to this time science had been wholly beneficent and really miraculous in the changes it had brought about. So much social good had never been achieved before as that which had resulted from it by the middle of the nineteenth century. The Pope's Syllabus of 1864, which is a wholesale denunciation of all that is modern and Liberal, was still undreamed of outside the Vatican; there was nothing yet to damp anyone's enthusiasms.

Despite the war, the ideology of internationalism and universal peace which had fired their youth was still dominant in the minds of the promoters of the second great exhibition. It remained the obvious aim of reasonable men; had the great wars of the twentieth century been foretold, none would have believed the dreadful prophecy. The establishment of peace seemed nearer than that, and men believed unhesitatingly in Progress as a continued upward road. As soon as the war was over, they thought, and the Russian autocrat beaten, the steady march of progress would be resumed. There was a curious faith in science, particularly in the quaint little railway trains of the day with their tall chimneys. These, combined with steamships, were enabling people to travel quickly, easily and cheaply from one country to another. Railway travelling, like all the fine inventions that had changed the face of society, had come into use in a peaceful age; they seemed connected with peace. When the Crimean War started it broke a spell of nearly forty years in which there had been no war between the Christian nations. It was popularly thought that war and discord had been caused in the past by misunderstandings, and that such misunderstandings would scarcely be possible in the future when science had finished linking all the nations together with railway tracks and telegraph wires.

The true implications of the return of Bonapartism were not popularly seen. Louis Napoleon was filled with Imperial ambition and the determination to restore the lustre of French arms. He threw dust in the eyes of the masses and persuaded them that military glory spelt peace and prosperity. Prince Napoleon, making himself for once the official mouthpiece of Bonapartism, declared that France, through holding an international exhibition while at war, was proving herself to be both "great in peace and powerful in war". So the emphasis was disastrously shifted from the ideal of peace, to the expedient of obtaining credit through a false use of the word "peace". And *Le Moniteur*, official paper of the state, said that France was "crowned at the exhibition, as elsewhere, with victories and saluted as Queen by the acclamation of the human race". It was not of national glory and prestige that Prince Albert had dreamed as he toiled at the task of preparing the Crystal Palace, nor was it of these the Saint-Simonites before him dreamed. The vision had been of a world that had grown up, that had outgrown the craving for glory and prestige. But already Europe's doom was closing in upon her, even while the sun shone in full brilliance. If Europe, if the world, chose to abandon the ancient religion to follow a new priesthood of scientists, it must abandon war; it could not afford both war and science; for science brings efficiency and regimentation in all things, war included. The first Napoleon gave a foretaste of what this horrid mixture of war and science would be. As the Industrial Revolution was beginning to regiment masses of men in factories he came to regiment the rest in barracks. A dreary and outrageous possibility for man was demonstrated, that the factory which was just springing into being could be nicely balanced against war and put to the service of death. Napoleon, the bringer of total war, was defeated by the coalition of Europe, and the world breathed again. But now, the second Emperor of that unhappy breed had arisen in Europe. And well meaning though he may have been, kindly and human though he undoubtedly was in the majority of his moods, he was the link between the old aggressive spirit and the new. The god Mars had run into bad times after the Congress of Vienna. By the time the 1840's came, with Victoria ruling in England, Louis-Philippe in France, the Saxe-Coburgs in many high places, with all rulers anxious for peace, there was a chance that good sense might prevail and fighting become a thing of the past. But Napoleon III came at the psychological moment to save the situation for the god of war. Bent upon a host of idealistic schemes, he was prepared to bring them about by force of arms. His reign was one long series of flashy military parades. Fine guards were for ever clattering up and down the streets of Paris, and his régime was one of constant sabre-rattling. As Karl Marx said, the device of France was changed from "Liberty, Fraternity and Equality" to "Infantry, Cavalry and Artillery". All those crack regiments, the Cavalry dashing gallantly hither and thither, the splendid uniforms,— all those "dear Zouaves" and "splendid *Cent Gardes*" by whom Victoria was so enthralled during her visit, were changing the face of Europe; they were fanning the flames of chauvinism in France and striking terror abroad. England, although in alliance during the Crimean War, was very uneasy both before and after and there were many invasion scares. Belgium was still more uneasy, the Germans were afraid. In this last lay the disaster; Germany, ready for union, was led in its fear of a militarised France to follow a strong man, and Bismarck was the answer to Bonapartism. Thus the humane ideals of Europe, that had steadily been gaining ground, were driven back without anyone's noticing what was happening until it was too late.

All the men who have laboured for peace since the Industrial Revolution began have laboured in vain thanks to Bonaparte and Bismarck and all that their deeds have led to. The men who were striving for peace a hundred years ago are now forgotten. Who thinks any more of the efforts of Prince Albert for the good of his fellow-men? The world still talks of the "military genius" of Napoleon I, and of the "brilliant statesmanship" of Bismarck. Worldly success is not achieved without faults, and both these men imposed their will on others with the aid of lies and deceptions. But for Albert who was the soul of honour, and a thousand like

him who strove to increase happiness in the world, the pages of
history have only faint praise.

In this summer of 1855 the dream of Peace and Progress was
part of the popular philosophy. And the Queen was held to be
in Paris not to promote a speeding up of the war, or for military
counsels, but to join with France in bringing about a higher
standard of life for all men. She had come, in the words of the
Illustrated London News, "to share with her great ally in the triumph
of industry, to aid in the development of those arts whose highest
aim is the increase of domestic enjoyment, the advancement of
commercial prosperity, and an addition to the happiness of all
mankind."

On the morning of Wednesday, the 22nd of August, crowds
assembled round the Industrial Palace with boundless enthusiasm.
Now only were they eager to see the Emperor and the Queen,
they derived tremendous satisfaction from the exhibition itself
which showed them all the wonders of science and seemed
to typify the very spirit of the new Empire. For the Empire was
popular at this time with almost all classes. The people were
happy and contented; things really seemed to be going well for
once. Paris, that most volatile, intelligent and difficult of cities,
considered at this time as the home of revolutions, had already
forgotten 1848 and its enthusiasm for Republicanism. The
workers thought no more of their champions, now in exile in
London and Brussels. The Empire provided them with work
and good wages,—or at least better wages than they had had
before; Haussmann, the Prefect of the Seine, had embarked on
plans that would provide work for as many years ahead as anyone cared to think of. It was a time of great expansion. Business
of all types prospered, and the industrial middle classes were
growing rich almost without an effort; Imperial fêtes and displays
were daily occurrences in the capital, and even the poorest felt
the benefit of the general wealth. With prosperity in the air, with
work, plenty to eat and plenty of amusement, men are happy
to forget about politics. So the working classes danced on fête
days in their own ballrooms, and with the utmost good humour;
and Bonaparte society danced and amused itself all the time.

For the latter it was a golden age; it had become the easiest
thing in the world to make money, and social problems were
being solved in a most agreeable manner. It was certainly
encouraging to find that a life of luxury and ease was really

philanthropy in disguise, and that the great balls and festivals and the extravagant needs of the rich all helped the poor, and kept them too busy and amused to occupy themselves with dangerous revolutionary theories. This was not entirely a vain and selfish delusion, either. A fair amount of genuine idealism was merged with the general self-seeking of society. The court was corrupt, but the Emperor himself was a genuine champion of the masses and was determined to improve their conditions; there were wealthy and influential followers of Saint-Simon living then who had generous theories as to how to deal with the possibilities of the industrial revolution. An effort was made to create prosperity in an ever-widening circle, and the ambition to bring plenty to all men was very real. The richer classes really believed they were interesting themselves in the well-being of the poor, even if they sometimes deluded themselves. The exhibition in the Champs Elysées was overflowing with humanitarian aspirations, from the hopes entertained of getting aluminium goods on the market at a low price, to the enthusiasms of the new shoe industry which was to be a blessing to the entire world. "No one doubts," said a journalist of the time, writing in the popular vein, "that our manufacturers think far less of enriching themselves than of creating happiness among the people." *Bon marché* was the word of the day, the goal officially set for commerce that was to raise the standard of life. And the shop of that name, the *Bon Marché* of Paris, had opened in 1852.

So far as anyone could then judge, men were on the right lines; for on a system of creating pleasure and social improvements France was growing rich. The opposite of a vicious circle seemed to have been set in motion: a beneficent circle in which pleasure created prosperity and more pleasure. All this was put down to the blessings of science which had suddenly descended on the world for its transformation to a Utopia; and but for the military tone of the Empire, the magic circle might have continued to work.

The modest, useful science of a hundred years ago, how pleasing it was to the world! The steam engines, the electric telegraph, gas lighting, electric light, photography, anaesthetics, the mass-produced goods, the false jewellery and electro-plate, the promise of luxury for all through the production of new and cheap substances, the promise of leisure for man while the machine worked— all this was a subject of delight which the presence of guns and steel from Messrs. Krupp, and artillery pieces invented by Louis Napoleon, did not in any way diminish. They were hardly noticeable among the vast array of beautiful and useful things in the Palace of Industry.

There was perfect confidence in the future and a feeling of unshakable security; individual troubles were toned down by a background of general satisfaction. Through the mists of time, indeed, our great-grandparents look astonishingly smug as we see them enjoying the delights of Paris. They should by rights have been struggling to establish a just society, instead of leaning back and waiting for a lot of lifeless machines to do it for them; they should have been thinking about democracy, instead of joining in the general hero-worship of Napoleon and the praise of his successful nephew. But however one might like to go back and give full vent to one's annoyance, it is impossible to disturb them in their sunny strip of time. There they are, beyond the reach of any reproaches, sitting outside Tortoni's, eating peaches and drinking iced wine. The men are in their newly ironed and excessively tall hats and their fancy tweeds, the women in glacé silk or embroidered muslin, with their hair done *à L'Impératrice* beneath their bonnets of flowers and feathers. They sit, happy or furious according to whether or not they have received tickets for the ball at the Hotel de Ville to-morrow night; and we, like the fools of the piece, are left among the ruins and desolation of Europe.

CHAPTER XI

THE QUEEN GOES TO THE EXHIBITION

LONG before ten o'clock there were many thousands in the neighbourhood of the exhibition, although the Royal visitors were not expected for another hour. People were crowding into all the entrances of the Palace of Industry, for although it had been decided (after Monday's lesson) that only season-ticket holders and exhibitors were to be admitted, it was easy enough to buy a season-ticket since they were for sale at the doors.

The weather was again brilliant and there was no cloud in the sky; the enthusiasm of the crowds, far from diminishing as the week went on, increased from hour to hour. There was nothing rigid about the rejoicings of the week; the decorations as well as the flowers were constantly changed and renewed. And the public were not separated by a row of bayonets from the Royal visitors and their hosts; private equipages and hired cabs were always passing up and down the roads when the Emperor and his guests drove along them, and there was a good chance for anyone to get a close view of the Queen. Nor were the people passively looking on at the pleasures of the few at the top; pleasure and fêtes abounded for all.

All night long workmen had been busy transforming the main entrance of the Industrial Palace into a great gold and velvet pavilion; a crimson canopy, broadly striped with yellow, now stretched far out into the road, and the steps were covered with a thick carpet. New masts and flagpoles had arisen all round, loads of flowers scented the warm air, and banners had appeared outside houses and shops of the district with greetings to the visitors: "Welcome to France", and "*Vive la Reine et Albert*".

The Champs Elysées was lively and animated from end to end. It was certainly very crowded, but not unpleasantly so; the *Morning Post*, in describing the scene, says, "the natural courtesy of the French prevents anything like inconvenient crowding". The paper goes on to complain of the conduct of the English visitors who, it seems, were rude and selfish. In fact, whereas in forming a crowd the French became an "assemblage", the English, apparently, became a "mob".

The Avenue des Champs Elysées was the pleasantest place in the world in those days. We know it now, given over to a straggling commercialism and a few tepid pleasures, with four brazen lines of irritable motorists speeding up and down when times are prosperous, and at other times wearing an air of over-sized emptiness. But in the days of the Second Empire it was gay and leisurely. Instead of the inhuman, dull and dangerous cars there were elegant carriages rolling up and down, and their occupants had time to watch what was going on about them; they did not hoot at and harass the pedestrians, they provided an agreeable parade for them to watch. On a quiet day, the people sitting on the green iron chairs, hired for two sous, had time to study the turn-out of the horses and the ladies' well displayed clothes, and to gossip about them as they passed. And spread up the length of the avenue were the hearty, if rather naive, delights of our Victorian forefathers. First and foremost, in the year in question, there was the exhibition; then there were musical entertainments of all kinds. On a serious level there was the miniature open-air theatre, the *Théâtre des Bouffes Parisiens*, where Jacques Offenbach was tasting the beginning of fame. Here the public listened to that light-hearted music which, becoming more brilliantly frivolous from year to year, was to be the apt musical accompaniment to the Second Empire and all its follies. There was music in the cafés, too, the café concerts of the *Ambassadeurs*, the *Café Morel* and the *Pavillon du jeu de Boule*. "The visitors," says an English guide book of the day, "are accommodated in the open air, and the singers under elegant kiosks, gaily painted and adorned with flowers." Near the Place de la Concorde was a large Winter Garden which, says the same book, was like the most luxurious regions of the East, apart from the welcome absence of the tiger. "Here the camellias, the yucca and the cactus meet the visitor's eye in juxtaposition with the palm tree, the arancania and the banana. An aviary filled with exotic birds is to the right; in the centre is a grass plot extending to a romantic grotto; while walls are completely coated with mirrors and lined with passiflores and other creeping plants." There were dances here at night, and children's balls were also held. And what with the rare flowers, pools in the form of enormous sea-shells, cascades, and groups of statuary, the spectator, we are told, could not help feeling that he was in Tasso's Garden of

Armida. We may be sure, however, that some of the cast-iron ornamentation, so dear to Victorian and Second Empire days, had found its way into the would-be Eastern scene.

There was dancing, too, higher up the avenue at the *Chateau des Fleurs* which, as its name implies, was noted for its profusion of beautiful flowers. These were "disposed in groves and recesses", and the place was lighted at night with Chinese lanterns, elegant candelabra and festoons in the trees. "A café and restaurant afford every desirable refreshment; there are besides, for amateurs, a *tir*, or shooting gallery, a *jeu de bagues*, Chinese billiards, and other pastimes. The company is good, and the pleasures of the dance are enjoyed with every regard to decorum." For those who had not come to Paris in search of decorum there was the *Jardin Mabille*, just off the avenue in the *Allée des Veuves*. Here, beneath "a profusion of gas lights suspended from artificial palm trees," the guide book warns the tourist that "the limits of propriety are frequently surpassed."

At the Rond Point there was a circus, the *Cirque de l'Impératrice*; Panoramas and Dioramas abounded, the latter perfected by Monsieur Daguerre. Beneath the shady trees were the toy stalls, the Punch and Judy show and the aerial ships; and a host of wandering entertainers lent colour to the scene. There were jugglers, tumblers and performing dogs, as well as the ambulant cooks and lemonade sellers. To-day only a few toy stalls and the Punch and Judy show remain.

Now it was eleven o'clock; groups of police in their cocked hats had been standing about before the Palace of Industry, and they now began to clear the entrance ready for the arrival of the Emperor and his guests. Mounted Dragoons cleared the space before the steps by making spectacular charges at the vehicles that were standing there. And now distant cheers were heard, and a military band began to play the national anthem.

Twelve carriages soon came into view, passing under the Arc de Triomphe with a large escort; the cheers and cries were tremendous. "Wherever the Queen goes," says the *Illustrated Times*, "she is received with an enthusiasm that almost amounts to worship." Now she was stepping from her carriage, assisted by Louis Napoleon. She was plainly dressed in white, with a blue shawl round her shoulders; but everyone noticed her radiantly happy expression,—good health and high spirits seemed to radiate from her. As the crowds cheered she turned in delight towards them, hesitated, then laughed and bowed with a friendly expression of gratitude. She delighted everyone, and as the cheers subsided, the flattering comments of the crowd could be heard.

Victoria walked forward, arm-in-arm with Louis Napoleon who, in morning dress, carried his stove-pipe hat which shone as brightly as his pomaded hair and his curled and waxed moustaches. Even he, schooled in impassivity and known as "the sphinx", was veiled and secretive no longer. Triumph overflowed from him, as pleasure overflowed from Victoria. The *Manchester Guardian* had been watching him, and had noted at the Opera last night that "when he spoke to her, his eyes sparkled with unwonted brilliancy and a smile curled about his lips. In that countenance, so difficult to read, one might plainly see, mixed with an unfeigned deference and respect for his illustrious guest, a sentiment of intense self-satisfaction at having gained a great political point at which he had long been aiming." And to-day, says the paper, the Emperor looked deeply gratified as he entered the exhibition, "being well satisfied, profound and astute politician that he is, that he never spent time so profitably or executed more refined diplomacy than during these hours of apparently delightful relaxation, spent in attentions to the greatest monarch of the world."

Prince Napoleon was standing at the entrance with a group of commissioners, and he led the party into the building. The Queen sat down for a short time in a reception room, and various jurors were introduced to her. Then, taking the Emperor's arm, and followed by Prince Albert, the children, and members of the suite, she began the tour of the building.

As the Royal party entered the main hall there was a ringing cry of "*Vive Victoria*" which made all the windows rattle, and the ladies gazing down from the galleries waved hundreds of handkerchiefs. The Emperor led his guests to the transept to see the general effect of the vast building. "To the left," says the *Illustrated London News*, "her Majesty perceived the majestic outline of the Dutch pulpit, Elkington and Mason's fine bronzes, Cain's bold eagles, and the great naval trophy of England. To the right lay the great lighthouse ornamented by Jérome, the great sheet of glass from Belgium, the gilt altars of France, the Austrian terra-cottas and the Bohemian glass." The rectangular building was a true commercial cathedral of Saint-Simonian dreams; it was divided into transept and aisles, and along its length ran nearly three hundred cast iron columns which supported the broad upper galleries. These galleries, too, had their rows of iron columns, and at each end of the building were stained glass windows whose subjects were: "France convening all Nations to the Exhibition", and "Equity presiding over the Increase of Exchange". With its bustling crowds all agog over the working machinery and its products, and their modern faith in a Utopia, what a far cry it was from the cathedrals of past ages, created for meditation on another world! Yet it aroused an equally fervid faith.

This building had none of the sparkling, fairy-like charm of the Crystal Palace, constructed of glass around trees. It was larger, and it was decidedly ugly. But it had a curved glass roof, and to-day this was deep blue from the summer sky. A dense throng of people was here, although for the moment they were mostly assembled in the galleries in order to look down and have a good view of the Royal entry. Apart from the numerous exhibitors and the many who already held season-tickets, over eleven hundred people had bought season-tickets this morning at the entrance. These people were mainly of the leisured class, so large in those days. They leaned on the railings above; the ladies wonderfully and impractically dressed with their flowing, frilly skirts, held out by half-a-dozen under-skirts. The gentlemen in morning dress carried the inevitable top hat, well ironed and very tall, and wore their uncreased trousers very tight. Their beards showed a wonderful variety of styles: most popular was the Imperial with its waxed moustaches and brief pointed beard; but there were others clipped closely in the Assyrian style, some that flowed all over the chest and some shaped like daggers.

Now, with the bands playing "God save the Queen" and a general bustle in the building, people began to come downstairs. The Royal party turned to the right and, with hardly a glance at the nave stalls of Parisian jewellery, millinery and fans, entered the court of French bronzes. Here Victoria stood for some time, gazing at a statue of Joan of Arc by Marie d'Orléans, the gifted daughter of Louis-Philippe whose early death was the first of the long run of misfortunes that had overtaken his family. As she inspected this work of art, journalists formulated all manner of interesting and melancholy thoughts with which to accredit her: for it added great piquancy to her visit to Louis Napoleon that she was the friend and relation of the family whom he had supplanted. According to the *Illustrated Times*, which had talked of her air of gaiety only a moment before, she appeared much

Between pages 112 *and* 113]

STATUE OF THE EMPEROR OUTSIDE ONE OF THE ENTRANCES TO THE EXHIBITION.
(*From a photograph.*)

depressed when she turned away. "Indeed, she passed by a stall of wonderful lace without even honouring it with a glance."

After the lace came gloves and dress materials and then the sections of the German states: Wurtemberg, Bavaria, Hanover, Saxony and Prussia. But it was not at all easy to see the exhibits, for the crowds had arrived downstairs and were surging close to the visitors. There had been a mistake in the organization of the visit, too; the jurors should have been stationed in their respective divisions, instead of which they had formed themselves into a procession which followed the commissioners and the Royal and Imperial suites. Seeing this procession, scores of the public joined it in their turn, hoping to pass as ladies and gentlemen in waiting, and this caused a good deal of confusion. It was also intensely hot; the sunlight bore down on the roof and the atmosphere was very stuffy. "And wherever the Royal party went," says one of the papers, "bands suddenly gave notice of their hidden positions by striking up 'God save the Queen'. No sooner had one group of performers ended than another began."

But the Royal party went on as best they could and now visited the Austrian and Belgian sections and then went on to that of England. Here "God save the Queen" was played upon the English organ of the musical section. England had been allotted the largest amount of space after France and the Queen lingered here for some time, particularly among the ceramic manufacturers—Rose, Copeland, Wedgewood. Here was a candelabrum that the Queen had ordered to be made for the Emperor, and another that Eugénie had given the Queen, an affair of hunting horns and antlers, supported by a Scotch ghillie, and just the thing for Balmoral. There was a dinner service presented to the Emperor by the Lord Mayor of London, and a copy of a toilet service that Albert had given to the Queen. Furniture, pianos, marbles, bronzes, embroidery (with its stalls of Berlin slippers), dress materials and a host of other things were looked at in a desultory manner, for the crowds were pressing inconveniently close and the Royal persons were frequently separated from their suite. There was a considerable fracas close at hand from time to time as the police and the employés of the building tried to keep unwarranted persons away from the group.

Now the English section was left and a group of objects classed as "Trophies of War" was inspected. Here were specimens of a new cannon that Louis Napoleon himself had invented, and that had been in use at Alma and Inkermann. Victoria was pausing to look at them, but always most polite and tactful her host led her away to spare her the necessity of complimenting him. Passing the trophies, the visitors went into the French printing section. "Here before the stall exhibited by the Emperor's printer, Monsieur Henri Plon, his Imperial Majesty was the first to notice a splendid expanse of white satin. Drawing towards Monsieur Plon, his Majesty at once enquired whether this satin, upon which were verses to the Queen by Barthélemy, was intended for presentation to her Majesty. At this moment the Queen came up, whereupon the Emperor presented the verses."

The visitors now went to the Panorama, the circular building which joined the palace by a passage-way to the annexe containing machinery. Here they began to look at the French furniture; but now the pressure of the crowd became greater than ever and "some rather serious scuffling took place". The Royal party was led into the inner court, and the police turned the public out, and with them the Marquis of Breadalbane and one or two other gentlemen of the Queen's suite.

In this central court were the finest things in the exhibition. The crown jewels were here, to see which the public usually had to wait in a queue. All round on the walls hung the tapestries and carpets of Beauvais, Gobelins and Aubusson; there was a big display of Sèvres china, and of electro-plate by Christofle. While they were here the Emperor presented Prince Albert with a beautiful Sèvres vase commemorating the Crystal Palace exhibition, and the Queen purchased a "pretty oxydised tazza".

The visitors sat and rested for a time, and they drank chocolate from exquisitely light and fine Sèvres china cups. After this Louis Napoleon led them up to something that particularly interested him, the display of aluminium. He had supplied funds from his own privy purse to have experiments made with this new metal which he hoped would be of great benefit to the poorer classes. It was on view in bars, and also made up into spoons, forks, tankards and other domestic articles.

From the Panorama they went to the Gallery of Industrial Design, and "'God save the Queen' was played on Du Croquet's large organ"; from here they passed into the Annexe, the gallery of raw products and machinery which had also been cleared of the public. Here there was a hum of working machines, here also was the Prussian steel exhibited by Krupp. But the party were hot and tired after the agitating walk round the main building, and they did not linger very long. They paused to admire a machine which wrapped up bars of chocolate, and another which made yards of "Alliance ribbon" before your eyes—Victoria and Napoleon in full colour, surrounded by flowers and flags. Then at last they turned away to leave the exhibition. Re-entering the Imperial carriages, they drove off in a blaze of sunshine and a chorus of applause to the Palace of the Tuileries where the afternoon was to be spent.

The Palace of the Tuileries, which was later destroyed during the revolution of 1871, was joined on to the Louvre and faced west, overlooking the gardens and the Place de la Concorde. Louis Napoleon had made it his principal palace, and when he had lunched with his guests he spent some time showing them round the building. First they saw his private rooms: his bedroom, with busts of his father, the one-time King of Holland, and of his famous uncle; and other rooms which contained Bonaparte relics in glass cases, and portraits of his mother Queen Hortense, and his elder brother who had died. The Queen was also shown many historical objects, among them the cabinet on which Louis-Philippe signed his abdication. Then they went up a small private staircase which led to the Empress's rooms; these were lavishly furnished and decorated and were greatly admired. From here they went to a more official room where the celebrated Prefect, Haussmann, was waiting for them. He had come to give the Queen an invitation to the ball at the Hotel de Ville to-morrow night, an invitation which was gracefully accepted. He also had a long address to read, with compliments from the Municipality of Paris; but the Emperor managed to put a stop to this. "The Préfet then asked whether they might call the new street leading to the Hôtel de Ville after me," says the Queen's diary, "on which I said '*Je serai bien flattée de cela*' then turning towards the Emperor, '*si L'Empereur le permet*,' on which he cordially gave his consent. I then observed upon the beauty of the city, and all that the Emperor had done for it."

After this interview, the Queen says, "we went to see the State Rooms, which are magnificent: the Salle Blanche, Salle du Trône, Salle de la Paix, in which there is a large statue in silver, of Peace, la Salle des Maréchaux, beautifully redecorated by the Emperor, who has had entirely to renovate the Tuileries after the horrors of '48. Then the Galerie de Diane, a long apartment, which has had to be divided, and the Chapel (nothing very particular, and resembling ours in the Palaces), and the Theatre, which is very pretty. Everything is on such a large scale, so truly regal. The view from the middle window of the Salle des Maré-chaux, looking up the Tuileries gardens, to the Place de la Concorde, is extremely fine. The Emperor thinks that the Obelisk spoils the view. . . ."

The Royal family separated during the afternoon; Prince Albert went out to pay visits to Prince Napoleon, Princess Mathilde and the Papal Nuncio; the Prince of Wales was allowed out shopping with his correct and unbending tutor, Mr. Gibbs, and the Queen and the Princess Royal remained with Louis Napoleon. Later in the afternoon, however, amid much laughter, the Queen and Prince Albert, with the Princess Royal and Miss Bulteel, entered a remise under the disguise of ordinary mortals. The Queen had sent to a shop for some "common bonnets", one of which was put on her own head and the others commanded to be put on the heads of her daughter and lady-in-waiting. She put on a black mantilla, and pulled a black veil over her face. "In going through the gates," she says, "the curious crowd looked very hard into the carriage which stopped for a moment, and we felt very foolish. However, we got away, and by help of my veil I was able to look out, and we took a charming long drive by the Rue de Rivoli, Rue de Castiglione, Place Vendôme, Rue de la Paix, all along the Boulevards des Capucines, des Italiens, Montmartre, Poissonnière, Bonne-Nouvelle, St. Denis, St. Martin, du Temple, des Filles-du-Calvaire and Beaumarchais, then by the Place de la Bastille (where stands the Colonne de Juillet) . . ."

Victoria was delighted with it all. Now at last she could have a good look at this most delightful city; now instead of looking at cheering crowds and bowing her acknowledgments as she drove, she herself was being entertained by those crowds as they strolled on the boulevards and sat enjoying their apéritifs and ices outside the cafés. It was all splendid. Even the hardware shops were far better than at home. Why, Victoria asked, could the London shops not arrange knives and scissors in big circles like those in the windows here?

From the Place de la Bastille they went down to the river, crossing the Pont d'Austerlitz "where," says the Queen, "we had a beautiful view up and down the river, and along the quays, everything there looking so light, and white, and bright, with great numbers of people and soldiers in bright colours, *marchands de coco*, etc., people sitting and drinking before the houses, all so foreign and southern looking to my eyes and so gay. We then drove along the Place Walhubert, to the Jardin des Plantes, then by the Marché-aux-Fleurs (very pretty along the quay), Halle-aux-Vins (a number of curious little houses in a sort of garden), Quai de la Tournelle, Quai Montebello, Quai St. Michel, then across the Pont au Change, opposite the old Tower of St. Jacques, and by the Quai de la Mégisserie, Quai de l'Ecole, Quai du Louvre. . . ."

But now the novelty was wearing off. Someone on the pavement glanced into the carriage and said that Victoria looked rather like the Queen, and she bridled and began to grow a little fidgety over being passed by as a person of no consequence whatsoever. She soon grew tired of not being a queen; obscurity was very entertaining in its way for a short time, but she began to feel lost without the attentions due to fame. When she looked round and said "They don't seem to know who I *am*," say the memoirs of Lady Ponsonby, it was a sure sign that she was beginning to be bored.

They reached the Palace of the Tuileries shortly before six. "We found the Emperor in the drawing-room below stairs," says the Queen. "We changed our bonnets, and immediately re-entered open carriages to return to St. Cloud, where we arrived at near seven." There in her rooms the Queen found all that she had singled out for special admiration in the Palace of Industry. The Emperor—that truly attentive and indeed quite fascinating man—had somehow contrived to remember each item and have it purchased as an offering to her.

A large banquet was held at St. Cloud that evening. The Queen and the Emperor had a long and interesting conversation about their ambassadors, the diplomatic conventions of Europe, and about the war. News had come by telegraph that day from General Simpson, saying that a vertical fire had been begun which was taking good effect. While the entertainments of the last day or two had been taking place in Paris, ten thousand shells had been thrown into Sebastopol.

When dinner was over, there was a play in the small, jewel-like theatre of the palace. *Un Fils de Famille* was given by the actors of the Gymnase. "But," says the *Illustrated London News*, "although the piece was excellently well played, the performance went off coldly. The actors felt the restraint of court, there was no applause. The Queen laughed good-naturedly, and the Emperor alone applauded when the curtain fell."

CHAPTER XII

VERY DECORATIVE ARTS

ON Thursday morning Victoria stayed at St. Cloud to do water colour sketches of the Zouaves in the lovely garden, to enjoy a stroll with the Emperor among the flowers and the fountains, and to write to Uncle Leopold. "I am *delighted, enchanted, amused,* and *interested,*" she said in her letter, "and I think I never saw *anything* more *beautiful* and gay than Paris. . . ."

But Prince Albert at an early hour was riding down the Champs Elysées in a char-a-bancs, accompanied only by one or two gentlemen. They were going without any ceremony to the Industrial Palace to make up for the lost chances of looking round yesterday. The Prince, having such an enthusiasm for art and industry, was anxious to examine some of the exhibits that he had noticed out of the corner of his eye.

He was received by a few of the commissioners at the entrance; Prince Napoleon was to have met him here, but was late. So after waiting in vain for some minutes, Prince Albert began his tour of inspection, untroubled by bands and crowds. First he went to the French section of the nave where every article of luxury was on view. Here were the stalls of the pre-eminent jewellers: Vechte, Froment-Meurice, Callot; here were the fans of Duvelleroy, the lace, the silk and the gloves which Paris makes so well. Here also were a host of hybrid metals and false gems; the age of imitations came fully into its own with this exhibition, and there was hardly a substance which was not imitated in the Industrial Palace and sold cheaply. It was all part of the praise-worthy endeavour—so typical of the Second Empire—to make luxury a universal commodity. But unfortunately the *nouveautés de Paris,* that host of superfluous ornaments which the gay, new society found essential to life, displayed a very riot of bad taste. Magnificent progress in physics and chemistry had been made, socially and economically the world had been transformed since the fall of the *ancien régime.* But when the head of Marie Antoinette was chopped off, good taste died in the world just as drastically. However wicked the old régime had been, it had upheld the traditions of European culture. Napoleon and Eugénie had no appreciation at all of the fine arts, and with them vulgarity settled down on Europe. Boule and Reisener were no more, and as vulgarity is always self-satisfied, the perpetrators of the new Industrial Art felt themselves to be marching ever forward and upward, with civilisation itself, to splendours undreamed of by artists of the past. Only this conceit could have enabled them to believe that their disgraceful Minerva resembled the work of Phidias.

However, a thousand delightful trifles were displayed side by side with the trash; even some of the fussy filigree ornaments and the brooches and bracelets containing hair were charming in their way. The sunshades, with handles of ivory, jade and coral, and covers of silk and costly lace, were a delight to the eye; the toys were wonderful, ingenious and highly finished; the dress materials showed a thousand new substances, from translucent gauze to heavy velvet, and were made in the season's colours: Garnet, Siberia, Violet, Acajou, Fumée de Londres, Myrthe, Tan d'or, Napoleon (which was bright blue) and Blonde (which was a pink shade). Hats showed a frivolous ingenuity unknown elsewhere, and there was a great variety of artificial flowers.

The Prince turned now to the glass section, where he particularly admired a lion in solid glass. It was noticed by one of the papers that the Prince, who had been so subdued at the Opera House, was in a gay humour here and seemed to be enjoying himself very thoroughly. Going up to a toy stall "he laughed very heartily at a baboon playing a fiddle". The baboon went by clockwork and made amusing grimaces as it played. No doubt he also looked at the talking doll, for it was one of the features of the exhibition.

While he was looking at some ornaments executed for Ali Pacha, Prince Napoleon arrived and they continued the inspection together. English exhibits from Sheffield were looked at, and then the musical wind-instruments. Sax, the inventor of the Saxophone, had a stand here; he was in his element in this new Bonaparte Empire which laid such stress on military music, and received a medal of honour at the exhibition. The Prince laughingly observed that some of his instruments reminded him of brass sea-serpents. Bronzes, enamelled cups and diamonds were admired, and silver, crystal and repoussé work was looked at. They admired the dinner service which the Russian ambassador had ordered before leaving the country, and then they studied a model of the newest screw-steamer for the *Messageries-Impériales*, called the *Danube*.

They spent some time among the bronzes, where the Prince made "critical remarks", and where he pointed out to Prince Napoleon the statues of Pomona and Ceres by Miroy which he had ordered for the Queen. And after that they went upstairs, pausing to admire "an ingenious apparatus of Monsieur Foucalt for demonstrating the movement of the earth". They walked along the gallery among the displays of French silk and lace, shawls, perfume, shoes and fans. They were now in the vicinity of the Empress's boudoir, and the most varied array of delightful clothing was displayed. All was inspired by the beautiful Empress. There were dresses, hats and shoes made for her, and copies of them cheaply reproduced for the middle class public to buy. These dresses were being manufactured in great numbers, and by the autumn would be on sale in most countries. Such advertisements as the following appeared in the English press:

NOW READY!!!

The Empress Eugénie's Robe, price 35s., from the Paris Exhibition, composed of real Cashmire, Merino, exquisitely fine, with woven Velvet or Peluche ombre, flounces, and full complement for Bodice included, produced by Messrs. Rumbell & Owen in the undermentioned new colours for winter, viz:

Lucine	Nieuwerkerke
Violet	Ruby
Marron claire	Alma
Black	Myrthe
Gris Protestant	Raisin d'Espagne

Another London firm announced its display of Paris dresses which included "flounced silk robes, interwoven with velvets, chènes, floss-fringed plushes, etc.; dinner and ball dresses of glacé silks, elaborately embroidered; mantles in every elegant design and shape, ornamented with rich trimmings of the newest plushes, or beautifully figured with needlework. Ribbons and ribbon-trimmings in endless varieties, together with every novelty upon which Imperial patronage or public approbation has bestowed any justifiable notoriety."

Prince Albert was taken to see the Empress's private boudoir; this was a lavishly furnished room, all velvet, gilt and flowers, its walls covered with historic tapestry that had been executed for Louis XIV. The Prince next walked to the end of the gallery in

THE ALLIANCE RIBBON

"This tasteful commemoration of the union of England and France is displayed in the Paris Universal Exhibition, where the visitors have the gratification of seeing the ribbon made in a loom worked by steam power, by a workman in the employ of Mr. James Hart, of Coventry. The ribbon was designed by Mr. Pratt, and draughted by Mr. Robert Barton. It represents Queen Victoria and the Emperor of the French. Our Queen is placed under the tricolour; Louis Napoleon is placed under the Union Jack; surrounded with the arms of both nations and wreaths of flowers, the words in English and French underneath, 'May God bless the Alliance.' The ribbon has attracted considerable attention, as a proof of the advancement made by this country in her appliance of steam-power to arts and manufactures."

(*Illustrated London News.*)

[*Face page* 120

order to obtain a good view of the transept with its crowded stalls, its palms and many decorations. This he pronounced to be most picturesque. Now, with his companions, he looked at more of the jewellery of France; here were the stalls of Payen, Lemoine, Maret, Albite and Dotin, and they showed jewellery, enamelled boxes, cameos and a great array of the fashionable filigraine ornaments; here also there was ivory, jade, coral and amber made into all manner of pleasing trifles.

The Princes walked downstairs again and crossed the transept to the Panorama. In the large outer court of this were the show-pieces of French furniture which they had been unable to look at yesterday because of the disturbing crowd; these they now studied with great care.

Here was to be seen Industrial Art in all its glory. Here was reflected the taste of the new-rich, led by Bonapartist "aristo-cracy". The wildest nineteenth-century dreams of outstripping the past in grandeur had found expression in this gallery, which contained the continental version of mid-Victorian furnishing. But the English, through an instinct to make themselves com-fortable, escaped the worst excesses of the period; English furniture, although dreadful enough, generally served some purpose. Here the hall-mark of superiority was that the object should be useless and costly, and that a wealth of carving and ornamentation should make it impossible to tell what it was meant to be.

Nothing was so well liked as the unexpected in those naïve days, and so *les meubles-surprises* had been invented for the general pleasure. The delighted visitor found *prie-Dieux* (kneeling desks for prayer at home, much used at the time in Catholic countries) which were really washstands in disguise; little boudoir-chapels made to look like writing desks; book-cases which when the doors were opened revealed not shelves of books but cabinets for coins, a wine-bin and a chiffonier.

Size was another essential attribute of the new furniture. The bigger the better, was the watchword, for the objects on view seemed to be made for palace use. And nothing was better suited to the type of snobbery that prevailed at the time, than to come to the exhibition on the "expensive" days (no one cared to be seen there when the admission was half price) and hover round these mountainous oak and mahogany pieces, catalogue in hand, as though considering a purchase. With few exceptions, there was nothing on view in this rotunda that could possibly have been used in rooms of reasonable size. And what a riot of fecund carving was here! What ebony sculptures, reliefs, mouldings, incrustations, what mother-of-pearl! What painstaking representations of historic scenes and famous architecture! There were copies of sculpture carved on sideboard pediments,—of the Industrial groups to be seen at the exhibition, and of statues from the Vatican: all reduced to the same insipid level of mediocrity. It was a veritable cabinet-maker's nightmare. And added to all was the incorrigible tendency of the age to moralise. All this furniture might be the reflection of the taste of upstart, speculating capitalists and their uncultured mistresses; it also belonged to the world of Progress and pious enthusiasms. Therefore improving inscriptions and carved object lessons abounded. In their new faith in themselves, born of scientific development, men could not resist expressing the grandeur of human evolution, and the divine purposes of Nature, even in walnut commodes and oak sideboards. There were sermons in mahogany, allegories in bookcases and morals in everything. With many of these pieces that were so elaborately carved, there went an explanatory catalogue so that the public should miss nothing of their intellectual purpose.

Round this gallery of Industrial furniture there now walked Prince Albert who spent a good deal of time in admiring, or at least looking at, the works on view. It is not likely that he found much to approve of here, although his name is usually associated with the taste of his time. He praised a *meuble de salon* by Grohé, the papers say; but Grohé was an exception: one of the few who adhered to the traditions of his trade. Apart from this, we learn that the Prince stopped for a long time examining a *buffet* by Ribaillier, but without informing the world of his opinion.

This *buffet* of Ribaillier's is worth describing, for it was one of the most popular and admired works of the exhibition, and is a typical Second Empire production. Four life-sized figures rested on its stylobate (for only architectural terms could be used in describing a work of such dimensions); they represented the four continents: Africa, in the guise of a woman leaning on a javelin, Europe, with a more serious expression, "teaching the Universe the precepts of the good and the beautiful", America, leaning pensively on an anchor which symbolised her maritime trade and rich future, and Asia nonchalantly holding a pipe from which emanated (according to the official description) imaginary and exotic perfumes. Behind each of these figures was a column made from different woods: oak for Europe, palm for Africa, and others suited to America and Asia; plants of the different continents were climbing up the columns, and carved on an entablature above was a group of infants representing the elements. On the panel at the rear of this sideboard there was an "apotheosis to famous men". On the top were the celestial hierarchy and the saints; in the centre were the great men of antiquity, and at the bottom were the moderns, with Voltaire and Rousseau at their head. There were about five hundred figures "representing all great men from the most remote times up to the eighteenth century: philosophers, mathematicians, legislators, prophets, historians, commentators, philologues, poets, chemists, inventors and doctors. This panel recalls to mind the sculptured reliefs of the middle ages, but in addition it has the superiority brought about by progress in modern sculpture." So said the catalogue, and someone must have laboured long on the instructive colossus. They made things solid and heavy in those days, and Europe will be lumbered with them for many a century to come, as it will be with the Industrial architecture of that prosperous time.

There was a true reflection of society in all these exhibits, that is to say, of the Imperial fête which set the fashion. The Emperor and his wife were international characters, knowing less of France than of Spain, Germany, England or Switzerland; about them at their court were foreigners of all kinds; speaking five languages well, the Empress always had in her entourage a certain number of Spaniards, Mexicans, Americans, Italians, Germans, Russians and Englishmen. This might have been a most useful League of Nations at the most influential court of Europe. But unfortunately it did not turn out that way; it was a court of adventurers, and the courtiers came mostly for what they could get, and it was at this period that Paris was transformed into a kind of permanent exhibition for the pleasures of all the world. Many of those pleasures were delightful, and a good deal of genius went to their making; but they were international. Offenbach, Meyerbeer, Worth,—such foreigners helped to produce that dazzling society that was presided over by the Empress Eugénie. But the old aristocracy lived in a dignified poverty; men of intellect followed their pursuits in obscurity and kept away from the court circle. The Emperor complained that there were no men about him whom he could trust; but his was not an accessible court for honest men, unless they were in the army. When de Morny, his half brother, was using his private political knowledge in order to enrich himself by deals on the Bourse, it was obvious that the majority of those at court would do the same. The Emperor and Empress were surrounded by the Bonapartes, the Camaratas, Caninos, Taschers, Murats, Mouchys, de Mornys, Walewskis,—and the new bourgeois capitalists, speculators and place-seekers. The society formed by all these was brilliant and showy; as though unconsciously doubting itself, its aim was always to make an impression by some kind of loud and grandiose display. All this had its reflection in art and commerce and in the lower grades of society. The demi-mondaines slept in carved ivory beds, and lined their rooms with satin, the bourgeoisie felt ashamed of anything modest and simple and were only at their ease when they had surrounded themselves with a host of cumbersome things that looked expensive. All manner of excellent people, of course, had a hand in industry; but it so happened at the turn of the nineteenth century, when science and industry were expanding their works on all sides and manufacturers of all nations were getting together, that this Second Empire arose in the most artistically influential country in the world, and the result was that throughout western civilisation there spread such an artistic decadence as can hardly have been seen before. How many decorative sideboards, the world over, may not Monsieur Ribaillier have inspired with his laboured *buffet* ! And in how many provincial houses and dreary hotels they linger on, as good as new.

The Prince had now finished his tour of the Panorama, and he crossed the transept again and went up one of the staircases to the gallery. Evidently in the mood for furniture, he paused to admire a table in the Australian section and liked it so well that he bought it; it was not an ornamental affair, like the pieces in the Panorama, but was made to display the highly polished wood of New South Wales. The courts of Tuscany and Turkey were visited next, and after this Prince Napoleon took his leave.

The courts of Sardinia and the Pontifical States were looked at, and then the Indian section where there was a Rajah's tent to be seen. And after this the Prince went to the English printing section where the most interesting object was a history of Balmoral, privately printed for the Queen. Irish stalls were next inspected; there was a fine stall of poplins, and the Prince "was pleased to express his approval of many of the specimens exhibited, especially a white robe, flounced with leaves of shamrock in green and gold".

Lithographs, photographs, and philosophical instruments were inspected in the English courts, and then the Prince went to the Belgian court and had a good look at the fine lace. After a visit to the Austrian section with its fine shawls and its musical boxes, he went to the Prussian court which was of rather special interest to him. During the Crystal Palace exhibition he and the Queen had entertained the Crown Prince and Princess of Prussia and had discussed the project of marrying their two children, the Princess Royal and Prince Frederick, the heir of the Crown Prince and of the throne. The Princess Royal had been ten years old at that time, and was not yet quite fifteen; but from this visit to Paris the Royal family were going almost at once to Balmoral where the young German Prince was to pay them a visit and where the matter was to be taken a stage further.

But in the Prussian section there was little to admire, although there was plenty to be seen. Here was the same over-ornamented taste of the Panorama furniture, without even a trace of the redeeming features to be found here and there in the French work. The crowded china stall was unattractive and the colours were crude; and the five mammoth porcelain vases on view, with their square pictures on oval forms, had none of the charm of Sèvres china. Into this room had strayed,—among all the china, the fringed plushes, the Berlin silver, the fans of Stolberg and the photographs and stereoscopes,—two great stone pinnacles for Cologne cathedral (which was not completed until 1880), looking strangely misplaced, frigid and uninspired. Prussia had also sent a bust of Napoleon executed in solid rubber, and plenty of eau de Cologne. The Prince spent most of his time studying prints and photographs, and when he had finished with these he went to end off the visit among the pleasant exhibits of Switzerland. Here musical boxes were playing, and jewelled birds popped out of chiming clocks to flap their wings and then retire again. There was wood-carving and fine embroidery; and all round the walls the pretty carved wooden clocks were cheerfully ticking. It seemed to be the reflection of a happy, simple way of living, and the Prince lingered as though unwilling to return to the splendour and ceremony that awaited him.

CHAPTER XIII

WHILE Albert enjoyed the exhibition and Victoria was painting in the park of St. Cloud, the crowds of Paris also relaxed; this morning there were no processions or ceremonies to watch, so they amused themselves as upon ordinary occasions. The cafés, the famous, delightful cafés along the boulevards, were thronged. Outside Tortoni's, La Maison d'Or, the Café Cardinal, the Café de Foy and a hundred others people were sitting, idly talking. Already the air was heavy with heat. Waiters were drawing down the striped awnings to give their customers a little shade; they brought out more chairs and small, circular green tables, and arranged them along the pavement, and then they scattered damp, yellow sand under them. Remises, carriages and cabs rolled lazily along the boulevards, the Auvergnat water sellers plodded along deliberately with their splashing buckets of water, the smart midinettes were hurrying about with hat-boxes. Groups of visitors from the provinces and abroad, here on holiday, were constantly arriving at the little green tables to sit down for half an hour for a drink or an ice while they decided how they could best amuse themselves.

There was a delightful air of leisure about the boulevards; no one was in a hurry, and there was nothing much to trouble about except how best to entertain one's self. Some of these laughing groups were planning to have an early lunch and then spend the afternoon rowing on the new lakes in the Bois de Boulogne, which owed their creation to Louis Napoleon's fondness for the lakes in London's parks. Others were going out to Versailles for the rest of the day and after a drink would take a bus or a train and arrive there in time for lunch. Many would spend the afternoon in the Champs Elysées where there was so much to be seen. The Industrial Palace would be dreadfully hot and glaring on such a day. A better proposition would be a visit to the Horticultural exhibition just opposite. Here, passing through a turnstile—*un tourniquet compteur*,—that horrible clanking contraption for turning men into ciphers that England had invented for the exhibition of 1851, and which our simple forefathers, far from execrating, thought worthy of many admiring exclamations and magazine engravings,—passing through the *tourniquet* you came into a delightful garden where there were fountains, conservatories, kiosks and ornamental tents. The finest tent, it is true, was not for you, unless you were a Bonaparte: made of silk and velvet, fringed with gold and elegantly furnished, it was reserved for the Imperial family. But in the others there was a varied array of rare flowers, and of fruit so perfect that you never knew which was made in wax and which was to be eaten. You could, too, visit the chalet containing stuffed birds, all in the most natural positions and surroundings.

Those with a real ardour for royalty would go presently to take their stand in the Jardin des Tuileries to watch the Queen arriving at the palace where she was expected for lunch. And those of quite opposite character who had advanced intellectual tastes could go and see Courbet's pictures in the Avenue Montagne. Annoyed by having his best pictures refused by the jurors of the exhibition, he had decided to hold a private show of his own works immediately opposite the Palais des Beaux Arts: a common enough thing in our day, but a daring departure from custom at the time. "Le Réalisme, G. Courbet" was written up over the door. But few people went to see these paintings by the most vital and modern artist of the time; the public who cared nothing about realism made a great joke of the affair, and the exhibition stood quiet and empty.

There was the evening to be thought of as well as the day; which ballroom or which theatre should be visited? Those who were lucky were going to the ball at the Hotel de Ville; but there was an immense choice of entertainment for everyone. There was dancing in all parts of the city, and at the theatres you could be entertained by the works of Auber, Offenbach, Halévy, Scribe, Alexandre Dumas fils, Emile Augier and a host of other competent writers and composers.

Before the boulevard cafés, how many languages were being spoken! Spaniards were particularly in evidence; since the success of Eugénie de Montijo they had been much in the mood to come to France. "One has no future in our country," a young Spanish girl had complained on hearing that Eugenia was to marry the Emperor; and now Spanish society was a marked feature in Paris, and with its intemperate love of the ornate and its strong passions, Spanish character made its mark on the popular taste of the day. Englishmen were as much at home on the boulevards as the French themselves, and there were crowds of Austrians and Germans. Bismarck was strolling about somewhere or other on this fine morning; there was no one more heartily ready to enter into Parisian pleasures than he was with his huge capacity for enjoyment. Italians, Swedes, Danes, Norwegians,—only the Russians were temporarily missing, and soon how eagerly they were to make up for lost time.

It was a tragedy for France that instead of a universal understanding coming about from the international fair created by Napoleon and Eugénie, the reputation of France was damaged. And this was the most unjust thing in the world, for the tone of Second Empire Paris was not set by France itself.

The old narrow streets of Paris, where the working classes had lived for centuries, were obliterated by Napoleon through the medium of his Baron Haussmann. The workers, the simple citizens, were driven out to the suburbs while the fine new streets of Haussmann were filled with immense houses for the new industrial rich and with rows of great hotels for foreigners. They were told, these people of Paris, that the Emperor was letting sunshine and air into their capital, and this was true. Baron Haussmann also provided Paris with water and with an admirable system of drainage, which was, doubtless, very necessary. Henry Cole, describing his visit to Paris to see the exhibition of 1849, says, "Digby Wyatt and I put up at the Hotel de la Ville de Paris. We were awakened at midnight by the stifling odour of emptying the cesspools, altogether a novel sensation which years have not obliterated from my mind." But one can pay too high a price even for fine drains. Paris became the capital of Europe, the most agreeable city that ever was, under the guidance of its joyous Spanish Empress and a largely foreign court. Here all the pleasures of the earth were concentrated in a small space; there had been nothing like it since the most luxurious days of ancient Rome. Here came the princes and wealthy epicures of all the world to enjoy an unrivalled freedom from interference. The air, says Lord Malmsbury, was like champagne. Thousands and tens of thousands came to have a really glorious time in Paris, from those enjoying the most intelligent pleasures, to others who came to indulge in extravagant excesses for which there was no opportunity at home.

The result was that, as the reign advanced, visitors to Paris, seeing the incessant round of gaiety, began to look on the French as a frivolous and pleasure-seeking race. Not only that; the immorality and wickedness that was becoming so blatant in the capital was also thought of as being typically French. When the exhibitions of a Castiglione, a Paiva and a Cora Pearl

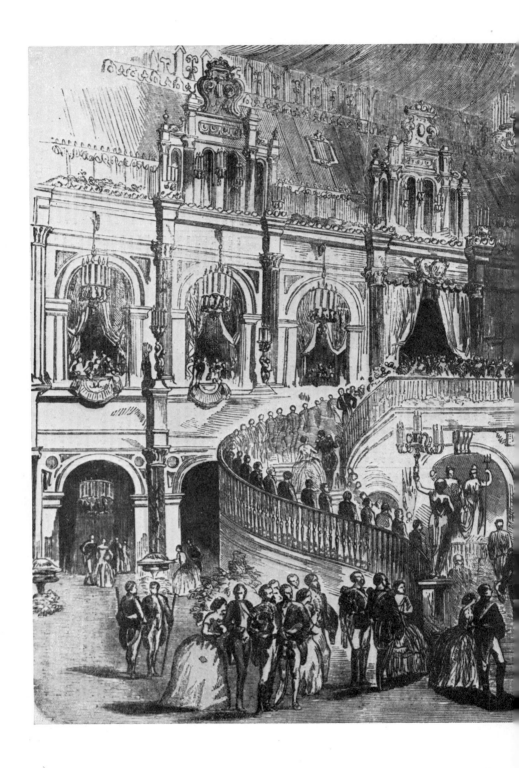

THE ENTRANCE TO THE BALLROOM.

disgusted the world, it was forgotten that they were not French and that the society supporting them was international.

In those fine new avenues, too, as the years went on, victorious armies,—back from the Crimea, the Italian campaign,—capered home with all possible clatter and colourful pomp. The Imperial display, the receptions of foreign Sovereigns and the public festivals were incessant, and were always accompanied by an impressive military ceremonial. As well as frivolous and corrupt, the French were ambitious and dangerous. Neighbouring countries grew anxious. In England Louis Napoleon was denounced by certain sects in the '60's as an anti-Christ, aspiring to rule the whole world, and Germany was very nervous about her own security. Germany in particular, in noting Parisian follies, became conscious of her own virtues; and by the time the Franco-Prussian war of 1870 was fought, the popular conviction was that Germany had every steady and honest quality to oppose the giddy French. Why should so decadent a country as France take the lead in Europe? With her patriarchal homely virtues, her sentimental feelings and all her culture, it was Germany's place to lead Europe and the whole world. Even Prince Albert did not really appreciate the French character, and always hoped for German ascendancy, although in a Liberal sense, with Germany ruled by a constitutional monarchy. Even the intelligent Princess Royal, by that time the Crown Princess of Prussia, had come to believe in the superior merits of German virtue and wrote rather sententiously in 1870:

"Gay and charming Paris! Our poverty, our dull towns, our plodding, hardworking serious life has made us strong—is wholesome for us. I should grieve if we were to imitate Paris and to be so taken up with pleasure that no time was left for self-examination and serious thought."

Poor, hard-working, conventional France! She was much more competent than Germany to lead Europe. First and foremost she had more common sense. She had a sense of proportion, entirely lacking in her earnest neighbours who, for all their tedious self-examination and their lumbering thought, invariably managed to miss the near and the obvious.

Prince Frederick of Prussia spoke in the same vein as his wife. He wrote in his diary during the siege of Paris in 1870:

"I cannot help myself at this crisis from thinking . . . of the plans which my late father-in-law (Prince Albert) as also the late King (Leopold I) of the Belgians, in conjunction with old Baron Stockmar, entertained for a united Germany under a monarchical head. God so willed that those men should conceive the notion of a free German Imperial State, that in the true sense of the word should march at the forefront of civilisation and be in a position to develop and bring to bear all noble ideals of the modern world, so that through German influence the rest of the world should be humanised, manners ennobled and people diverted from those frivolous French tendencies. . . ."

The truth was that the frivolity of Paris was based on great merits. If the world found the Parisian pleasures unrivalled, if it found Paris supremely gay and exhilarating, all this was due to great French qualities. The French were unequalled as cooks, and far from being frivolous and thoughtless, they were utterly conscientious and hard working in this fine art, prepared to spend many hours in the preparation of a meal and ready to despair if the result were less than perfection. They made the finest wines. But corruption was not in the vineyard. There you would rather meet with the warm, glowing welcome that Laurence Sterne received when he dropped in accidentally on an old peasant farmer and his wife and shared their lunch of bread and wine. There was much natural gaiety among the people of France, but they worked hard. They made wonderful liqueurs in their old monasteries; and the reason their products were so excellent in quality was that they were thinking not so much of making profit as of doing something well. As milliners and dressmakers they excelled because they would have things just right. Clothes must fit, they must be finely sewn. They were good hairdressers because they took a lot of trouble. And they were a courteous race who knew how to make a stranger feel at home. Better than all other people they knew how to mind their own business. They knew, too, how to do things easily and pleasantly; in their hands nothing was heavy and dreary as it became elsewhere. All the luxury and frivolity of Paris rested on the labour of a race like this which was good humoured and conscientious, whose qualities created conditions ideally suited to attracting wealthy foreigners. Not the most fabulous expenditure of wealth could create a city as delightful as Paris once was, without the underlying qualities of a superior and enlightened race to work on; the character and goodwill of the people gave it its unique charm, and the most humble helped to create the atmosphere that drew foreigners back again and again. The correspondent of the *Illustrated London News*, writing from Paris during this August of 1855, speaks thus of the waiters of the boulevards:

Civility appears to be the motive power of his life. That wonderful fleetness with which he dashes through the café into the open air, and threads his way through the rows of lounging customers at the green tables, carrying on the tops of his four fingers and thumb an immense pile of cups, liqueur glasses, tumblers, bottles of iced water, and lumps of sugar, which are the glory of childhood in Paris—appears to be the noble effort of a chivalrous nature. Ask him for a light and he produces lucifers from any pocket. Although people are calling him or hissing to him in various directions, he finds time to light two or three lucifers and even to hold them till the fumes of the sulphur have passed away before he presents them to you. He pretends to be a judge of the weather; he has his opinion, of course, on the conduct of the war; he knows by heart the last despatch from Pelissier; he is "up" as the phrase runs, in the closing prices of the public funds; and he is voluble about the theatres. He is free with you; he has a light retort for any attempted joke; but he is never familiar—never rude. You may forget his *pour boire* when you pay, and he will receive the exact sum of the little bill without an observation. On the other hand, even when you handsomely acknowledge his services, he is dignified. He thanks you—but not with that painful submission, that torturing obsequiousness peculiar to the overpaid waiter in a London tavern. As customers crowd into the café—invade every table—every man raising his hat to the splendid lady at the splendid counter as he enters—as the hissing of impatient customers increases—the waiter's energy rises to the level of the occasion. He dashes about with a tremendous impetuosity; he shouts to the man whose life is passed carrying a huge coffee-pot in one hand, and an equally large milk can in the other, to the various tables of his master's establishment, to pour out at numbers 7, 8, and 10; he calls for a dozen ices in one breath; he answers the questions of one table while he satisfies the wants of another. Doing three or four distinct things at once, he is yet never confused, and he seldom blunders. Order four ices—one, half vanille and half lemon; the second, half pastiche and half raspberry; the third, half orange and half strawberry; and the fourth, half pineapple and half currant,— and the chances are that he will bring them to your table, together with an equal number of different combinations for your neighbours, without making a single mistake. The reader who wishes to study the Parisian waiter in perfection, should choose a fine summer's night, and take his seat outside the rotunde in the Palais Royal about eight o'clock, in the midst of about 300 people, served by about eight waiters, who caper, loaded with crockery and newspapers with an activity that any Harlequin might envy. The number of people who visit some of the well-known Paris cafés in the course of a summer's day is astonishing. For instance, the director of Pergod's Neapolitan ice establishment, expects to sell every fine summer's evening, no less than one thousand ices. If the consumption falls short of this estimate he is discontented with his waiters.

It was not the Paris waiter who was frivolous. One can imagine the hours he worked in 1855. The Empress Eugénie was frivolous with all her court ladies, and Bismarck, perhaps, who was constantly gallivanting down to Paris; but not the ordinary French citizen, and not the hard-worked class whose cheerful labour provided the agreeable atmosphere of Paris. We know the French waiter still after nearly a hundred years. But three times he has been dealt a staggering blow by his virtuous northern neighbour. And to-day he is no longer the same. He is not so mercurial as of old, not so happy and friendly. The urbanity of the French, once so noted, is no more. The French have endured too much. They have become a tired and cynical race, and the world feels the loss. Someone once said that when France sneezes all Europe catches cold; and it might be said that when France is exhausted the whole world yawns. For they have the key to the old civilizations, and have so much to transmit from the past to the present, so much that is indispensable and complementary to the traditions of England, whose roots are also deep and living. They understand the art of making life a pleasure in an intelligent way, and the world will hardly be happy in a satisfying way until France is itself again, and its culture lies open to all men.

Yet in 1855 it was natural enough that Germans such as Prince Albert and King Leopold should wish for a strong Germany; for Germany then was a land of quiet, domesticated people, where savants and virtuous pastors abounded and stood in high esteem, and where everyone was peaceful. One could hardly have thought otherwise than that this country would exert a good influence, when once it was harmoniously organised. The last thing that was expected or desired was that the entire people should lend themselves to Prussian reaction and become a nation of virtual slaves; France was then the military nation, and it seemed inevitable that a strong Germany, friendly with England, would ensure peace and progress in Europe. To that end the Princess Royal was being trained in all good Liberal principles to take her place at the head of Germany with Prince Frederick.

If such plans were natural and sensible in their day, it was not unnatural either that Louis Napoleon should Haussmannise Paris: for that, too, viewed from a commercial standpoint appeared to be a good thing for the prosperity of the country. It was the military side of the picture that did the harm, the sabre-rattling that caused mistrust of France. But even this was never so serious as it seemed in its day to foreigners. No one in the middle of the last century wished to ruin Europe. On the contrary, everyone was eager to make it a better place. It seems that the devil has somewhere taken a hand in the affairs of men.

CHAPTER XIV

HAUSSMANN'S BALL

PRINCE ALBERT and his two gentlemen were now bowling along the Champs Elysées again in their char-a-bancs. The air was sultry with midday heat, and they watched the lazily strolling crowds who occasionally noticed them and saluted them as they passed. They crossed the Place de la Concorde, drove along the rue de Rivoli and then turned into the Palace of the Tuileries.

In the public gardens of the palace thousands of people had gathered to watch the Emperor and the Queen arrive from St. Cloud, and there was a continual rushing about from side to side as rumours arose that the cortège was coming. Despite the torrid glare of the day, enthusiasm conquered fatigue and everyone was alert. At last the Royal carriages, the outriders and the troops arrived. Quickly and splendidly they drove through the garden entrance of the palace; for a moment they were there, amidst the roar of applause, and then they were gone. But the crowds remained, hoping to catch a glimpse of the Royal persons during the afternoon.

There was just an occasional fleeting glimpse of the Queen and the Emperor later in the afternoon, as they looked down from the windows of the Louvre. The Queen was looking round the great picture galleries, and now and then the Emperor led her to one or other of the windows to show her a view of the quays and the Pont Neuf or the Place du Carrousel. The whole party,—the Royal family with their suite, and the Emperor with a numerous body of court officers, had entered the Louvre from the Palace of the Tuileries soon after lunch, to be received there by various Ministers, the Comte de Nieuwerkerke, who was the Director of the Imperial Museums, and the Comte de Viel-Castel, author of a racy diary of the period and a man of high artistic culture whose fame was known to the Queen.

It was between three and four o'clock. The public were in the galleries as usual this afternoon. But the visit of the Emperor and his guests had not been widely spoken of and the attendance was small. It was really far too hot a day for looking at pictures.

"The pictures are beautifully arranged," says the Queen, "and one goes through endless galleries and rooms, with splendid collections of the old French, Italian and German schools, by the most celebrated Masters, such as Raphael (la belle Jardinière) quite exquisite, magnificent Paul Veroneses, in particular the Supper of Cana, etc., etc. . . . The weather being so very hot, and the Ball at the Hotel de Ville before us in the evening, I and two of the Ladies went about in little chairs."

The rest of the party walked round in the exhausting heat as well as they could, and were rather glad when, at four o'clock, the attendants called out to the public that it was closing time. As people were going, it might possibly suggest the idea of leaving to the Queen as well. The Emperor was particularly hot and bored, and was hoping to get away from the tedious pictures quickly. The great galleries emptied, the outer doors were closed; and the sudden silence seemed only to make the place still more oppressively hot. But to the general consternation, instead of allowing herself to be pushed quickly through the remaining schools of painting, the Queen jumped up from the Bath-chair, took off her cloak and bonnet and dropped them on to it, and remarked with a smile that now, since the public had gone, they could really start to look at the paintings properly and at their ease.

Now there began a thorough-going inspection of canvases, and everyone had to look minutely at the great series of Rubens' adulatory paintings of Marie de Medicis, the "Rubenses", as the Queen called them. She enjoyed them all very much; but those accompanying her felt frizzled up by their heavy, oily colours. On and on they went, up and down the slippery floors; and the Queen became more and more interested and enthralled. After the paintings they looked at prints and drawings, and then they went downstairs to the sculpture galleries. "I recognised the originals of many of the casts which are in the Crystal Palace, in particular the Venus de Milo," says the Queen's diary. But, while she stood there, pointing out the statue to Prince Albert, and smilingly remembering the Crystal Palace, one of the members of the Imperial household, a fat elderly man whose uniform was thick and hot and who was beginning to limp, whispered to his neighbour that he would gladly give the Venus de Milo, and everything else in the place as well, in exchange for a glass of lemonade.

Even the Queen said that when they passed a doorway which stood open to a courtyard "the heat rushed in as from a furnace";

but she was lifted out of herself by her interest in all she was seeing; the others had all seen the Louvre many times and could come again when they liked; but for her it was new and wonderful. The heat which she normally disliked so much seemed not to touch her to-day; her eyes remained clear and sparkling while those of her companions burned, and she continued to lead the way on and on and backwards and forwards, trying to see in a few hours those collections that it would have taken days to look at had she been free to please herself.

At last the visit ended; it was seven o'clock and the sun was sinking low. And now the Queen was back in the palace again, sitting in the Empress's rooms where, it had been suggested, she might like to take a rest. She was busy writing her diary at one of the fine windows that overlooked the garden of the Tuileries. But with the great windows flung open and all the pleasant sounds of summer coming in, she was overcome with a sudden and unusual melancholy. It was all so gay, she wrote. A band was playing in the gardens; she looked out, and there lay those bright gardens so full of flowers; there rose the silver fountains, and just as straight and fine the obelisk from Luxor. And beyond lay that broad aristocratic avenue, the Champs Elysées whose gradual upward slope, so perfectly measured, had been artificially created in the days of Louis XV, and at the head of which stood the Arc de Triomphe. Above this widespread picture of beauty the sky glowed with unclouded vivid light. And now the Emperor appeared and was walking up and down in the small private garden of the Tuileries, and the people cheered him joyously. All was beauty and perfect happiness before her eye; but it was the sudden remembrance that nothing could last that made Victoria feel sad, the sense of the fleeting moments that carried all away. "The band made me feel *wehmüthig* and melancholy," she wrote. "All so gay, the people cheering the Emperor as he walked up and down in the little garden; and yet how recently has blood flowed, a whole dynasty been swept away, and how uncertain is everything still! All is so beautiful here, all seems now so prosperous, the Emperor seems so fit for his place, and yet how little security one feels for the future!"

But there was not much time for such introspection; soon the Queen had to dress for the great ball at the Hotel de Ville. The children had been sent back to St. Cloud, where they were going to spend the evening with the Empress, and Victoria and Albert dined at the Tuileries with the Emperor and one or two friends, including General Canrobert. "We had a nice quite *vertrauliches* little dinner with the Emperor," says Victoria's diary. "We talked most cheerfully together, and he was in high spirits. We laughed much at a fine old-fashioned Imperial cafetière, which would not let out the coffee in spite of all the attempts of the page to make it do so."

Victoria talked about the works of art in the Louvre, of which her mind was full, and she told General Canrobert how fond she was of pictures and how she liked to paint in water-colours. "The Queen told me," say the General's memoirs, "that she had been able to do a few paintings during her visit; one of them was of the band of the *Guides*, playing during the lunch at the Trianon; another showed a group of Zouaves talking in the Park of St. Cloud. She had had time to make quite a finished study of this one and was very pleased about it: 'For I love the Zouaves,' she said; 'they are the comrades of those who fought with my own soldiers at Alma and Inkerman. And I love their picturesque uniform with its bright colours.'"

After dinner the Queen, Prince Albert and the Emperor walked over to one of the big open windows and looked out. The sun had set, and the stars were coming out in a mild, soft sky. "We stood," the Queen says, "and I thought at the time how very extraordinary it was, and how much had happened in these very Tuileries,—with the Emperor, all three looking out of the window, which opened on the garden, the sound of music, of carriages, and people being heard in the distance, talking of past times. The Emperor said he knew Madame Campan, who had been one of the dressers of Marie Antoinette. . . ."

At nine o'clock the heat of the day had not diminished and the air was motionless. It was now almost time for the Imperial cortège to leave the Palace of the Tuileries for the great ball, and a serried mass of people had collected at the gates to watch it come out. A line of carriages well over a mile long was moving very slowly towards the Hotel de Ville, and above the moon shone calmly in a deep blue sky. The rue de Rivoli was transformed with new flags and banners, and special illuminations shone on every house. For hours that evening workmen had clambered along housetops and had hung over balconies and windowsills lighting up the fairy lamps, the Chinese lanterns and the stars of gas. But the most interesting feature of all the illuminations was the *tour St. Jacques* which had been lighted by electricity.

For the Occasion of the Great Ball the Hotel de Ville was Lighted with Thousands of Hissing Gas Jets and with Pyramids of Variegated Lamps: "The Air was as Luminous and Hot as that Over a Furnace from the Blaze of Gas."

Facing page 136]

At half-past nine the Imperial cortège made its way very slowly through the great crowds at the gateway. There were eight carriages surrounded by an escort of *Cent Gardes* in their magnificent full dress; they turned into the rue de Rivoli and drove along to the Hotel de Ville, enthusiastically acclaimed as they went.

The Grand Place before the Hotel de Ville was one of Louis Napoleon's new improvements to the city, and it was wonderfully decorated for the ball. The main ornaments in the square were "sixteen gigantic pyramids illuminated from the base to the summit with variegated lamps". The lamps hung thickly together, the *Illustrated Times* says, and resembled "mounds of crumpled gold leaf, burning with a dull rich brilliance". Between the pyramids were mounted Cavalry; Venetian masts and immense banners had been put up, and the Hotel de Ville itself, a fine early Renaissance building (which was destroyed in 1871) was hung out with banners and festoons. Heavy garlands of flowers were looped over garlands carved in stone, and the whole façade of the building was lighted after the manner of the time. Gas jets ran all along its architectural lines, and here and there in hissing flames, cast slightly to one side by warm currents of air, were the Royal and Imperial initials. As one approached the entrance, say those who went, one could smell the flowers that were densely massed round the entrances and feel the heat thrown out by the lighting. "The air," says the *Illustrated Times*, "was as luminous and hot as that over a furnace from the blaze of gas."

The Emperor and his guests arrived at a special entrance that was reserved for kings and princes of the blood. It was surrounded by a tent-like edifice made of blue velvet, dotted over with gold bees. Passing through, they entered the Louis XIV courtyard which had been entirely transformed for the night. The Prefect Haussmann saw things on a large scale and spared neither time nor money nor trouble to produce his grandiose effects. The courtyard, recently roofed in with glass, was thickly carpeted. As one entered there was a perfume that drugged the senses, coming from a million flowers; one was only kept from falling into a trance or sleep by the cold sound of cascades and fountains, or by the interest of gazing at the mighty. A temporary staircase had been erected, leading straight up to the throne room on the first floor. It rose in a double curve, copied from the staircase at Fontainebleau, and beneath it were large sheets of water, into which two reclining statues of naiads, representing the Thames and the Seine, were pouring their waters out of marble urns. A fraternal group of England and France stood above the water, and marble dolphins and water-lilies added to the scene. The staircase had gilt balustrades, entwined with flowers, and the handrails were of velvet; on the landing at the top there waited the wives, daughters and sisters of those municipal authorities who stood in solemn dignity on the carpet below, ready to bow to their Emperor and the Queen. Behind the ladies, who flashed and shone in satin and diamonds and carried bouquets in their hands, gilt trellis work was seen, covering the walls up to the roof and supporting a wealth of pink and white roses.

All round the splashing of water could be heard, falling from cascades or vases into marble pools. White statues shone against the red velvet draperies that hung on the walls; cupids and water nymphs emerged from reeds and lilies, and golden chandeliers hung aloft with thousands of lighted candles. There were luxurious fringed curtains and gilded ornaments wherever one turned, yet it was "all in the very best taste", the Queen declared. But it was the mass of flowers that caused the greatest wonder in that week of glorious floral displays. Where had they all grown? Had all the conservatories of the continent been rifled? A John Keats would not have survived the first intake of this heavily scented air where all the ladies too had come well perfumed.

Needless to say, no hypersensitive poet had been invited to this grand municipal ball, so no one's life was carried away on an attar of roses and heliotrope; on the contrary, all remained very alertly interested as they watched the Queen and the Emperor. They came slowly up the staircase arm in arm, chatting with Haussmann who had met them below and had given the Queen a bouquet in a costly jewelled holder. Behind them came Prince Albert with Princess Mathilde, various minor royalties who happened to be in Paris, and a host of courtiers. At the top of the stairs they acknowledged the curtseys of the waiting ladies, and then passed into a private salon.

At the general entrance, where other guests arrived, there was a vast throng of people, a hum of conversation and an impressive display of decorations. Thousands of square envelopes, that had contained invitation cards, lay scattered on the scarlet carpet, and people followed each other slowly up the stairs to the ballroom which was already very crowded.

Now the entry of the Imperial party was announced, and a passage-way was formed for them. They crossed the room and took their places on a raised dais, and there listened to the National Anthem and the Emperor's March.

There followed various presentations, and everyone stood about watching, or admiring the general effect of the great room. All round the room were fountains reflected to infinity by the great mirrors behind them, and at each corner there were stone nymphs in ponds of water, surrounded by flowers. The Queen's dress, the *Illustrated London News* says, "consisted of white silk, covered with lace, embroidered with geranium flowers etc., enriched at every possible point with diamonds". The Koh-i-noor diamond was flashing in her heavy diadem, and another renowned diamond, the Regent, glowed as brightly in the hilt of the Emperor's sword.

The other guests,—and there were eight thousand of them,— seemed hardly less resplendent. Jewellery, feathers, military gilt and municipal silver made a fine show. The hairdressers of the city had been rushing from one client to another during the afternoon and evening; dressmakers had been slaving away at the finest embroidery and sewing for weeks. "All the ladies were dressed in the latest fashions that the Paris dressmakers have invented in honour of the Royal visit," says the *Illustrated Times*. "How wonderfully were the different ribbons twisted about and fastened in the most marvellous and effective designs. The Empress by wearing full skirts has made them become fashionable. Some of the ladies appeared like soft balls of lace, so entirely were they embedded in fluttering flounces. Others passed by in crackling silk that almost growled as it was dragged through the crowds." The men were as brilliant and varied. A Greek was covered in gold, "as though he had been rolled in it," a Turk, dressed in white, sparkled with diamonds and looked like crystalline and liable to crack. There were Arabs in white and red, ambassadors in velvet jackets, British and French officers in full ceremonial dress.

Everyone was assembled; but such affairs are tedious enough when all is said and done, except to those who can continue to enjoy spying out the famous for a whole evening. However, the celebrated Herr Strauss was now tuning up his orchestra, and soon it began to play the "Quadrille of Honour" which he had composed specially for the occasion. Dancing began, but only for eight. "The Emperor and I," the Queen writes, "with Albert and Princess Mathilde, opposite Prince Napoleon and Madame Haussmann, Prince Adalbert and Lady Cowley."

Everyone gathered round to watch the dance, and there was some surprise over Victoria's skill. It was the fashion then to be somewhat lackadaisical over dancing; it was not thought in very good form to look at all interested in what one was doing, particularly at an assembly such as this to attend which one had been ready to commit murder, and where to appear other than blasé might suggest that one was new to such splendours. But the Queen was prancing to and fro with all the vigour of enthusiasm. "That's exactly how her soldiers fight," said Canrobert who was looking on. "It's easy to see that in England they do everything with conviction." The Queen was naturally good at dancing and had been taught by Taglioni. She was not going to spoil the enjoyable exercise to match the silly languor of others.

The quadrille over, the Royal persons returned to their dais and the evening proceeded with more presentations, compliments and the occasional dancing of a waltz to Strauss's pleasing music. Some of the Eastern dignitaries who were brought up to be introduced showed an embarrassing desire to grovel at the Queen's feet, others kissed her hand, and it was altogether very tiring having to be troubled with so much ceremony on a hot night. When the Emperor felt that she needed a change from the crowded scene, he led her away to show her some of the most famous rooms of the Hotel de Ville. With her historical taste she was soon pondering on the events these rooms had seen; in one Robespierre had been wounded, in another Louis-Philippe was proclaimed and in another Lamartine had made a long speech from the window in 1848. "This happy night will wipe out all sad memories," said the Emperor who was plying her with sympathy and compliments to-night as always.

The heat was terrible. Outside the dark summer sky became horribly white from time to time as sheets of lightning flashed across it. The Emperor led the Queen back to the ballroom which seemed quite airless and where several ladies had recently fainted. Everyone was in search of ices and something to drink; but it was not always easy to get what one wanted in this great crowd. Eugène Delacroix says in his diary that he had to walk three times round the Hotel de Ville before he could find a glass of punch. *Quelles insipides réunions!* and *Quel chaleur!* are the only other observations he has to make.

The Queen walked about arm-in-arm with the Emperor, smiling and bowing now and then to someone whom she knew, and she had some most gracious words to say to that very clever man, Horace Vernet, who came up to make his obeisance. There were one or two more dances, and then it was time to go. At half-past eleven the Emperor and his guests left the building and entered their carriages; first they drove to the Tuileries where the Queen took off her diadem, and then they went out to St. Cloud where they arrived soon after midnight. But crowds remained at the Hotel de Ville until the morning, dancing among those wilting flowers which had gleamed for a brilliant hour and now died silently and uncomplainingly.

CHAPTER XV

HOMAGE TO NAPOLEON

BY Friday morning the heat had reached a climax of intensity. Gone was the deep blue vault that had so far roofed the triumphal week; instead the sky swirled with electric currents and looked like a vast expanse of mother-of-pearl.

A large review of the troops had been arranged for the morning; but owing to the weather it was put off until the evening. Instead, the Queen spent a peaceful morning at St. Cloud, and the Emperor took Prince Albert and the Prince of Wales out to the Chateau de Vincennes, a military establishment where all manner of experiments were carried out. Accompanied by a select attendance of French and English officers in civilian dress, they set off in a post-chaise and were received at the chateau by the General in command.

Here the Emperor was in his element among all the machines of war, and among those experiments that were already harnessing modern science to the art of killing. The main item of interest was the Minié rifle, invented by a Captain Minié who now stood high in the esteem of the Emperor and had been handsomely rewarded. The guests spent some time in watching rifle practice with the new weapon. Six bullets out of ten struck the bull's eye at a distance of a quarter of a mile, and the last to be fired was a flame-producing ball which burnt up the target. Many other demonstrations followed, and the Prince was told about the most original of all the recent experiments, although there was not a demonstration to-day as very special conditions were needed. This was nothing less than the dropping of bombs from the air. Balloons, filled at a gas works of the neighbourhood, were sent up with projectiles on board to be dropped on to the earth from above. So far the attempts had not been very successful. Each time a balloon had been sent up it had met with misfortunes; trees had torn it, it had caught in gates and had never arrived over the object to be attacked. But although military men, always suspicious of new methods, took little interest, the Emperor was determined that the experiments should continue. Next time, he told the Prince, pure hydrogen was to be made on the field, to obviate the accidents that had hitherto been met with. He himself was coming to watch the experiment; several fire-balls for igniting buildings would be taken up and a number of thirteen-inch shells which were to be fired and dropped by means of electricity.

Perhaps it was bound to come. Ever since the days of Leonardo da Vinci men had been struggling to conquer the air, and Leonardo, probably, would not have cared much how his flying machines were used, so long as he had succeeded in making them work. But the actual scientific founder of aeronautics, Francesco Lana, who was born in 1631, was a pure scholar, content with an intellectual exercise; he was without desire to see his plans and diagrams materialised into reality. Having invented an aerial ship, the excellent man, a Jesuit priest, concluded that God would never permit the machine to be used, since it would destroy all security. "Where is the man," he wrote, "who can fail to see that no city would be proof against surprise, as the ships could at any time be steered over its squares, or even over the courtyards of dwelling houses, and brought to earth for the landing of its crew? And in the case of ships that sail the seas, by allowing the aerial ship to descend from the high air to the level of their sails, their cordage could be cut; or even without descending so low iron weights could be hurled to wreck the ships and kill their crews, or they could be set on fire by fire balls and bombs; nor ships alone, but houses, fortresses and cities could be thus destroyed, with the certainty that the airship could come to no harm as the missiles could be hurled from a vast height." Here was a man who did not believe in the wisdom of rulers, and Bonaparte had come to justify his fears.

Among the weapons studied by the Emperor and his guests some pieces of Swedish artillery were found to be particularly deadly and admirable. "Some new grenades," says the *Illustrated Times*, "which take away human life with the most marvellous facility, were also much admired." One feels rather surprised, on looking through the papers of the day, by the flippant tone often adopted towards military matters at a time when the men in the Crimea were facing so much misery and horror. Quite cheerfully and gladly the public saw new and more deadly weapons devised and sent out to the front to supersede the old trundling cannon ball. Men who had not the least idea of what the fight was about, men whose courage and loyalty were being exploited for the ends of those above them, were now to terrify, torture and destroy each other with these new scientific weapons or be shot for disobedience. And for what? To appease the pride of Stratford Canning who had a grudge against the Czar, to satisfy the Czar's pride, to satisfy Louis Napoleon's offended vanity, to satisfy waves of popular emotion caused by incomplete knowledge,— for a variety of reasons not one of which justified a single hour of the anguish of those who were maimed and died in torment, or the anguish of their wives and mothers. The people of the west were clamouring for an age of peace, convinced that it was practically upon them; yet they raised no outcry against the carrying out of scientific military experiments, and did nothing much in an active way to bring about an end to warfare.

This little group of well-dressed men stood calmly watching the demonstrations of different means of violently killing innocent men. The Emperor, who would not have hurt a dog, represented a society that was enthusiastic for science. Saint-Simon and his followers had realised that science should not be developed without the universal abolition of war; but the Emperor's head was clouded with romantic Napoleonic dreams, and men in general became blind from that time on with regard to science. Science was to be pushed to the utmost limit, and yet was also to assist as a matter of course in the inventions of war. How that polite group would have recoiled, pale with horror, at a demonstration of poison gas and the atom bomb. How wicked they would have declared it to be and how insane. Yet the guilt and madness lies as heavily on them, for it is not a million times more wicked to kill a million men than to kill one man. It is the same thing seen under a magnifying glass.

Prince Albert at least had a clear conscience with his constant efforts in the cause of peace. As they all drove back to Paris in their post-chaise he may well have harangued the Emperor on the folly of war, as well as congratulating him on his military establishment, for he was much given to moralising, it is said. But if he did the Emperor without a doubt talked back like a very apostle of peace. No one more earnestly wished for peace than he did, subject to certain modifications in Europe absolutely essential to the cause of justice. A war could not conceivably ever be his fault.

After this instructive morning the gentlemen joined the Queen and her ladies at the Palace of the Tuileries for lunch, and afterwards the Royal family paid a last visit to the Industrial Palace.

Between pages 144 and 145]

THE QUEEN AND THE EMPRESS WATCHING A MILITARY REVIEW IN THE CHAMP DE MARS.

"A review is rather like a ballet," says the *Illustrated Times*; " accordingly it is a sight well suited he eyes of ladies who thus have the horrors of war merely suggested in the distance, while all the gnificence of spectacle is placed immediately before them."

This time the authorities, tired of the confusion caused by crowds, gave up the attempt to be popular and democratic and ruthlessly shut out the public of all categories. The Queen was given her usual warm welcome, however, all the way along from the Tuileries. Paris was by now quite under the sway of England; English notices were in the shop windows, and everyone interspersed his sentences with English words. The Queen had appealed by her domesticity, by the way her two nice, well-mannered children went about with her and by her reputation as an excellent wife and mother. It was in this week that the French, to the displeasure of those who care for the purity of language, took up those two dreadful expressions "le home" and "le confortable", generally with only a hazy idea as to how they should be used. There were even such notices as "comfortable pastry" to be seen in the windows. The whole city, in fact, was mad on England, and no one talked of anything but the Queen. Everybody gave his opinion of her, from the private of the Guards on duty at the palace, who said: "She's no worse than my wife is," to Prosper Merimée who admired her grand manner but thought her a little too imperious.

The afternoon was overcast and stifling, although the air was dry. The flags hung limp round the exhibition, but the spectators waved their hats, their handkerchiefs and the small Union Jacks they carried. The visit did not last very long. Toys were bought for the Osborne nursery, and the Queen made two purchases for herself and the Prince. One was a bronze cast of a lion, the other was one of Duvelleroy's beautiful fans, which cost £60 and was painted with a picture of the Empress as a child distributing alms to the poor.

They returned to the Tuileries for tea, and afterwards set off for the Champ de Mars for the military review which was now to take place. The carriages this day, say the papers, were entirely new and shone with white harness and gold ornaments. "The Emperor, it has been observed, has new carriages almost as often as the ladies of the court have new dresses." The Empress, being a lover of military displays, was out on this occasion. She sat beside the Queen; and the Emperor and Prince Albert, on horseback, rode one on each side of their carriage. Behind was Prince Napoleon, and Prince Adalbert of Bavaria who attached himself to most of the functions of the week; the military escort was unusually large and brilliant. Crowds had gathered to watch the procession, and on the Pont d'Iéna there waited Marshal

Vaillant, Marshal Magnan and General Canrobert who fell in with the cortège.

On the Champ de Mars about fifty thousand troops were assembled,—"each regiment with its own good, powerful band," wrote the Queen in her diary, "and their fine commanding *tambour majors,* their stalwart bearded *sapeurs* (those of the *Voltigeurs de la garde* have yellow *tabliers*), and the very picturesque and smartly dressed *cantinières,* all cheering, and the bands playing 'God save the Queen!' The cortège had become immense as we drove down the lines (only in the middle as it would have taken too much time otherwise) having been increased by the *Maréchaux-Généraux* and the picturesque Arabs. We first passed down the Infantry, then the Cavalry, which are beautiful, then the Artillery. This over, we drove into the *Ecole Militaire,* the Emperor alone dismounting and handing me upstairs to the large balcony, in front of which the Emperor, Albert, and the rest, took their station. There we found Princess Mathilde and sat down. Then the troops began to *défiler* in quick time, which took three quarters of an hour; a beautiful spectacle, such fine troops! . . . The clothes of all the men are infinitely better made and cut than those of our soldiers, which provokes me much. The drums, too—brass ones —are much finer. It was a magnificent sight. Albert regretted, and so did I, that I was not on horseback."

Big drops of rain were now beginning to splash down heavily from the sky; but pleasure was undiminished. Victoria, with the "dear Empress" and Princess Mathilde sitting beside her on their gilt chairs, and "the Ladies" standing round about, watched the performance enthralled. All of them were delighted with the variety of the colours, the fine, solemn, military, bearded faces and the exhilarating cavalry charges in fancy dress. How easy it was to lean back admiring the pretty display, without giving a thought to its actual implications. A review is rather like a ballet, says the *Illustrated Times.* "Accordingly it is a sight well suited to the eyes of ladies, who thus have the horrors of war merely suggested in the distance, while all the magnificence of spectacle is placed immediately before them."

The review lasted until half-past six, and then the Empress parted with them and the Emperor took his English guests to the Hotel des Invalides. This home for wounded soldiers had been built by Louis XIV; under the revolution it had very typically been re-named the "Temple of Humanity". But when the early hopes and ideals had been lost in terror and disorder Napoleon came along to call it, equally typically, the "Temple of Mars" and to fill it with injured men to attest to his powers. But after his time it had gone back to its original name, and had been less ominously filled.

The Queen wanted to see the tomb of the great Napoleon and they drove up to the church of St. Louis. The heavy drops of rain still fell down, and a towering bank of rolling clouds, shot with yellow, started up from the earth to the zenith, dwarfing everything below. As the carriages crossed the courtyard the old pensioners from the Napoleonic wars stood round, holding flaming torches, and drums rolled. The Queen descended from her carriage and was led past the pensioners, followed by her family, Princess Mathilde and a number of officers. They entered the church and went straight to the new tomb prepared for the great man.

It was Louis-Philippe who had brought back the remains of Napoleon from St. Helena in 1840, just fifteen years ago. In that same year he had locked up the nephew, Louis Napoleon, in the prison of Ham for attempting to seize power from him. What, one wonders now, was the peace-loving Louis-Philippe thinking of, when he aroused the fires of Bonapartism in this way? He is supposed to have thought that by paying respect to Bonaparte he could please those sections of the people who remembered the days of "military glory" with a certain amount of nostalgia, and appease them for any disappointment they might feel at his own determination to keep out of wars. Or perhaps he thought that Napoleon's remains were safer under his own eye in Paris than far away from the country where the Bonapartists might make them a centre of pilgrimage. Whatever he had in mind, he sent his son Joinville to fetch them to France. It was all done far too well. Napoleon trundled down the Champs Elysées in such a catafalque as never was. Of colossal, unwieldy height, surrounded with trophies, standards, heavy fringed draperies and mourning statues, it was pulled along by four rows of horses, four abreast, all heavily caparisoned, with great sable plumes waving on their heads. In front there walked a single white horse carrying Napoleon's own saddle. A shiver ran through the watching crowds when they saw it. "It is Napoleon's battle horse," they whispered, not pausing to think that in that case it must be well over thirty years old. The impression made was profound. The cortège in all its gloomy pomp was like some terrible engraved procession by Durer; looking back to it in the light of subsequent

events one can see in it a horribly ominous thing—a re-intro-
duction of militarism into Europe, a ghostly Trojan horse bearing
the seeds of tyranny. The solemn event captured the popular
imagination. An inexplicable and hysterical emotion spread
through the silent crowds. The Napoleonic legend was given a
tremendous impetus, and by exploiting it Louis Napoleon was
able to come to power eight years afterwards. There were thirty
years of revived Bonapartism—from the year that Napoleon's
body was brought to Paris to the year of France's defeat by
Germany in 1870. Midway between these dates was 1855, the
zenith and the triumph of Bonapartism, and the Queen of
England had come to pay homage to the Corsican family.

The great well-like tomb was not yet completed, and the
coffin of the Emperor lay in a side chapel. The Queen and Louis
Napoleon leaned on the marble balustrade, looking down into the
gloomy circular vault and studying the statues of Pradier which
represented the campaigns of Napoleon. It was cold and repelling,
even on a hot summer day. Louis Napoleon said it looked like a
marble pool and that one expected to see water in it.

The visitors then went on to the side chapel of St. Jerome.
All round stood the old soldiers who had fought under Napoleon,
lighting the place with torches; and in the centre was the coffin,
covered with black velvet embroidered with golden bees. A great
bronze eagle stood above, and at the foot were the hat worn at
Eylau and the sword of Austerlitz. The walls were hung with
purple velvet. It was oppressive and ghostly, and everyone stood
by in silence.

"There was not a word," say Canrobert's memoirs. "Everyone
contemplated the coffin in silence. Prince Albert was in front
of me, in the red coat of a field-marshal; beside the Queen stood
the Prince of Wales in Highland dress, with his velvet jacket, fur
sporran and kilt; to the right was Princess Mathilde, whose fine
features were accentuated by the light of the torches and recalled
the face of her uncle.

"After a moment of meditation, of absolute silence, the Queen,
with a respectful, calm and severe expression, turned to the
Prince of Wales and putting her hand on his shoulder said,
'Kneel down before the tomb of the great Napoleon.' At that
moment a terrible storm, to which the torrid heat of the last few
days had been working up, burst forth. Great peals of thunder
shook all the windows of the chapel, and their sound went
echoing round the vaults. Rapid and ceaseless flashes of lightning

gave an almost supernatural aspect to the moving and solemn scene, by continually lighting it with an unnatural brilliance.

"As far as I was concerned, at first I was absorbed, and then deeply moved, almost breaking down; I began to see nothing.

"Waterloo, St. Helena . . . the English alliance . . . England in the person of her Queen and of her future King who was kneeling before the remains of Napoleon: all that made my senses reel. I was overcome with giddiness. I was near the door and was obliged to retire through it hurriedly. I could no longer control myself and was obliged to weep."

The Queen herself was equally impressed. "There I stood," her diary says, "at the arm of Napoleon III, his nephew, before the coffin of England's bitterest foe; I, the granddaughter of that king who hated him most, and who most vigorously opposed him, and this very nephew, who bears his name, being my nearest and dearest ally! The organ of the church was playing 'God save the Queen' at the time, and this solemn scene took place by torch-light, and during a thunder-storm. Strange and wonderful indeed. It seems, as if in this tribute of respect to a departed foe, old enmities and rivalries were wiped out, and the seal of Heaven placed upon that bond of unity, which is now happily established between two great and powerful nations. May Heaven bless and prosper it!"

This heartfelt prayer has been granted. Never since then have the two countries fought each other as they had so often done in the past, and such a thing is inconceivable now. The Queen was not always to be so well pleased with the French, not always so utterly trustful of the Emperor. But the prayer had its answer in the Prince of Wales, who grew up with such a love for the French and in the gradually changing sympathies of the English people.

At half-past seven the Emperor, the Queen and the Prince returned to the Palace of the Tuileries and the children were sent back to St. Cloud.

Again, the Queen says, "we had our nice *vertrauliches* little dinner with the Emperor, and we talked a great deal about the war. Some despatches, up to the 14th, had arrived, and Albert showed the Emperor the *Morning State* and spoke of the reports which we had received. The servants being still in the room, the Emperor began to talk in English. He lamented bitterly the want of invention and energy in both our commanders from the first, and the absence of any great genius. He then spoke very openly and frankly of the defects of *our* generals; and *we* told him equally frankly what was objected to *his*; and nothing could be more satisfactory than the conversation, or more straightforward or honest than the Emperor's observations and propositions. It was just as if we had one and the same army; and so, in fact, it is, but it is very pleasant to find this so in another sovereign."

As they had done last evening, they stood looking out of the windows after dinner, although now it was pouring with rain. It was dark, and the air, which was pleasantly cool, carried the smell of damp earth and wet leaves up from the gardens. Now they heard the bugles being sounded in the gardens as a signal to the public that the gates were about to be shut for the night; and from the rue de Rivoli there rose the sound of wheels and horses' hooves. Then, rather late, and quite privately, they went to the *Opéra Comique* to see Auber's *Haidée*. They sat in the Emperor's stage box, and the Queen was happily recognised.

"The first act was over when we arrived. After the opera, before the curtain dropped, 'God save the Queen' was sung; I was obliged to show myself and was loudly cheered."

CHAPTER XVI

A DAY IN THE COUNTRY

IN the morning all signs of storm and cloud had vanished and it was obvious that the day was to be perfect. It was warm, although the air had lost its heaviness and was clear and sparkling; the sky was intensely blue and not a cloud was to be seen. That legendary weather that was supposed always to shine on the Queen's holidays and ceremonies was back again. Brilliant sunshine, in fact, was enjoyed during the whole of the visit, and gilded the ceremonies with a happy warmth, becoming obscured only on the occasion of the visit to Napoleon's tomb. A correspondent of the *Illustrated London News*, writing from Paris after the Queen had left, says:

"Your readers are fully aware of the almost superstitious faith with which people talk of the Queen's weather. Her Majesty's previous experiences have been repeated throughout her French visit; for with the exception of the evening on which the Royal party went to the Opéra Comique, the most beautiful skies heightened the effect of every festival given by the Emperor in her Majesty's honour. The day after the Queen left Paris, however, the fine weather broke up, and it has been showery, even chilly at times, ever since."

To-night the finest festival of all was to take place, the ball at the Palace of Versailles; but the day was to be spent quietly in the country. The Queen had romantic feelings for the Stuarts and had expressed a wish to see the chateau of St. Germain where James II had died in exile and was buried; and soon after breakfast she and her family set off with the Emperor in open carriages, and the suite followed in chars-a-banc.

They drove out through the park of St. Cloud, emerging into quiet and delightful country; and at each village they passed, a crowd of rustic spectators had gathered under arches of evergreens with flowers and addresses to present. Bougival, the Queen writes in rather incoherent haste, was "full of people who presented bouquets, generally 'les autorités', le Curé etc. being amongst them, and arches, banners and all sorts of kind mottoes". The sky was so deep a blue, and the detail of the wooded hills and the white houses was so sharp and clear, that Albert said he felt he was in Italy.

At mid-day they reached the town of St. Germain. At the entrance to the principal avenue stood a large arc de triomphe decorated with banners and surrounded by tall flag masts painted in brilliant colours. A blue streamer floated lazily from the tallest of these, and on it was inscribed in gold letters: "The inhabitants to their Majesties."

While the Queen listened to an address of welcome read by the Mayor, the horses were changed. The fine thoroughbreds, which looked so splendid in the Imperial carriages, had done enough, and a relay from the *Poste Impériale* was brought out. But these were very different animals. Round, fat and strong, they were immense beasts with thickset necks; and their tails were tied up into round balls. They looked decidedly odd when they were mounted by the postilions in their powdered wigs, green and gold jackets, yellow breeches and tall, highly polished boots. The Royal party having thanked the citizens of St. Germain for their welcome, the carriages were re-entered for a drive through the forest. "The appearance of the procession was extremely grotesque," says the *Illustrated Times*; "and as it dashed off with jingling bells and cracking whips, the people gave a shout of delight heard a mile off."

The forest was entered by the Porte Dauphine, and the cortège drove along fine shady avenues towards La Muette where lunch was to be taken. There was no one to be seen, and the only sounds were those made by the carriages and escort themselves and by the rustling of leaves high up in the great trees. The Queen thought it was hot. "It was dreadfully dusty, the soil being so sandy," she says. "The sun had come out and it became oppressive." But the same event, seen through the medium of different minds, can have many aspects; and the *Illustrated Times* correspondent, who awaited the arrival of the party at La Muette, reported that the showers of Friday had laid the dust and that it was pleasantly cool beneath the trees.

La Muette was a small hunting lodge, and when the Royal party reached it they were met by Marshal Magnan, Count Edgar Ney and Monsieur de Toulongeon, all in huntsman's dress,—dark green velvet with red waistcoats, high boots and cocked hats. Other huntsmen stood round, dressed as in the days of Louis XV, their dogs beside them. A fanfare of horns was sounded, and the dogs jumped excitedly, imagining that a chase was about to begin. "Her Majesty honoured the dogs by patting their heads," says the *Illustrated Times*. "They seemed deeply grateful for the distinguished attention and licked the Queen's feet and wagged their tails in the most approved courtier-like style."

Now through the dark shadows of the trees there came a procession of young girls all in white, carrying flowers, and led by monsieur le curé who was all in black. The pale figures of the girls, with wreaths of white roses in their hair, gleamed among the dense trees; but the smiling curé was scarcely visible in his sombre gown to those who stood in the sunlight. Beyond there was a military band which played "God save the Queen", and the brass instruments sparkled in the shafts of sunlight which found their way through the branches above. The Queen, the Emperor and everyone present turned to the little deputation of village girls as it emerged from the trees, and the band stopped playing.

"*Grande Reine*," began the foremost young girl. And there followed a long and monotonous speech about the Royal visit, the Anglo-French alliance, war and peace, science and industry, and universal exhibitions. On and on went the high-pitched voice, while the Emperor and his guests occupied themselves with their inner thoughts,—apart from the Queen, no doubt, who was perfectly capable of listening to it all: great with the great, Victoria had also the grace to be simple with the lowly, and could always turn a sympathetic attention towards them. But presently the voice came to an abrupt end. "Suddenly she stopped," in the words of the Queen's diary, "exclaiming, '*Ah, mon Dieu!*' The Emperor and I proposed to relieve her by taking the nosegay from her and thanking her, but she would not give it up, and said, '*Attendez; je vais me rappeler?*' which nearly set us off. But she persevered, and *did* recollect it for some sentences, when she broke down a second time. Then the *curé*, who had evidently composed the speech, burst forth with the finale of '*Vive la Reine d'Angleterre!*' which set the girl right again, and she continued: '*Vive la Reine d'Angleterre, vive sa Demoiselle, vive son Prince Albert, vive l'Empereur, vive l'Impératrice, vive tout le monde!*' We laughed much afterwards at this little episode, for the effect was most comical; and yet the poor girl was much to be commended for her courage and perseverance; she looked so frightened . . ."

The Emperor now led the Queen indoors for lunch. Outside the band played selections from Verdi's "Les Vêpres Siciliennes", a favourite opera of the Queen's. Everyone was extremely cheerful.

The conversation at dinner last night, so long and outspoken, had left an impression with Victoria—and even for the moment with Albert—that a complete understanding existed between themselves and the Emperor who had talked with such sincerity; his affection for all of them seemed to be genuinely unfeigned, his admiration for Victoria incapable of diminishing. The Queen was very happy. Friendship with the Emperor and his most kind and welcoming people was assured; Vicky was about to create a lasting bond with Prussia by becoming engaged, if all went well, to Prince Frederick William; the war would soon be won, and then indeed they could all hope for a good future. These were the reassuring thoughts in the background that made the present moment with its light and trivial conversation pass so merrily.

When lunch was over, the Queen and the Prince were shown round the house and the stables, and then were brought round to the terrace for a rest. This was one of those moments, which were all too rare, when a quick sketch could be made; and the Queen was soon painting one of the pretty views into her album. The Prince took a chair near to one of the gentlemen, and the Emperor lit his cigar and strolled about on the lawn. But presently the band, which was still playing, struck up a lively tune, and on the terrace there now danced Napoleon III, the future Empress Frederick and the future Edward VII. They leaped about with a gay abandon, laughing merrily at each other; and the Queen closed her album to watch them.

At half-past three there was another drive through the forest, and it ended at the Palace of St. Germain. As they were driving along the great, wide terrace here, the Queen spied someone painting, and the unfortunate artist found a most formidable group of interested spectators descending upon him; for the Queen, her head full of her own recent attempt, insisted on going to have a look.

After this they entered the palace, which had been built by François premier for Diane de Poitiers. It was all very disappointing, however, all sad and neglected. The Queen was taken to the rooms which James II had occupied, but she was not tempted to linger. In these dingy, uncomfortable apartments there was nothing to inspire dreams of past historic lives, nothing that suggested romance. It was a house no longer loved or wanted, a place where desolation reigned.

They were now taken to see the apartments of Louise de la Vallière. To reach these they had to cross a courtyard which contained about five hundred prison cells. Here the political prisoners of 1848 and 1852, the year of the *coup d'état*, had been confined; they had recently been removed to other French prisons or deported to Cayenne, but were mostly to be pardoned at the birth of the Emperor's son in the following year. Here the party glanced into some of the cells, and saw that the unhappy prisoners had passed the time away by drawing on the walls. They all laughed very heartily over a caricature of the Emperor which was discovered.

The rooms of la Vallière were dark, damp and full of cobwebs; the place was utterly depressing and the Queen was glad to turn away; in fact the atmosphere of the place was so gloomy that she did not even go to the tomb of James II in the church. It was nice to come outside and drive off again into the warm sunshine.

They returned to St. Cloud by a different route, passing Malmaison. There was just time for a fleeting visit to this house, which had belonged to the Emperor's grandmother, Josephine. Here the Emperor had many interesting reminiscences to recount; for this was where he had seen the Empress Josephine as a small child. He had lived here, too, for a time while Napoleon was in the island of Elba; his grandmother was dead by that time, and the allies were in Paris. Here, in his nursery, the small Prince Louis had met the sons of the King of Prussia, and had frequently seen the kindly Czar Alexander who had been so good to his mother. But there was not time to linger at Malmaison. The party re-entered the carriages and drove home past the fortifications of St. Valerian. Still, as they went along, villagers met them with flowers and greetings, and there were decorations everywhere. The Queen admired the many vineyards that they passed, which glowed in the early evening light.

When they reached St. Cloud, they found the Empress had already left for Versailles. She was to be present at the ball, but so that she should avoid the crowds and all possibility of fatigue, she had gone in advance to the palace where she would prepare herself at her leisure.

The Emperor dined quietly and early with his guests; their cheerfulness was undiminished, and the children were particularly excited, as they too were going to Versailles, and there was to be a big firework display. The great ball had been eagerly talked of all the week, not only at court but by the whole of Paris. For it was the first time, since the old kings fell, that such an event had taken place in the Hall of Mirrors.

CHAPTER XVII

THE FÊTE AT VERSAILLES

THROUGHOUT the day crowds of sightseers had been pouring into the town of Versailles; thousands were staying there for the night, and many who had not booked rooms had been going from door to door, with carpet-bags in their hands, hoping to find a resting place, and offering high prices for an arm-chair or even a table on which to pass the night.

Tens of thousands had spent the afternoon in the park and had watched men at work, fixing lamps in the trees and round the palace and the fountains, and generally preparing for the night. At six o'clock they were turned out by the soldiers, and retired to the cafés and restaurants, there to await the setting of the sun; for when it was dark they were going back to the Lac des Suisses at the end of the gardens where the firework display was to be held, and where there were to be wonderful illuminations.

As daylight faded people began to assemble in the avenues that led up to the palace; *marchands de coco* wandered among them, their bells jingling as they moved, and gingerbread sellers were doing a brisk trade. Lights now broke from coloured paper lanterns at every window; stars in gas shone over all the doorways; and illuminated words of welcome stood out clearly against the gathering darkness. Now workmen were clambering about among the trees and soon thousands of coloured fairy lamps, hung in graceful festoons, were lighted up. Chains of lights joined all the trees together, and the leaves looked transparent and luminous. The houses soon seemed as pale as alabaster and looked like stage scenery with their lanterns swaying in the breeze; and light was cast upward in a fan-shaped halo into the darkness of the night.

Crowds of people now poured along the side of the palace and turned towards the borders of the Lac des Suisses. As they passed they saw the men busy at the illuminations of the great building. Lights were flying along the lines of its architecture, and soon lights began to glance from the great open windows. By the time it was fully dark, the palace was ablaze with flaming gas jets without, and with thousands of wax candles within. The fountains began to rise in the air, pouring forth illuminated and coloured water, boats and gondolas were lighted up with brilliant lamps on the Lac des Suisses, and dragoons took up their position before the entrance to the *Cour d'Honneur*.

The first carriages began to arrive, setting down ladies glittering with jewellery and gentlemen covered with orders. The crowds and the excitement began to increase, and before long endless lines of carriages were coming up to the entrance, following each other very slowly. The spectators were looking out for celebrities, and there was a murmur of excitement when Canrobert appeared, when Horace Vernet stepped from his carriage and a party of Arab sheiks arrived on foot.

Now, driving up from St. Cloud, there came the Imperial cortège with its splendid escort. The crowds raised a tremendous cry of welcome, the drums in the courtyard rolled and the air rang with shouts of "Present arms!" The Royal party descended from their carriages to the sound of an impressive rattling of swords, and the Emperor gave the Queen his arm and led her into the building.

Going in by their own private entrance, the Royal visitors were soon ascending the grand staircase through heavily perfumed air. Masses of exotic flowers were arranged up the sides of the thickly carpeted marble stairs, and at the top there stood the Empress Eugénie waiting for them,—a dream of beauty even in a day when society women were exquisite in their lovely clothes and their sheltered idleness, and were trained to all the graces that kept them in the clouds for a race of gallant men. She seemed perfection itself, with her finely made figure and her lovely face, her gold hair, her small and even white teeth. One could see no fault in her, and to that flawlesss grace there was added a lively charm of manner and a glowing happiness. She was in all the magnificence of an Empress's robes; but with her flair for clothes, she looked as neat and elegant as she did in the most dashing of her fashion creations. The good Victoria, so far removed from this amazing ability to cut a dash in heavy satins, velvets and jewellers' show-pieces, gazed with admiring smiles at the vision which almost defied description in the Royal diary, which says: "The dear Empress . . . was looking like a fairy Queen or nymph, in a white dress, trimmed with branches of grass and diamonds,—a beautiful *tour de corsage* of diamonds round the top of her dress, and all *en rivière*, the same round her waist, and a corresponding coiffure, with her Spanish and Portuguese Orders."

The Queen also heard the Emperor say to his wife, "How beautiful you are!" At this time he was still deeply in love with her, and she was very happy with him. Not that she would have been attracted to him as an ordinary man; but she had been educated to the Bonaparte legend, and the Emperor now had all the glamour of greatness and success about him; he was something of a hero in her eyes, and since he worshipped her and was the most generous, affectionate and tactful of men, she was contented and at her best.

From the head of the stairs the Emperor and Empress led their guests through various apartments of the palace; Imperial relations and courtiers followed,—Prince Napoleon, usually bored and disagreeable at such functions; Princess Mathilde, intelligent and good-hearted, the best of the family; de Morny, the illegitimate brother of the Emperor, unscrupulous but considered the prince of exquisite breeding and *bon ton*; Colonel Fleury, General de Montebello, Madame de la Bédoyère, and all the rest of members of the household. They passed with Royal dignity, far from the throng of ordinary guests, through brightly lighted rooms lavishly adorned with flowers; some of these fine apartments were hung with heavy pale blue silk, embroidered with golden bees, others with azure velvet or with white and gold. And at the end of them they came to the Hall of Mirrors, lighted with many thousands of candles. The gold floor shone, a deep layer of flowers lined the walls, and the assembled guests displayed an untold wealth of jewellery and glittering regimentals. There was a dais at the centre of the room where gilded and brocaded chairs awaited the Royal visitors; but they walked straight up to one of the windows.

It was a balmy night and the whole row of great windows were flung widely open. The Emperor and his guests stood looking out at the decorations in the garden,—the fairy lamps, the shining Royal initials, the fountains turned to pink and blue and green, the parterres, terraces and marble stairs illumined, and the gondolas in the distance outlined with light. Now there came a salute of guns. The firework display was about to begin. The Royal group was led to an adjoining room and on to a balcony to watch it. The Queen asked where General Canrobert was, and an aide-de-camp was sent to fetch him. Down by the Lac des Suisses, where the fireworks were to be sent up, was a dense mass of people, and on the water, beside the gondolas, there now appeared fairy boats with illumined sails.

At the Fête in the Palace of Versailles.

[*Face page* 158

There followed a lavish display of rockets like frosted silver, great fiery columns of gold and purple, revolving wheels, coloured balls, girandoles, fiery sprays, vivid bouquets of rainbow colours, and all the other types of firework in existence. The grand finale was a picture of Windsor Castle which appeared against the deep blue sky in gold fireworks, while the military bands below played "God save the Queen!" "A very pretty attention," was the Queen's bland comment. But the effect was slightly marred by the row of dumpy little Crimean cannons which fired an accompanying salvo, the smoke from which hid most of the picture from those in the palace. This caused great chagrin to the Empress who had designed the whole entertainment, fireworks included.

Now the Royal and Imperial party returned to the Hall of Mirrors and stepped on to the dais, which was richly draped with scarlet velvet. Here, as if posing for Winterhalter, they took their places: the Queen, in thick white satin embroidered with gold and wearing a weight of diamonds, sat next to the uniformed Emperor who wore his jewelled sword; Prince Albert, in uniform and orders, was next to the Empress beside whom was the Princess Royal in the simplest of white dresses and with a wreath of roses round her head. The Prince of Wales, in his full Highland dress, was standing a little apart, and behind them all sat Prince Napoleon and Princess Mathilde with a few minor royalties. Only Prince Napoleon spoilt the resplendent group. He had turned up in riding boots at this grand affair where only court breeches and full dress uniforms were de rigueur. He was an original character of republican tendencies, and although he wished no one to forget he was a prince, the Winterhalter aspect of royalty had no appeal for him.

He danced with the Queen, however, in his noisy boots, in the second of the Royal Quadrilles: for the dancing now began. At each end of the vast hall was a fine orchestra, hidden by a screen of palms and flowers; one was presided over by Strauss, and the other by Dufresne. As at the ball at the Hotel de Ville, Strauss had composed special music. The "Welcome Quadrille" was played, and then the "Prince of Wales' Polka".

This fête at Versailles, the first since the days of Louis XVI, and said to rival the entertainments of the great Louis XIV, had created a stir among the visitors to Paris. Every foreigner had been most eager to come. Paris was full of notabilities at this time, and nearly all the city seemed to have a claim to be invited.

The Emperor, too, was the kind of man who liked to share his own pleasures and entertainments to the greatest possible extent. Therefore an enormous number of tickets had been given out, and the fine firework display had been arranged where all the world could watch it. Spacious though the Palace of Versailles is, the crowding was colossal, and a dignified and easy entry had only been possible for royalty. For the rest it was an evening of queues and confusion, as well as of pleasure in the fine spectacle of the Hall of Mirrors come to life. There had been a slow-moving two-mile queue of carriages at the entrance, and there were queues to cloakrooms and up staircases. Many visitors had wandered out to the spacious gardens to watch the fireworks; now they were crowding back again towards the ballroom, and there was another queue in which one moved about a yard every ten minutes.

Passing the time by admiring celebrities and foreign uniforms, the great throng moved almost imperceptibly past statuesque guards, and up staircases, making their way through the great halls of *Hercule*, *Abondance*, *Venus*, *Diane* and *Mars*, and hearing the music of the ballroom growing a little more distinct above the murmur of voices as they advanced.

"The ladies gave little screams," says the *Manchester Guardian*, "as every now and then they felt a sudden check, and on looking round beheld an immense *carabinier* assiduously attempting to disengage his spur from a tremendous rent in one of the gay dresses upon which a whole previous week of taste and labour had been exhausted; while at every second moment some remarkable personage was observed struggling faintly with the billows; now it was the venerable Czartoryski, for whom everyone attempted to make way; then it was General Narvaez, covered with orders and ribbons, and who seemed very well able to make way for himself; now someone pointed out General Canrobert . . . and then Horace Vernet. The great point of attraction was the grand ballroom, the far famed *salle de glaces*, where it was understood the two Sovereigns were holding brilliant court. This magnificent salon, supposed to be the finest ballroom in the world, is nearly 250 feet long by 40 feet in width and about as many in height . . ."

There was no hope of dancing, the writer says. "Nobody could turn round, much less dance, and to the volatile Frenchman, with whom the waltz and polka are pastimes only varying in their degrees of intensity, to play him the finest music in the world while he was thus pinioned, was only adding insult to injury. There was only one consolation; we were slowly approaching the

THE HOSTS.

Between pages 160 *and* 161]

THE GUESTS.

Imperial dais, and should see Queens and Emperors and heirs apparent and princes of the blood dancing like any ordinary people. On approaching the sacred boundaries the great officers of the Imperial household in their magnificent scarlet embroidered coats, might be seen resolutely keeping the ground by leaning diagonally against the intruder, as we see beams put up against old houses, and expostulating with the invaders with more or less of civility, as the pressure became more or less inconvenient. . . . I stopped to see two or three Quadrilles in which the Queen, the Emperor, Prince Albert, Princess Royal and Princess Mathilde took part, and then moved on to make room for other sight-seers. . . ."

The Royal dancers tripped about where Marie Antoinette had been the last queen to dance, where Louis XIV had shone in his brilliance; and the gleaming floor reflected their diamonds, their satin dresses, scarlet uniforms and the wax candles that hung above them. Now they returned to the dais and sat laughing and talking among themselves, or receiving a guest who was brought up to be presented.

How happy a night that was! Personal troubles everyone might have, but life flowed on securely, and would continue to flow on in the same way when they had gone. The old virtues, the old loyalties, the respect for truth and justice and the faith of men in each other,—all these things seemed an imperishable part of nature. There was no reason for things to go amiss in the future, nothing to cast a shadow over the universal faith in progress. Victoria and Albert were good and conscientious rulers, and they were young and happy together. It was Albert's birthday to-morrow, and he would only be thirty-six. He was virtually the ruler of England and it might be expected that his beneficent influence in Europe would continue for many years to come. The Emperor, too, was happy in his domestic life and still had the upper hand with his highly strung wife. His political plans, if ambitious, were also humane and generous; he would have liked nothing better than to have made all men rich and to have freed all men from oppression. The Empress, too, who was to play havoc with his policy many a time in the future, was capable on this August night of doing very well. Having gained her point, she was prepared to shine in her position. High-spirited, fiery, intemperate in her views and ambitions,—those qualities were now in abeyance and the better side of her nature shone during this brief and happy period of her husband's love for her and of her own satisfied ambition. She had many virtues and had the character to learn by experience as she grew older; and in the end unanimous opinion voted her a noble old lady of very great qualities. In fact, seeing the picture of her days of exile, and the picture of the first years of her marriage, one is astonished that so attractive and clever a woman had such a phase of madness in between and brewed such a lot of mischief for France. On this night she meant to do well, and only a run of misfortunes utterly undreamed of then brought out the worst in her in later years.

As far as Queen Victoria was concerned, her views were identical with those of Prince Albert. Their children were educated in a liberal manner, as believers in peace and justice, the Prince of Wales for the English throne, the Princess Royal for the throne of Germany. This proposed marriage of their eldest child to the Prussian prince was preoccupying their thoughts more and more now that they were on the eve of the actual engagement. It was a heavy sacrifice to give up so young a child to the responsibilities of such a great position; but Prince Albert had always had great faith in her abilities. He knew she would be equal to the task. Vicky, in fact, consoled him for all the silly, flighty ways of Bertie; she had inherited her father's intelligence and absorbed the Stockmar training with ease and enjoyment. Philosophy, literature, science and art,—all these were dear to her in a rather Germanic way, and she had a remarkable comprehension of politics for a girl of her age. Her engagement next month was not to be the inauguration of a time of pleasure and of planning a fine wardrobe; it was to be marked by intensive history lessons each evening, extra study of all kinds and the writing of essays. Prince Frederick, too, was a good and broadminded young man. In the next year or two, how often the Prince Consort was to stroll up and down with him in the gardens of Buckingham Palace or Windsor, earnestly discussing the future of Europe and the government of Germany. A united Germany under a liberal, constitutional monarchy: this was the aim, and since it would all be in the family, a close association with England was inevitable. Here lay the world's best hope. In the East there was always danger while the Russian people were serfs, living in dark and powerless ignorance under the autocratic Czar. France was a potential danger with the revival of Bonapartism, and the corruption at its court. But Germany was peaceful and honest, and with England would make a strong combination to resist the despotic countries; Belgium, Holland, Denmark and Switzerland would join them, and in time France would inevitably return to more liberal ways and be attracted to the alliance; and the rest of the world would gradually evolve to join the peaceful union. Such were the plans and hopes of the hour. Louis Napoleon's plans were different; but they might have been made to fit in with those of England and Germany in a peaceful way. The Emperor fell in with the best European spirit by acknowledging that Liberalism should be the ultimate goal of a despot, and at the end of his reign he instituted liberal reforms, thus proving that in his case absolute power had not corrupted absolutely. He liked Prince Albert more than the Prince liked him, and once said of him that after being with him one felt more inclined to do good. He too meant to co-operate in an ever-improving Europe in 1855.

All was well on this night of August the 25th, as Strauss played his waltzes and the ancient glories of the Hall of Mirrors were revived. And yet some evil genius seemed to preside at the fête, for now there appeared on the dais a tall and vigorous man in a white uniform, and Herr von Bismarck was presented first to the Emperor and then to the Queen.

If the Queen and Prince Albert had not met Bismarck before, they had heard about him and knew of his influence with the old King of Prussia, and knew that he was using that influence to their disadvantage and in favour of Russia. Prince Albert, who always talked about serious affairs, either at a ball or anywhere else, was soon taking Bismarck to task about this while Bismarck parried half jokingly. With their delight in irony the fates had put Bismarck in white, and Albert (whom Victoria always swore was really an angel) in dead black. "For this occasion," says Canrobert in his memoirs, "the Prince Consort had donned a uniform which was entirely black, and it suited him to perfection, making him seem even more handsome than he was." There the two Germans stood, attired in black and white; and their souls were equally in contrast, black and white. For although they were both concerned for the destiny of their country, one strove for the happiness of men, and the other cared not a rap for men's happiness and strove for the supremacy of a militarised State. They were striking figures. Bismarck was a massively athletic man, overflowing with jovial high spirits, a man who had drunk deeply at the fountain of civilisation and seemed too intelligent for his own creeds. The Prince, looking like a well-groomed Hamlet, was sizing up the Prussian diplomat and could see the barbaric depths; he was already feeling a dislike for him and he was courteous but remote.

Bismarck found Victoria rather more polite. "At that ball at Versailles," say his memoirs, "Queen Victoria spoke to me in German. She gave me the impression of beholding in me a noteworthy but unsympathetic personality, but still her tone of voice was without that touch of ironical superiority that I thought I detected in Prince Albert's. She continued to be amiable and courteous, like one unwilling to treat an eccentric fellow in an unfriendly way."

Victoria and Albert, the Princess Royal and Prince Frederick, —all these were in powerful places and understood the European tradition; by what disastrous circumstances were their hopes and beliefs to be defeated? In a few years' time Bismarck was to say, "It is not with speeches or with parliamentary resolutions that the questions of the day are decided, as was mistakenly done in 1848 and 1849, but with blood and iron." For the rest of the century he never deviated from the principle of force as the foundation of government, and the German people accepted the creed.

Where was the carefully trained Vicky in these later years of the century? She was submerged under Bismarck's hatred of all that she stood for and by a mass of Berlin intrigues and suspicions. In the end she did little but fume, and might well have been spared the heavy part she was made to play and allowed to stay happily in free and peaceful England. But who was to know that in 1855? The plans were bravely made in the hope that much good would come of them, and they were more likely to succeed than to fail. But all went wrong. Prince Albert, although he was younger than Bismarck, died soon after his daughter's marriage; but Prince Frederick's father did not die. The Emperor of the French began to make disastrous mistakes; Eugénie lost all faith in him and went her own headstrong way, her political influence growing stronger and more disastrous as his will grew weak. Bismarck was there to exploit every folly, until at last he had engineered the war of 1870 and had brought about the union of Germany. Vicky's father-in-law, the Emperor Wilhelm I, relied utterly on Bismarck after these triumphs; he did not share the more scrupulous view of his son. Prince Frederick wrote in his war diary of 1870: "Bismarck has made us great and powerful, but he has robbed us of our friends, the sympathies of the world and—our conscience."

By the time Bismarck had achieved this triumph the Germans were growing far away from the sympathy with England that Prince Albert had expected to arise from his daughter's marriage; but *The Times* predicted in 1874 that when Prince Frederick, "the consistent friend in Prussia of all mild and liberal administration", succeeded to the throne all obstacles to Anglo-German friendship would disappear. But Prince Frederick's father lived on and on. And when at last he died, his son too was a dying man. It was the grandson, Wilhelm II, who inherited the position. The Prince Consort's hopes had come to nothing. By the end of the century the old friendliness of the West was gone for ever. In 1899 Vicky, by now the Dowager Empress Frederick, wrote:

"For Germany and England to go together—it would want the undoing of Prince Bismarck's work of *brouille* at which he was such a master. He wanted distress and enmity, and he *knew* how little political understanding and independent opinion there is in Germany, and kept waving before their eyes to *madden* them, the red flag of England's enmity and falseness, greed and ambition, etc. The seed Prince Bismarck sowed for years is now springing up. Who shall unravel the tissue of falsehoods and intrigues with which German public opinion has been worked upon and is hoodwinked?"

It almost seems that no one could attempt to unravel it now that Bismarck's process of sacrificing anything and everything to military might has been carried to a logical conclusion. He so loved the military State that he would sacrifice conscience for it; and now in the Germany he united there is no clear cut faith left; the ability to believe the word of others, the ready trust in another man, the old sense of honour, all these have been trafficked away in exchange for a miserable and demented theory of blood and iron, and only confusion remains. It is strange and sad to look back and see how very easily things might have gone a different and a better way had Bismarck and his unhappy gifts not been in the picture of 1855. But there he was, amusing himself in Paris as the guest of Count Hatzenfeldt, the Prussian ambassador, who had invited him to come for the great exhibition.

"I little thought," says Canrobert, speaking of this first meeting with Bismarck, "of the fate he reserved for Germany and for our own country. And I am sure that at the time he had not even dreamed of it himself."

To-night such things were undreamed of, and Bismarck thought only of pleasure. Yet instinctively he was summing up the weak points of men, instinctively he had his eye on the military muddles and the deficiencies of organisation in the Crimea and formulated ideas of an efficiency in war that was more wicked than any blunders of ineptitude. In this broad and glowing Hall of Mirrors, where now he danced and laughed and joked, Otto von Bismarck was to bring Prussian militarism its supreme hour. Here he was to stand in 1871, a spiked helmet in his hands, proclaiming the German Empire. Here the picturesque arrogance of Louis XIV, painted all across the walls and ceilings in vain-glorious, historic scenes, was to be answered with a more heart-felt and unredeemed arrogance.

But now the arbiters of human destiny were dancing; the Queen with the Emperor who, she said, "waltzed very quietly", the Princess Royal with Prince Napoleon, Prince Albert with Princess Augustenberg. And as Johann Strauss filled the hours with melody, the mild air of a glorious moonlit night came in the great windows and outside all the fountains played.

At half-past twelve the Royal party went in to the theatre of the chateau which had been converted into a supper room. "We waited," says the Queen, "till all the company had gone into supper, and then began our procession, the Guards, officers, etc., walking before us. We walked through a number of fine rooms and a long gallery to the theatre, where the supper was. The sight it presented was truly magnificent. The whole stage was covered in, and four hundred people sat down to supper at forty small tables of ten each, each presided over by a lady, and nicely selected, and all by the Empress's own desire and arrangement. There were many garlands of flowers, and the whole was beautifully lit up with innumerable chandeliers. The boxes were full of spectators, and a band was playing, but not visible. We sat at a small table in the centre box, with only the Emperor and Empress, the two children, Prince Napoleon, Princess Mathilde and Prince Adalbert. It was one of the finest and most magnificent sights we had ever witnessed; there had not been a ball at Versailles since the time of Louis XVI, and the present one had been arranged after a print of a fête given by Louis XV."

This rather official description does not fit in with some of the accounts given which speak of the noise and disorder of the supper room and of a shocking lack of organisation. Bismarck describes how he was given no less than three tickets for supper, while many others had been left out altogether; how the visitors were put into different categories for the meal and how there were altercations over this, collisions among the crowds and a general confusion and lack of good manners. But perhaps the noise of guests arguing and clamouring for tables was not noticed from the Royal box, or seemed to be lost in the general splendour of the entertainment.

After supper the Royal guests returned to the ballroom and there was another waltz which "the Emperor danced with Vicky". It was nearly two o'clock when Napoleon and his guests drove back to St. Cloud, cheerful and yet rather sad that the last great festival was over. For the Queen and her family were going home on Monday. "It's terrible that there's only one more night!" the Emperor said, and the Queen agreed in the most heartfelt manner, but told him that he must soon come to England again. "It was past two when we got home, much delighted, and the children in ecstasies, and past three before we got to bed." That hour was spent in planning future holidays together. "You will come back, won't you," the Emperor said. "Now that we know each other, we can visit each other at Windsor or at Fontainebleau without any ceremony, can't we?" The Queen eagerly agreed. She went on to say with her good, hearty laugh that she would come back next year as an ordinary traveller; with her bag in her hand she would jump out of the train, take a cab to the Tuileries and ask for some dinner. And so the night ended, with friendliness, and hope and confidence in the future.

CHAPTER XVIII

FAREWELL

THE morning dawned after the brief night, and Victoria awoke to wish Prince Albert a happy birthday and lead him to the table where, in the German manner, she had put his presents, surrounded by a wreath. Louis Napoleon had spent his birthday in London, during his visit in the spring, and now the Prince's birthday was being celebrated in Paris. "May God ever bless and protect him for many, many years to come, and may we ever be together to our lives' end!" wrote the poor Queen who was to lose him at such an early age. On the table was the bronze statue which she had bought on Friday, and "some very pretty Alliance and Crimean studs", one of which was left blank, ready for the word "Sebastopol".

"The Emperor joined us and we breakfasted," the Queen writes. "Immediately after breakfast the Emperor said that he had some music of his own composition in honour of Albert's birthday. He took us to the balcony of Albert's dressing-room, which overlooks the courtyard, where were assembled three hundred drummers, with their several tambor-majors. Upon our appearing the Emperor gave them the signal, '*Commencez!*' on which they all, as if they were one man, began a splendid roll of drums in a particular manner, which is only given upon the *jour de l'an*. They repeated this twice, and then went away cheering. It was very fine, and very kind of the Emperor. He is particularly fond of it."

As he had done last Sunday, the Emperor took the Royal family out for a drive round the park. Again Victoria drove with him in his private phaeton and enjoyed an hour of the refinements of gallantry. Day after day the Imperial homage had been paid to the Queen to her great content, and Louis Napoleon was keeping it up until the last moment. It was not love-making in any popular modern usage of the word; not a pretence of the physical instinct and desire that goes by the name. It was love-making in a courtly tradition inherited from the seventeenth and eighteenth centuries, a homage to a woman raised to the status of goddess; it involved an apparent forgetfulness of self on the

168

part of the cavalier, a constant attention to the lady's every mood, a forestalling of her slightest wishes. It was all as mannered and as artificial as the graceful music of the old minuets, and it added considerably to the charm of life, particularly when practised with such an air of unfeigned sincerity as the Emperor assumed.

However, serious subjects were also touched upon during the drive; for the Queen wished to explain her feelings towards the Orléans family. They were now living in England, and she had been told that her friendly visits to them were displeasing to the Emperor. She wished to know if this were true. They were closely related and were her friends, she said, and she could not drop them in their adversity; but they were very discreet, and during her visits the subject of politics was not touched upon. The Emperor replied very cordially that she was right; one could not abandon those in misfortune, and he would be the last person to wish it.

Since they were on such good terms, the Emperor now ventured upon that really dreadful subject, which had so upset Victoria and Albert: the confiscation of the Orléans property in France. He would like to explain why he did it, he said. He had no feelings of animosity towards the family, and at first had wished to leave all Orléanist employés in their places. But he had discovered that their agents were constantly trying to upset his authority, and had realised that it simply was not safe to leave the family with large possessions in France which would give them power against the government. However, he had no unfriendly feelings, and hoped that Queen Marie-Amélie, who was shortly going on a visit to Spain, would not hesitate to travel through France.

This was a subject on which the Queen felt rather strongly; and it is a proof of the very special fascination that Louis Napoleon had for her that they got on so splendidly together. For she entirely accepted the Orléans family's version of his behaviour—which was not always strictly impartial—and never ceased to regard him as a man who had broken his word to them: not a thing that she could lightly pass over in any ordinary mortal. But she had been swept off her feet. "There is something fascinating, melancholy and engaging," she said, "which draws you to him in spite of any *prevention* you may have against him."

She ventured now to say that the Orléans had felt the confiscation very much, and as a result were far more bitter than they would otherwise have been. "I praised the Princes, and the Queen, their discretion, etc. The Emperor said, in conclusion of his explanation about the confiscation, that their agents were in constant communication with his enemies, even 'avec ceux qui prêchent l'assassinat.' I said I could hardly credit this. They were, I was sure, incapable of such conduct. I, however, added that naturally all exiles were inclined to conspire, which he did not deny, and which indeed he had practised himself . . ."

"I was very anxious," the Queen wrote, "to get out what I had to say on the subject, and not to have this untouchable ground between us. Stockmar, so far back as last winter, suggested and advised that this course should be taken."

The awkward subject was now successfully surmounted and the Queen could go on to the main preoccupation of her mind: her desire to visit the chapel of St. Ferdinand, put up in memory of the Duc d'Orléans. Having gone in state to the tomb of Napoleon on Friday, she now felt entitled to go privately on this more personal pilgrimage. The Emperor offered in the most friendly manner to take herself and Albert to the chapel that afternoon; he was really very generous towards his political enemies, the Queen thought; and upon the acceptance of his offer they drove back to St. Cloud where the Embassy chaplain had come once more to deliver his brief sermon.

After this, Louis Napoleon and Eugénie gave their birthday presents to Albert. They were a picture called "Le Rixe" by Meissonier, from Napoleon, which the Prince had singled out for special admiration at the exhibition, and which Victoria therefore declared the finest thing there, and a handsomely mounted carved ivory cup from Eugénie.

It was a day of presents and thoughts of the homeward journey to-morrow. The Emperor and Empress produced many gifts for the smaller children at Osborne, and Vicky and Bertie examined all the lovely things they had bought at the exhibition on Friday, and particularly their favourite toy, an example of the wonderful mechanical devices made at the time for children. It was a French grenadier, holding the Malakoff tower between his knees. When wound up he would open his mouth, take a deep breath and draw up from the tower a perfect model of a cossack which disappeared down his throat, whereat the grenadier made a smiling grimace and then continued the process.

Early in the afternoon Napoleon I's only surviving brother, King Jérome, called upon the Queen to pay his respects. He was the father of Prince Napoleon and Princess Mathilde, but he had been absent during the week with a diplomatic illness.

There had been some difficulty on the subject of precedence, and he had also disapproved of the Queen's visit to his brother's tomb at the Invalides. But now that that ceremony was safely over, he was back home in the Palais Royal.

It was not until the evening that the Queen was taken to the memorial chapel to the Duc d'Orléans. "We drove through the Bois de Boulogne," says the Queen, "which was full of equipages and people, so gay, and the evening so fine,—alas! our last."

They came out of the Bois at Neuilly and drove to the scene of the Duke's death; he had been thrown from a carriage in 1842, and the chapel was erected on the spot where he had died. Here the Queen made the pilgrimage that she knew would so much please her friend, the ex-Queen of France who had been through so many sorrows. It was all very pathetic, she found, with the chapel in black and white marble, the *prie-Dieux* in black and silver, embroidered by the poor Queen and her daughter, Louise, and the figure of an angel "with hands stretched upwards as if imploring Heaven for mercy", carved by Marie d'Orléans who had also died very young. The monument to the young Duke and other carvings in the chapel were by Triquetti and seemed very beautiful to Victoria. When Albert died this was the sculptor whom she chose to design the decorations of the memorial chapel at Windsor.

Victoria and Albert lingered for some moments; the chapel was silent, it had been empty when they arrived. They remembered the shock that all the family had felt on the death of the French King's heir, and reflected that events would have taken a different turn in Europe but for this unhappy accident. Louis-Philippe's abdication, in fact, had been ill advised and unnecessary, his eldest son had been a good, intelligent man whose presence would have changed the whole situation. Here in this quiet chapel was the key to that downward trend that things were taking in Europe, all unnoticed at the time. It was the Duc d'Orléans' death that cleared the way for events leading to the return of the Bonaparte Empire and of militarism in Europe; from that simple accident what disasters were to ensue!

As they left the chapel, a woman from a house near by came out with commemorative medals for sale; the Emperor bought two of them and presented them to Victoria. On one was the head of the Duc d'Orléans, on the other that of his son, heir to the throne, the Comte de Paris; on the latter were the words to the effect that the boy was the hope of France, and the Queen was surprised to find that they were being sold, and still more surprised that the Emperor should buy them.

This, the last evening of the visit to Paris, ended with a large dinner party which was followed by a concert. The occasion was rather sad for the Queen; the week had been so brilliant, so delightful from start to finish; she had been the object of such attentions, such tactful, deferential flattery, and she had received so many friendly ovations from the French people, so many wonderful gifts of lovely things not to be found elsewhere,—that she could not bear to think the holiday was over. She had been astonished, too, by the magnificence of France. Once, eleven years ago, she and Albert had visited Louis-Philippe at the Chateau d'Eu; but the short visit had given her no indication of what the country was like. Louis-Philippe and Marie-Amélie were almost excessively homely, the visit to d'Eu had been an affair of country excursions in chars-a-bancs, cold collations taken in marquees, and private musical evenings. This time she had seen the splendour of French monuments, the brilliance of French traditions, and had been royally entertained. All the show and ceremony had fascinated her, and she had enjoyed every minute of the week. Now it was ending; they sat listening to classical music, "which Albert was much pleased with, but which bored the Emperor"; and soon this too was over, and they said good night.

For the last time the Royal guests awoke in their light and cheerful rooms at St. Cloud, hearing the sounds of the muster of the guard. They were to leave at ten o'clock; Victoria rose early, and was soon at her desk. "I must write to-day," she wrote in her diary, "and here in my lovely dressing room, in this beautiful St. Cloud, with the cool sound of the fountains in my ear, a few parting words. I am deeply grateful for these eight very happy days, and for the delight of seeing such beautiful and interesting places and objects, and for the reception which we have met with in Paris, and in France generally. The union of the two nations, and of the two Sovereigns, for there is a great friendship sprung up between us, is of the greatest importance! May God bless these two countries, and may He specially protect the precious life of the Emperor, and may this happy union ever continue for the benefit of the world!"

Having dealt with the subject as a monarch, the Queen turned away to look once more at her lovely surroundings; and her next entry was in a more personal vein. "A beautiful morning," she says, "which made the dear place look only more lovely, and the departure even more sad . . . Everything in my lovely room was so beautifully arranged. The Toilette of the finest *point d'Angleterre*, with choice ornaments, on the washing-stand beautiful modern Sèvres china, with my monogram, and gold glass bottles and tumblers, which the Emp^r. and Empress insisted on my taking away with me, as I could not buy any. In the sitting-room, charming light green satin furniture and a beautiful *escritoire* (at which I have been writing) . . ."

It was terrible to have to tear one's self away from this charming palace and its attentive owners. The Queen's regrets, however, were nothing to those of her eldest son. To Bertie the visit had been a revelation. It had shown him a glimpse of a world that seemed actually to be run for purposes of pleasure, for getting as much fun as you could out of life, instead of for self-improvement and the acquiring of stores of knowledge. He felt it was his own world, a promised land. He was tired to death of edification and would have liked to settle down for ever among the Parisians. If only he could have stayed! He had tried his best, he had dared to ask, but it had been no good. Vicky had said she wanted to stay, too. So they had gone to the Empress and had asked her if she would persuade their parents to leave them behind. The Empress had said that she was afraid it would be impossible, as their parents could not possibly do without them. But the Prince of Wales, who knew he was a constant source of irritation to them, was incredulous. "Not do without us!" he exclaimed. "Don't fancy that, for there are six more of us at home, and they don't want us." But no argument had availed, and Bertie was now in his Highland dress, waiting to drive to the station.

The Princess Royal's admiration for their Imperial host and hostess was as great as her brother's, and for the moment she too loved everything French. She particularly liked the wonderful Empress, and Eugénie had been specially kind and attentive to her both at Windsor and ever since. After the visit to England, Eugénie had sent the Princess a lavish gift. She had obtained Vicky's measurements from a dresser in their minutest details, and on returning to Paris had had a fashion doll made exactly to the size. This had been fitted out with a perfect trousseau showing examples of the finest Parisian skill: dresses, mantles, bonnets, *coiffures*, boots, gloves, *lingerie*, trinkets,—everything that could possibly find a place in a young lady's toilet, and the whole thing was sent to the Princess Royal. But it was the Empress herself, rather than her many fine presents, who filled the young princess with a dazzled wonderment; she was enraptured by Eugénie's beauty and elegance, although she was not tempted to imitate her. The impression was to fade quickly. It was a fleeting passion that was to be forgotten in the new emotions of love. For in exactly five weeks' time Prince Frederick was to propose to her in Scotland, and she was to accept the proposal.

Now it was really time to leave. The Emperor came to the Queen's rooms, and with that easy familiarity which, because she scarcely ever met with it, had won her heart, said that Eugénie was in her room and ready, but could not drag herself away. "If I would come to her room," says the Royal diary, "it would make her come. When we went in, the Emperor called to her, 'Eugénie, la Reine est là'; and she came and gave me a beautiful fan, and a rose and heliotrope from the garden, and Vicky a beautiful bracelet, set with rubies and diamonds, containing her hair, with which Vicky was delighted."

Now they all entered carriages to drive to the Palace of the Tuileries, from which point they were to make a ceremonial progress to the station.

"The morning was more beautiful than ever, though intensely hot," the Queen continues. "The crowds great everywhere, beginning with the town of St. Cloud, where we generally (as also in other places) saw some poor wounded soldiers from the Crimea, including some of my favourites, the Zouaves. Along the whole route there were immense crowds, all most friendly. The Arc de Triomphe, under which we drove almost daily, had never been driven under before, except, I think, on one great occasion by the Emperor himself, and when the 'cendres de Napoléon' passed through it. All these things are striking and valuable, as indicating the altered feeling of the country."

At the Palace of the Tuileries they said good-bye to the Empress and changed into state carriages. Since the French public had been so enthusiastic over the Queen's visit, it had been decided that the last drive in the capital should be a spectacular procession, moving at a walking pace so that the people should have a good view of it. And now there set out from the great archway of the Tuileries, first a squadron of mounted *Chasseurs*, then a staff of generals, and then a military band in scarlet uniforms. Then came outriders and the long line of carriages containing both French and English courtiers, followed by troops. A state carriage, all gold and glass, carried the Prince of Wales and Prince Napoleon, the heirs apparent and presumptive of England and France; and at last there arrived the Emperor and the Queen, Prince Albert and the Princess Royal, in a coach drawn by eight elaborately caparisoned horses, each led by a running groom who held a gilded bridle. This was a spectacular coach of glass and gilt, and the cheering crowds were as delighted as if at the theatre. It was the coach in which Napoleon I had driven to his marriage with Marie-Louise: on that occasion the gilt crown which surmounted it had detached itself and fallen to the ground. Napoleon and Eugénie had driven in the same coach to their wedding at Notre Dame, and the same crown, regilded, had once more rolled down ominously into the dust. But to-day there were no unhappy portents, and the coach proceeded smoothly on its way, followed by many fine detachments of soldiers and by another band.

Slowly the cortège went through the boulevards, with drums beating and trumpets sounding their flourishes. The troops along the roadside presented arms as the state coaches passed, and the enthusiastic crowds shouted and waved flags. Above, ladies in their white morning wrappers, then the newest fashion in Paris, looked down from open windows; and gentlemen in gay morning gowns or jackets of brilliant hue, looked over their shoulders. Now the procession turned into the Boulevard de Strasbourg, leading up to the station. The Queen looked back through the glass window. "Alas!" she says, "it was our last sight of that gay brilliant town, where we have been so kindly received, and for which I shall ever have an affect^{ate} feeling."

The station was reached at last to the sound of saluting guns; its decorations had been renewed, and it was ablaze with brilliant autumn flowers. The initials of the Queen and Prince confronted them, enormously large and entwined in white dahlias, against a bank of vivid green; and all round were curtains of heavy silk and velvet, flags and streamers. The train was waiting; the usual deputations gave their bouquets and parting words, and the Emperor assisted the Queen to enter her carriage. She called General Canrobert up at the last moment, for a few cordial words of farewell, a few more words about the war, and then the Emperor, Prince Napoleon and various members of the French court followed the English guests into the train, which slowly puffed out of the station while ministers raised their hats, generals saluted, and the bands played "God save the Queen".

There was a triumphant five-hours' journey down to Boulogne. Once more country people had assembled all along the route to wave, and to present flowers wherever the train stopped. Deputations, bands and salutes of guns awaited them at the principal stations, and farewell messages and bouquets were given. Boulogne was reached at half-past five, and here bands and soldiers led them to the *Hotel du Pavillon Impérial*.

A great review of the troops was to be held this evening before the Queen and her family embarked on the *Victoria and Albert*, and the Emperor soon took his guests down to the beach in carriages and on horseback. Here were ranged about fifty thousand men,—Cavalry, Lancers and Dragoons. The Queen was driven along the lines, and the Emperor, Prince Albert and Prince Napoleon rode on horseback. The sun was now setting, and there was, says the Queen, "quite a forest of bayonets. The effect they produced, with the background of the calm blue sea and the setting sun, which threw a glorious crimson light over all —for it was six o'clock—was most magnificent."

The Emperor then decorated some of the men, after which there was a march past and the Queen turned her thoughts to the past. Her yacht lay out at sea, and a squadron of the fleet was standing by. Once, she remarks, "at this very place, on these very sands, Napoleon I reviewed his army which was to invade England, Nelson's fleet lying, where our squadron lay, watching that very army. Now our squadron saluted Napoleon III while his army was filing past the Queen of England, several of the bands playing 'Rule Britannia'!"

Far from being bored by this ceremony, Victoria thoroughly enjoyed it all. "The sight of the troops," she says, "as they filed off in their separate battalions of eight hundred each along the sea-shore, the setting sun gilding the thousands of bayonets, lances, etc., was indescribably beautiful." She had no yearnings after a stroll on a quiet beach, no feelings that it was sad to see these thousands of human beings regimented like slaves. With sparkling eyes she laughed and joked with the Emperor who exerted himself, as usual, to keep her amused and was in very good form. Prince Albert remained calm and quiet; he was wondering where Napoleon's ambitions would end, thinking how close this gathering military might was to England. What did the Emperor propose to do with these fine armies which provided him with such a magnificent hobby? Would he not in the end, in spite of all his assurances, use them to enforce his will on others? Napoleon was

THE FRENCH ARMY WAS THE FINEST IN THE WORLD. IT

Between pages 176 *and* 177]

IPEROR'S PASSION TO WATCH IT MARCHING TO AND FRO.

an ally now; but how long would it last? Would not England in due course need to fortify her coasts and see to her defences? Such questions rose in his mind and preoccupied him as the finely-equipped battalions marched past.

Now the whole party entered carriages and drove out to the camps of Honvault and Ambleteuse. "I had a *cantinière* called up to the carriage," says the Queen, "and looked at her dress and her little barrel. She was very tidy, clean, and well-spoken. I wish we had them in our army. They must always be married, and if they wish to remain in the regiment, and their husbands die or are killed, they must marry again within the year."

The most interesting feature of the drive was at Honvault, where, high up on the cliffs they watched some demonstrations of rocket firing. The Emperor interested himself greatly in rocket-propelled explosives, and one of these, as the Royal persons watched, travelled two leagues before it burst.

"Some day," says the *Illustrated London News*, jokingly, "we may hear of the possibility of bombarding Dover from Calais!"

But now it was late. "The moon was rising like a crimson ball," says the Queen, "and giving beautiful effect to the darkening sky and dim twilight." They drove back to the Imperial Pavilion Hotel where they had a leisurely farewell dinner. And at eleven o'clock they re-entered the carriages and drove down to the quay. "The streets and houses of the town were one blaze of illuminations and fireworks," says the Queen. "There were salutes, bands playing, great cheering, and, to crown all, an exquisite moon, shining brilliantly over everything. It was a very fine and moving sight. The Emperor led me on board, followed by his whole suite, as he wished to go with us a little way out to sea. We glided out of the harbour, I with a heavy heart. . . . ."

Louis Napoleon was shown round the new yacht, and was astonished by its size and beauty; he would like one just like it, he said, only smaller. Why not the same size? the Queen asked. And the Emperor, tactful and gallant to the last minute, said that although such a splendid yacht was just right for the Queen of the seas, it was much too fine for a mere terrestrian like himself.

But now he had to leave, or it would be impossible for his own small yacht to re-enter the port. The Queen was considerably upset; it had been a week in which, through her attachment to Louis Napoleon, she had enjoyed herself in rather a special way. These were some of the happiest days of her life, she said afterwards. They had formed a dazzling interlude in which her

Royal solitude had been bridged by Napoleon's constant homage to her as an attractive woman. There was a sympathy between them; there was something in the Hanoverian side of her character that responded to the dashing, adventurous man of the world who had gambled and succeeded; she delighted in the touch of romance and excitement it had brought for a moment into her staid life. Now it was slipping away from her for ever, and with it the dreams of idle youth were going,—those dreams that the Emperor had revived for a few glorious, crowded days, making her feel as young and carefree as in the days before her marriage. Youth itself was vanishing, for she was going home now to see to the betrothal of her own daughter. She knew, despite all the plans of Saturday night, after the wonderful ball at Versailles, that the same happy circumstances would not arise again, and that the perfect hours could never return.

"I embraced him twice, and he shook hands very warmly with Albert and the children. We followed him to the ladder, and here I once more squeezed his hand and embraced him, saying, '*Encore une fois, adieu, Sire!*' We looked over the side of the ship and watched them getting into the barge. The Emperor called out: '*Adieu, Madame. Au revoir*'; to which I replied, '*Je l'espère bien.*'"

So the Imperial and Royal idyll ended. The Queen's feelings for the Emperor changed considerably in the course of the next few years, although she was a constant friend to the family in their later days of exile.

"We heard the splash of the oars, and saw the barge lit by the moon," says the Queen. They leaned over the railings, watching, as the Emperor was rowed to his yacht, the *Ariel*, and climbed on board. They watched the Imperial yacht sail past, waving handkerchiefs. The sailors cheered and sent up rockets,—"and then all was still, all over!"

"The night when we left I felt so unhappy," wrote Victoria to Lady Cowley, the wife of the ambassador to France. "It was with a heavy heart that I lay down in my cabin after we had left the shore of a country which had been so hospitable to us."

It had been a perfect holiday, the weather dazzlingly fine, the entertainments lavish and yet so skilfully arranged as always to be a pleasure and never a burden. The people had been happy, and there had been no mishap of any kind. And how white and shining Paris was, how beautiful the Palace of St. Cloud! For a time life had seemed to be not as it really was, an affair of constant irritations, work and difficulties, but an imaginary life where all was well and as one would like to have it.

"Now that those bright days are past," the Queen wrote, "they seem to be only a vision or dream, so lovely that we can scarcely believe it."

The Royal visit was over. Louis Napoleon returned tired but well pleased to the Imperial Pavilion Hotel, and all the white houses of Boulogne were silent. The Queen's yacht sailed away peacefully on a glassy, moonlit sea, into the mists of the hot August night, and into the mists of time.

BIBLIOGRAPHY

The details and incidents of this book have been taken from the first list of books below, and from the French and English guide books and newspapers for 1855, and in particular the *Illustrated London News*, the *Illustrated Times*, the *Morning Post*, the *Manchester Guardian* and *Illustration*. The second list is of some general history books giving a background of the subject.

F. Adolphus, *Some Memories of Paris.*
Paul d'Ariste, *La Vie et le Monde du Boulevard.*
Germain Bapst, *Le Maréchal Canrobert.*
André Bellesort, *La Société Française sous Napoleon III.*
The Bernstorff Papers.
Prince von Bismarck, *Bismarck, the man and the Statesman.* Translated by
    A. J. Butler.
Hector Bolitho, *Albert the Good.*
                    The Prince Consort and his Brother.
Henri Boucher, *Souvenirs d'un Parisien.*
A. M. Broadly, *The Boyhood of a Great King.*
Sir Henry Cole, *Fifty Years of Public Work.*
Emily Crawford, *Victoria, Queen and Ruler.*
Ernest II, Duke of Saxe-Coburg-Gotha, *Memoirs.*
Letters of the Empress Frederick.
The Greville Diary.
Comte de Hübner, *Neuf Ans de Souvenirs.*
Raymond Isay, *Panórama des Expositions Universelles.*
W. Blanchard Jerrold, *On the Boulevards.*
                    Imperial Paris.
Sidney Lee, *Queen Victoria.*
              King Edward VII.
Earl of Malmesbury, *Memoirs of an ex-Minister.*
Theodore Martin, *Life of the Prince Consort.*
Karl Marx, *The Eighteenth Brumaire of Louis Bonaparte.*
Sir Herbert Maxwell, *Letters of the Fourth Earl of Clarendon.*
Prosper Mérimée, *Lettres à la Comtesse de Boigne.*
Mary Ponsonby, *A Memoir, some Letters and a Journal.*
Imbert de Saint-Amand, *Napoleon III et sa Cour.*
Charles Simond, *Paris de 1800 à 1900.* Vol. II.

BIBLIOGRAPHY

Lady Augusta Stanley, *Letters*.

Queen Victoria's Letters. (Between the years 1837 and 1861.)

Further Letters of Queen Victoria, edited by Hector Bolitho.

Albert Vandam, *Undercurrents of the Second Empire*.

Comte Horace de Viel Castel, *Memoirs*.

George Villiers, *A Vanished Victorian*.

Henry Vizetelly, *Glances Back Through Seventy Years*.

Henry Richard Charles Wellesley, 1st Earl Cowley, *The Paris Embassy during the Second Empire*.

Sir Victor Wellesley and Robert Sencourt, *Conversations with Napoleon III*.

General Sir Evelyn Wood, *The Crimea in 1854 and 1894*.

Octave Aubry, *L'Impératrice Eugénie*.

Edmund B. d'Auvergne. *Napoleon the Third*.

Ferdinand Bac, *Le Mariage de l'Impératrice*.

Augustin Filon, *Recollections of the Empress Eugénie*.

Comte Fleury, *Memoirs of the Empress Eugénie*.

Comte Fleury and Louis Sonolet, *La Société du Second Empire*.

Pierre de la Gorce, *Histoire du Second Empire*.
Napoleon III et sa Politique.

Philip Guedalla, *The Second Empire*.

Blanchard Jerrold, *The Life of Napoleon III*.

Pierre de Lano, *L'Impératrice Eugénie*.

Frederic Loliée, *La Vie d'une Impératrice*.

Robert Sencourt, *The Life of the Empress Eugénie*.
Napoleon III. The Modern Emperor.

F. A. Simpson, *The Rise of Louis Napoleon*.
Louis Napoleon and the Recovery of France.

Comte de Soissons, *The True Story of the Empress Eugénie*.

Clara Tschudi, *Eugénie, Empress of the French*.

CHRONOLOGY

1804   Napoleon crowned Emperor of the French.

1808   Birth of Louis Napoleon (Napoleon III) son of Louis Bonaparte, King of Holland, and of Queen Hortense, daughter of the Empress Josephine.

1811   Birth of the King of Rome (Napoleon's son).

1814   Napoleon abdicates and is banished to Elba. Louis XVIII King of France.

1815   Napoleon returns from Elba. Battle of Waterloo. Napoleon banished to St. Helena. Congress of Vienna. Bismarck born.

1819   Birth of Victoria (May 24).
Birth of Albert (August 26).

1821   Death of Napoleon at St. Helena.

1824   Death of Louis XVIII. Accession of Charles X to French throne.

1826   Birth of Eugénie, wife of Napoleon III.

1830   Revolution in France. Charles X abdicates. Louis-Philippe proclaimed King of the French.

1832   Death of the Duke of Reichstadt (Napoleon's son).

1836   Louis Napoleon attempts insurrection at Strasbourg.

1837   Queen Victoria comes to the throne.

1840   Marriage of Queen Victoria to Prince Albert. Louis Napoleon attempts to incite insurrection at Boulogne, is taken prisoner and imprisoned at Ham. The remains of Napoleon brought from St. Helena to Paris. Birth of Princess Royal (November 21).

1841   Birth of Prince of Wales (November 9).

1842   The Duke of Orléans, heir of Louis-Philippe, killed by a fall from his carriage.

1846   Louis Napoleon escapes from Ham.

1848   General revolutionary movement throughout the continent. Louis-Philippe abdicates from French throne and flies to England. Louis Napoleon elected president.

1850   Louis-Philippe dies in England.

1851   Crystal Palace exhibition in Hyde Park. Louis Napoleon seizes reins of government by a *coup d'état*: dissolves the National Assembly, declares a state of siege, arrests the leaders of the opposition, constitutes a new ministry. Orders the restoration of universal suffrage and an immediate election by people and army of a president to hold office for ten years. The army strongly in his favour. The election, under various controlling influences, results in the confirmation of his presidency for ten years by a vote of about seven out of eight millions.

1852   The President Louis Napoleon orders the confiscation of the Orléans property. Louis Napoleon proclaimed Emperor of the French, with title of Napoleon III.

1853   Marriage of Napoleon III and Eugénie de Montijo.

1854   Crimean War begins.

1855   Emperor and Empress of the French visit the Queen at Windsor. Great exhibition in Paris, May-October. Visit of Queen and Prince Albert to Paris.

1856   Peace treaty signed at Paris. Birth of the Prince Imperial.

1857   Indian Mutiny.

1858   Marriage of Princess Royal and Prince Frederick of Prussia. Attempted assassination of Napoleon III by Orsini. Meeting between Napoleon III and Cavour at Plombières where an alliance between France and Sardinia is decided upon against Austria on condition of Savoy and Nice being ceded to France. Queen Victoria and Prince Albert visit Napoleon III at Cherbourg (August 4–5).

1859   France and Sardinia declare war on Austria. Empress Eugénie made regent during Emperor's absence. Austria defeated at Magenta and Solferino. Peace treaty of Villafranca. Prince Napoleon marries Princess Clotilde, daughter of King of Sardinia.

1860   Nice and Savoy ceded to France.

1861   Death of the Prince Consort.

1863   Prince of Wales marries Princess Alexandra of Denmark. French in Mexico. Maximilian of Austria made Emperor of Mexico.

1864   German ultimatum to Denmark on Schleswig-Holstein question.

1865   Victoria's uncle, Leopold, King of Belgium, dies.

1866   Prussia and Italy declare war against Austria. Austrians defeated at Sadowa.

1867   Schleswig-Holstein annexed to Prussia. Second Empire outwardly at height of brilliance. Great gathering of monarchs and princes in Paris for an international exhibition. But attempt is made on life of Czar while riding with the Emperor Napoleon through the streets; and at the height of the festivities news comes of the execution of Archduke Maximilian whom the French had supported and then been obliged to abandon. General signs of dissolution behind the brilliant façade.

1869   Eugénie opens the Suez Canal.

1870   Franco-Prussian war. France defeated. Surrender of Napoleon III and his army at Sedan. Eugénie flies to England.

1871   Imperial family living at Chiselhurst. Commune in Paris. Third Republic.

1873   Death of Napoleon III at Chiselhurst.

1877   Queen Victoria declared Empress of India.

1879   Prince Louis Napoleon (son of Napoleon III) killed in Zululand.

CHRONOLOGY

1887   Queen Victoria's Jubilee celebrated.

1888   Death of William I of Prussia (March). Death of Emperor Frederick, Princess Royal's husband (June). Accession of William II.

1897   Queen Victoria's Diamond Jubilee.

1898   Death of Bismarck.

1899   Boer War.

1901   Death of Queen Victoria (January). Death of Empress Frederick (August).

1910   Death of King Edward VII.

1920   Death of the Empress Eugénie.